Tales of the *Sea Cloud*

Number 168

Williams-Ford Texas A&M University
Military History Series

Texas A&M University Press
College Station

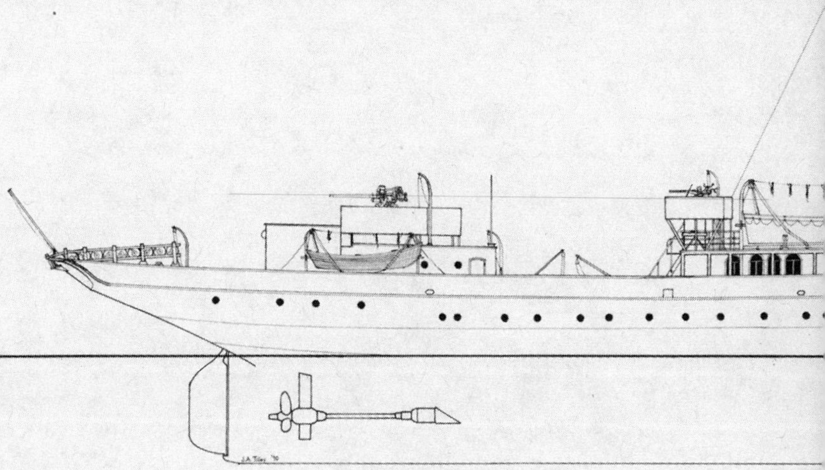

TALES OF THE SEA CLOUD

Luxury Yacht, Integrated Naval Vessel, Legendary Ship

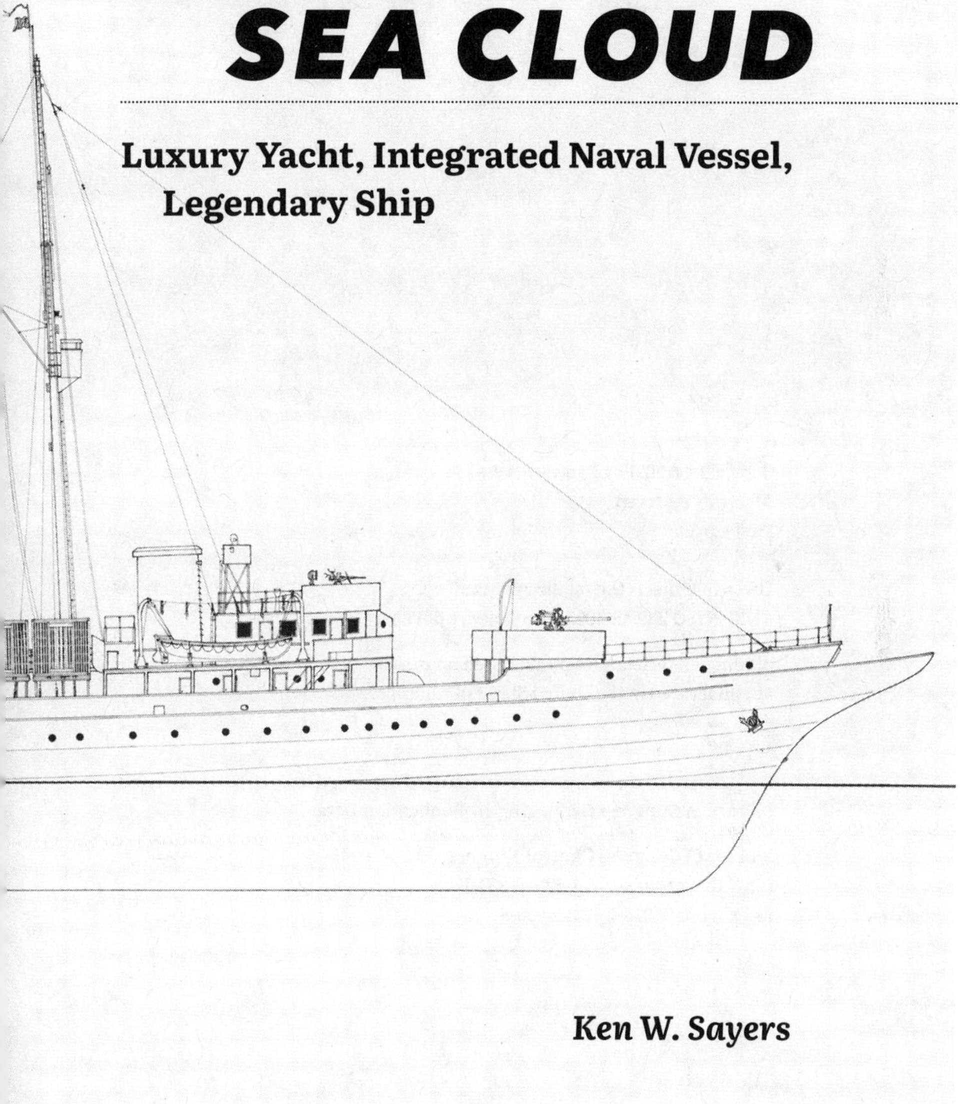

Ken W. Sayers

First edition

This paper meets the requirements of
ANSI/NISO Z39.48–1992 (Permanence of Paper).

Binding materials have been chosen for durability.
Manufactured in the United States of America.

Library of Congress Cataloging-in-Publication Data

Library of Congress Control Number: 2021941024
ISBN (hardcover) 978-1-62349-934-1
ISBN (ebook) 978-1-62349-935-8

For Rose

Contents

Foreword

I remember the day well. It was on March 6, 1973, that I first learned about the *Sea Cloud* during a conversation with my first "Sea Daddy" in the Coast Guard, Chief Boatswain's Mate Harold J. ("Sonny") Wise. Chief Wise was a burly, strong African American coast guardsman stationed at the Coast Guard base on Governors Island, New York. I had only been in the Coast Guard for a little over seven months and was serving aboard the cutter USCGC *Dallas* (WHEC-716).

Back in that period, the Coast Guard had few African American personnel. No one had the actual statistics, but it was estimated that less than 5 percent of coast guardsmen were defined as "Black." So it was rather easy for Chief Wise to spot me as one of the "newbies" on the base.

A chief petty officer in the Coast Guard (as well as the navy) is considered to be more than just a senior enlisted man or woman. The rank is also distinguished because only a few get to that level, and all who do are regarded as strong leaders and mentors. Thus, we use the term "Sea Daddy" (and "Sea Mommy" for women) for those experienced people whose sage advice and wise counsel help us through our careers.

While Chief Wise did not serve on *Sea Cloud* when the vessel was under the flag of the US Coast Guard during World War II, he knew several of the crewmembers who did. The chief proudly told me of *Sea Cloud*'s illustrious history as the first US military unit to operate with a completely integrated crew; where both blacks and whites worked together in a variety of jobs, lived in integrated quarters, and functioned in all aspects of an equal opportunity environment. Needless to say, that was quite unique during World War II. In fact, it wasn't until after the war, when President Truman signed Executive Order 99801 on July 26, 1948—which fully integrated the

US military services—that blacks and whites would work together without any restrictions in occupational specialties because of race. Little did anyone know back then that *Sea Cloud* had already accomplished this—three years before President Truman's directive.

Chief Wise believed it was important for me to learn about this bit of history, of which very few coast guardsmen knew back in 1973. He wanted me to appreciate the legacy of the men who served before me, those who had paved the way for both of us to have the privilege and satisfaction of working in any Coast Guard job in which we were interested and qualified to perform. Chief Wise related the story of *Sea Cloud* to me with such emotion and conviction that as I write this today, his words are still as clear, vivid, and meaningful as they were when he spoke them. Let me say that after that discussion with my new "Sea Daddy," I couldn't have been any prouder than I ever was to wear the Coast Guard uniform.

In 1998, a little more than twenty-five years after my education about the *Sea Cloud* from Chief Wise, I became the first African American in the US Coast Guard to be appointed as the master chief petty officer of the Coast Guard—the most senior enlisted person in the entire service. Not only was this a most prestigious position, but it was also a very important one. I now had the responsibility of serving as the principal advisor to the commandant of the Coast Guard on all matters involving quality of life, health and well-being, and personnel issues for the entire Coast Guard workforce.

In 1999, my first year in that post, I had the honor and pleasure to meet the man who was responsible for the integration of the US Coast Guard in World War II—the former commanding officer of the *Sea Cloud*, Commander Carlton Skinner. I just couldn't help but feel a deep respect and reverence for him. He was a true legend and inspiration, both for the Coast Guard and for our country. Commander Skinner proved to be every bit the person I had imagined from all that I had heard and read about: forward-thinking, kindhearted, and a true pioneer in implementing his vision for opportunity and racial equality at a time when such opportunity and equality were almost impossible for blacks to attain.

Skinner lit up like a Christmas tree when I shook his hand and he saw me in uniform. The position of master chief petty officer of the Coast Guard did not exist at the time he was in the service, but he told me he had read the news article when I was selected in 1998. He told me how good this made him feel and that it was one of his proudest moments: over fifty years later he had lived to see the real success of his efforts on board USS *Sea Cloud*. I'll have to admit, we both had watery eyes as we gazed at each other in amazement and mutual respect. Just as on the day when I met my first "Sea Daddy," I was glad to meet my "Sea Granddaddy!"

For those who have gone to sea, especially for the lucky ones like me to have had the honor and privilege of serving in uniform, we sailors have a very sentimental attachment to the ships we served on as well as the history of our service. The little-known story of *Sea Cloud* and the man who was at the forefront of integrating the American sea services during World War II is brilliantly told in this book. And it's about time—because Carlton Skinner has not received the credit he deserves for his trailblazing role in American history. Because of what he achieved on *Sea Cloud* in 1944, this black kid from the inner city of Detroit was able to become the master chief petty officer of the Coast Guard fifty-four years later. For me and so many others, Carlton Skinner made it possible to live the American Dream.

VINCENT W. PATTON III
8th Master Chief Petty Officer of
the US Coast Guard, Retired

Acknowledgments

Unlike novels, short stories, or poems, which are the singular products of an author's imagination and creativity, almost every work of nonfiction is assembled from multiple sources of information and benefits from the assistance of other people. This book is no exception. It exists in large measure because of the aid and support I received from friends and strangers alike. Those men and women include the following:

Solange Petit Skinner, who generously shared with me her memories, impressions, insights, and family photographs of her late husband. She was from the very beginning of this project an enthusiastic collaborator, a spirited interlocutor, and the lens through which I was able to see the kind of man Carlton Skinner was. I only hope that she is pleased with this portrait of him and the ship he loved so much.

Vincent W. Patton III, retired master chief petty officer of the US Coast Guard and now vice president for leadership of NewDay USA, was extremely helpful to this project. He contributed a wonderful foreword to the book with his authoritative assessment of Carlton Skinner's role in the integration of the nation's sea services, along with his first-person impressions of the man. Dr. Patton also pointed me to key sources and recommended several avenues for additional research. From his unique place in Coast Guard history, Vince served as a vital link between Skinner and the African American sailors of the past and those of today.

Julia Eble, manager of public relations at Sea Cloud Cruises GmbH, provided invaluable information about, and extensive photography of, the early history and current operations of *Sea Cloud*. As a consummate media relations practitioner, Julia was both exceedingly responsive and extraordinarily gracious in fielding my many queries and requests.

Susan Strange of StrangeArchives.com furnished much of the documentation and imagery dealing with USS *Sea Cloud*'s service in World War II. Researching at the National Archives in College Park, Maryland, and at the Coast Guard Historian's Office in Washington, DC, Susan uncovered rare photographs of the ship's crew taken by Lt. (j.g.) Joseph Charles Jenkins, the ship's navigator, and provided key extracts from *Sea Cloud*'s log books, Skinner's notebooks, and other fascinating facts, figures, and materials. I only wish that we had had the space to incorporate all of the treasures Susan found and sent my way.

Ian P. Hurley, the social media manager at Duquesne University in Pittsburgh, conducted a thorough baseline interview with Solange Skinner that became a cornerstone of the book's account of her husband's early life and postwar career. I will always be grateful to Ian for his significant contribution to the Skinner biography.

Rachel Saliba, director of institutional stewardship at Tilton School, Skinner's alma mater, was truly remarkable in her support of the project. She dug through old yearbooks and school records to help illustrate and describe the governor's teenage years at an institution for which he had much affection throughout his life.

A. D. Baker III, who edited *Combat Fleets of the World* from 1977 to 2003, is widely known for his columns, articles, and extremely precise illustrations of warships. Dave very early on encouraged me to write this book and, with no prompting at all, selflessly sent me information about *Sea Cloud*'s wartime operations. An aside: Dave steered me to a wonderfully detailed three-inch model of IX-99 as it appeared when Skinner was its captain, and that model now sits on my desk as an inspiration.

Karen Kazzi, the interlibrary loan coordinator of the Ridgefield Public Library, tracked down and put into my eager hands some rather obscure publications, including a copy of Skinner's account of Guam's transition to civilian government and an oral history he provided to the John F. Kennedy Presidential Library and Museum. Karen was not only proficient in locating and obtaining various materials that I had requested but also patient and cheerful in doing so. She is a great resource for authors and researchers in my town and beyond.

At the Hillwood Estate, Museum and Gardens, Estella Chung, curator of American material culture and historian; Elena Stuart, head of archives and special collections; Margaret Huang, archivist/librarian; Jaime McCurry, digital assets librarian; and Abby Stambach, archivist/librarian, were very helpful in supplying information and images related to Marjorie Post's ownership of *Sea Cloud*.

Neil Harvey in England enhanced some unique personal photographs he had taken of *Antarna* while it sat neglected in Panama and kindly sent them to me while seeking neither credit nor compensation. Chris Howell of Southern Shipping Services Limited in New Zealand also contributed an image of the yacht's forlorn years in the 1970s.

Anna Kleiser, a researcher in the German documentary film production company Florianfilm GmbH, furnished several leads and information about *Sea Cloud* and *Angelita*. She was a valuable pathfinder in the early stages of my own research, as was Ashley Trujillo, an archives associate at the History Miami Museum who located and offered several images of *Antarna* in Miami.

From time to time over the years Wendy S. Rehnberg, a librarian and researcher at heart, has bailed me out by exploring some of the back alleys of the World Wide Web and providing pertinent materials that I had tried but failed to find myself. And she did so again for this project by locating some excellent material.

Clark Broadbent, a retired certified professional yacht broker and photographer, is also an expert sailor and skipper of the sloop *Euphoria*. I drew from his knowledge and experience to navigate some of the specialized terminology and nomenclature of sailing, especially as it applied to a large sailing vessel like *Sea Cloud*.

Nicholas Rossi served aboard USS *Sea Cloud* as a seaman in 1943. He reached back in his memories more than seventy years to provide firsthand anecdotes and information about what it was like for enlisted men aboard the ship during World War II. I am so glad I was able to talk with him.

Obviously a volume like this one needs a publisher to nurture, improve, reproduce, and distribute an author's words. I have been very fortunate to have received the support and counsel of Jay R. Dew, director of Texas A&M University Press. His genuine enthusiasm for this project and his trust in its value have meant a great deal. I can't thank him enough for giving *Tales of Sea Cloud* a home and a harbor from which to reach you.

Luckily for me, I have had close at hand for many years a proofreader, a copy editor, a literary critic, and a multifaceted one-woman focus group. All four of these skills and capabilities reside in the person of my wife, Rose. She has been significantly involved with this book, even before I put the first proposal on paper in 2013 and right up to the day I dispatched the completed manuscript to College Station. Her sharp eyes, keen editorial judgment, and candid opinions about language, tone, and format were enormously helpful to me. Rose, who is a master multitasker, constantly amazes me and our family with what she accomplishes professionally and personally day in and day out—and with no time off for good behavior.

Tales of the *Sea Cloud*

introduction

This is the story of Sea Cloud and Skinner—one of them a ship, the other a man.

The ship—*Sea Cloud*—is a barque (or bark, if you prefer), a four-masted sailing vessel with three fully square-rigged forward masts and a fourth fore-and-aft-rigged mast at the stern. It is also sometimes called a windjammer, tall ship, motor-sailing yacht, and square-rigger. Among the many superlatives applied to the ship are luxurious, majestic, iconic, spectacular, legendary, beguiling, and incomparable. At various times since its launch in 1931, *Sea Cloud* was the largest privately owned motor-sailing yacht in the world, an oceangoing residence of the wealthiest woman in America, the extension of the US embassy in the Soviet Union, a naval weather ship in the North Atlantic, the presidential yacht of a Dominican strongman, a floating schoolhouse, a decaying virtual derelict in Panama, and now an upscale cruise ship in the Mediterranean and Caribbean.

The man—Carlton Skinner—was born in 1913, the son of college professors. During his ninety-one-year life he worked as a reporter in the nation's capital, government official in the Roosevelt and Truman administrations, Coast Guard officer and wartime ship commander, territorial governor, business executive, and US and foreign diplomat. He has been described by people who knew him as "an outstanding man with great ability," "a man of conviction, not ambition," "a man of integrity with a great sense of humor, foresight and sensitivity," and a "fighter of injustice." Skinner could also be called a social pioneer, a trailblazer, a humanitarian, a barrier-buster.

As we shall see in these pages, *Sea Cloud* and Skinner steered very different courses during the first years of their respective careers. But then, in November 1943, in the middle of World War II, their separate tracks intersected when the man reported for duty aboard the ship—he at the age of thirty, *Sea Cloud* then just twenty-two years old. They soon were to make history together (see appendix A for a chronology).

Sea Cloud in the 1930s was the embodiment of privilege, luxury, and opulence. Yet in the early 1940s it was just one of the more than 500 auxiliary vessels in Uncle Sam's navy, manned almost entirely by white officers and sailors. But less than a year after Skinner's arrival, he had successfully transformed the ship into a one-of-a-kind test-bed to demonstrate the effectiveness and benefits of staffing and operating a naval ship with a fully integrated crew of whites and blacks. It was a radical change—for the ship and for the navy. What had been originally a showboat for the ultrarich and famous was converted into a showcase of equal opportunity and racial integration in the nation's sea services.

As we look back on it now from the perspective of a country that has elected an African American as president—twice, Skinner's achievement on *Sea Cloud* hardly seems notable today. But we need to remind ourselves that just seventy-five years ago the US Navy and Coast Guard were largely segregated organizations, where Jim Crow kept black sailors apart from whites and confined African Americans to servile roles such as food-handlers and servants for white officers. Black sailors were not allowed to work in typical naval occupations, such as quartermaster, machinist, boiler tender, boatswain, electrician, signalman, gunner, or yeoman. But Skinner changed all that on *Sea Cloud*. He brought on board some African American line officers and a sizable contingent of black enlisted men. He saw to it that these men were trained in various general service specialties and opened the door for them to advance in those specialties. The black officers and sailors were fully integrated with their white comrades. All hands, regardless of color, ate, slept, and operated the ship—and fought the common enemy—together. And USS *Sea Cloud*, with its unique (for that time) racially integrated wardroom and crew, performed as well as its all-white counterparts in the Atlantic Fleet.

Carlton Skinner believed that as a matter of efficiency, common sense, and decency the United States should draw on and apply the talents, skills, and abilities of all of its citizens in uniform equally and without regard to their race. He proved on *Sea Cloud* that this approach would work. And within just a few years the navy, and ultimately the country's political leadership, agreed and mandated the full integration of the armed forces of the United States.

Of course, there is much more to the story of *Sea Cloud* and Skinner than the historic "experiment" they performed in 1944. Many significant events and developments occurred in the lives of both the barque and the man in the years before the war and in the peacetime decades after the hostilities. So, to fill in some of those holes in the record, this book also answers such questions as the following:

- How did an obscure Coast Guard lieutenant commander become "the George Washington of Guam" and what did he accomplish on that Pacific island?
- Why did an elegant yacht owned by an American heiress end up in the hands of a brutal Dominican dictator? Was the yacht really used later to smuggle his corpse out of the country?
- How did a one-time US diplomat—appointed by Presidents Kennedy and Johnson—become the honorary consul general of the Republic of Nauru in the Central Pacific?
- Why did *Sea Cloud* spend seven years as a virtual hulk in the steamy waters of Colon, Panama?
- What were all those kids doing on the ship in 1972? Were they child laborers?
- Why and how did a twenty-eight-year-old woman with a dream pursue litigation against one of the yacht's owners for more than a quarter century?
- What celebrated American artist painted some of his most famous canvases while serving during World War II as a steward's mate on USS *Sea Cloud*?
- How did a German citizen with a passion for windjammers save the yacht from probable destruction and restore it to former glory?
- What was the yacht of a US ambassador doing in Leningrad before war broke out in Europe?
- What do Marjorie Merriweather Post and Donald J. Trump have in common?

Taken as a whole, this work is the chronicle of both an extraordinary ship—*Sea Cloud*—combined with a biography of a most exceptional American—Carlton Skinner. While the core of the book is devoted to the historic role that Skinner and *Sea Cloud* played in the racial integration of the US Navy and Coast Guard, it also covers the antecedents of that singular achievement and the subsequent postbellum histories of the yacht and its wartime skipper. Clearly, each of the two principals—the ship and the man—warrant an exclusive volume for themselves. Yet I hope that this somewhat condensed and combined account of *Sea Cloud* and Carlton Skinner is worthy of the subjects it covers and that the reader will enjoy reading it as much as I enjoyed writing it.

1 From *Hussar* to *Sea Cloud*

The Yard

Human beings have been building boats for millennia, and the ancient craft of shipbuilding has become a worldwide occupational trade and global industry. Although the industry's techniques and technologies have evolved over time, the basic fundamentals remain the same. A builder lays down a keel—the ship's spine, erects longitudinal frames perpendicular to the spine, constructs interior decks and compartments, fashions and attaches steel plates to the frames, and thereby forms the ship's hull. At the same time shipyard workers install machinery, equipment, and engines within the hull and build deckhouses atop the main deck.

In recent years some builders have adopted an assembly-line approach by piecing together various modules or major subassemblies of the ship (some of which are fabricated off-site) and then carefully joining them together sequentially to form the complete vessel.

Once the ship is essentially constructed, the builder launches the vessel—sometimes sideways, other times stern first (usually after the bow is traditionally christened with a bottle of bubbly smashed across the stem), and still other times by using a wheel-on-rail transfer system to roll the ship into a dry dock or onto a platform, which is then deballasted so the ship floats out (thereby forgoing the usual slide down the shipway into the water).

By whatever technique or technology, since 1900 many thousands of maritime and naval vessels have been constructed in hundreds of shipyards around the world, primarily in North America, Asia, and Europe. One of those European yards was Friedrich Krupp Germaniawerft, a prolific builder of naval vessels, merchant ships, and yachts in the first half of the twentieth century. Located in the harbor of Kiel, Germany, the shipyard occupied more than sixty acres laid out on nearly a half mile of the waterfront. It had several large building berths, some of which could accommodate vessels more than 700 feet long, along with a number of workshops covering about nineteen acres and an iron foundry.[1]

Just before World War I, Germaniawerft employed some 4,000 workers, and during World War II the yard workforce more than doubled, to approximately 10,000 personnel, a number of whom labored there quite involuntarily. Between 1902 and 1945 the shipyard produced six battleships, two cruisers, eight destroyers, and 215 submarines for the German navy, along with additional submarines for Russia, Norway, and Austria-Hungary.[2]

But not every vessel that left the Kiel shipyard carried guns or torpedoes for the German Kaiserliche Marine or Kriegsmarine. The yard was also well regarded as a builder of large, luxurious yachts—both sail- and motor-powered. The kaiser himself, Wilhelm II, had acquired two racing yachts constructed by Germaniawerft, and several very rich Americans, including Vincent Astor, William L. Mellon, and William K. Vanderbilt II, owned splendid yachts built at the Krupp yard. But it was another American multimillionaire and his four-masted barque that figure prominently in the pages that follow.

First Owner and His Lady

It has been perhaps too frequently said that if you have to ask how much a boat costs, you can't afford it.[3] Well, Edward Francis Hutton certainly never had to ask. But if in 1930 he did happen to inquire about the cost of his next yacht, *Hussar* V, he would have been told that he would be paying about $1 million—more than $15.3 million in today's dollars.[4] He well might have replied: Fine. No problem.

Hutton was born on September 7, 1875, in New York City. He married his first wife, Blanch Horton, on October 9, 1900, and four years later he, along with his brother Franklyn Laws Hutton and Gerald M. Loeb, launched E. F. Hutton & Company, a highly successful and well-respected brokerage firm. (According to the firm's television commercials in the late 1970s, "When E. F. Hutton talks, people listen.")

Even as he and his firm were prospering, Edward Hutton suffered two grievous personal losses. His wife Blanch died from influenza in December

Edward F. Hutton was a yachtsman, stockbroker, and financier and the second husband of Marjorie Merriweather Post. (Sea Cloud Cruises GmbH)

1917, and three years later his son Halcourt was killed in an accident while riding a horse.

In 1920 Hutton married Marjorie Merriweather Post. She was born on March 15, 1887, in Springfield, Illinois, and was the daughter of Charles William Post, who owned the Postum Cereal Company. Young Marjorie had married Edward Bennett Close in 1905, and nine years later, at the age of twenty-seven, she became the owner of her father's business when he died in 1914 and left her an inheritance estimated at $25 million. Close and Post divorced in 1919, and she married Hutton the following year. Three years after that, Hutton was named chairman of the Postum Cereal Company, which grew through business acquisitions into the General Foods Corporation in 1929. Ultimately, Post was considered to be the wealthiest woman in the United States. Her personal assets have been estimated at a quarter of a billion dollars (more than $3 billion today).[5] One of her biographers wrote of Post that "she possessed a sharp mind, a beauty that increased with age, and the kind of fortune that embarrasses the most enthusiastic capitalists."[6]

After inheriting a large fortune from her father, C. W. Post, Marjorie Merriweather Post later became the owner of the largest motor-sailing yacht built for a single individual. (Sea Cloud Cruises GmbH)

The Hutton-Post wedding in 1920 thus formed a union of two people possessing high intelligence, formidable business and financial savvy, and vast wealth. In other words, Edward and Marjorie might be readily defined today as a "power couple." So it should be no surprise that such a pairing would naturally participate in the elite pastime of yachting.

In 1923, three years into the marriage, Hutton purchased a three-masted schooner he named *Hussar* IV. He had previously owned *Lady Baltimore*, his first boat, and then, in order, *Hussars* I, II, and III. The 202-foot *Hussar* IV had been designed by Cox & Stevens of New York City and built at the Burmeister & Wain yard in Copenhagen, Denmark.[7] It was a very fast boat, breaking a transatlantic crossing record of ten days and twenty-one hours. But as the couple sailed in Long Island Sound, the idea must have taken shape in their minds that, as nice as *Hussar* IV was, they wanted, needed—and probably deserved—something bigger and better, a yacht of spectacular dimension and quality that would truly impress and bedazzle their tony friends and fellow members of the prestigious New York Yacht Club.

Enter *Hussar* V

So it was that Hutton and Post retained the maritime architects of Gibbs & Cox to design what would become the largest privately owned motor-sailing yacht of its time. The firm, which was founded in 1922, later designed such notable ships as SS *United States*, the world's fastest passenger liner. (Today Gibbs & Cox is "focused on growth in emerging maritime programs in systems engineering, platform design, sustainment and life-cycle extension for both government and commercial market sectors."[8])

Gibbs & Cox was not the only designer on the project. Marjorie Post Hutton, who had been thinking hard about the future yacht's interior spaces, spent two years developing detailed plans for the staterooms, salons, galleys, and companionways. She was so dedicated to—and possibly obsessed by—this task that she directed the ship's cabins to be replicated in full scale in a rented Brooklyn warehouse.[9] That arrangement enabled her to develop the interior configuration in detail and lay out the vessel's furnishings in advance of their actual installation.

Preliminary work on the yacht was begun in 1926 by the Friedrich Krupp Germaniawerft shipyard in Kiel. The yard constructed a hull 315 feet long (with an overall length of 359 feet, the new vessel was about the same size as a contemporary navy destroyer) and a 49-foot beam. Workers installed ten watertight bulkheads and a double bottom to contain any leaks caused by ruptures in the hull. In the event of water penetration, the bulkheads could be shut and secured from the bridge by a mere push of a button. In their account of the yacht's construction, authors Kurt Grobecker and Peter Neumann noted: "To avoid reminding guests of the unpleasant possibility that such a system might have to be used in an emergency, Ed Hutton had all the bulkheads in the main hallway leading to the cabins disguised as elevator doors."[10] Deep within the hull were four six-cylinder Krupp diesel-electric engines producing 3,200hp. The engines in turn were mated to dynamos that were coupled to two 1,350 bhp electric motors. The motors turned twin nine-foot, six-inch-diameter propellers capable of moving the yacht at 14 knots.[11] (For a summary of the yacht's specifications, see appendix B.)

Newly christened as *Hussar* V, the black-hulled yacht was launched, minus its masts and rigging, from the building shed in April 1931. After it was afloat, *Hussar* was brought alongside a pier to be fitted with four masts, sails, ropes, and cables (totaling some 82,000 feet of standing and running rigging and weighing about 110 tons).[12] Its thirty sails encompassed 32,000 square feet of canvas. The steel masts stood 177 feet above the main deck—about the same height as an eleven-story building.

The ship's owners could now boast to friends that their yacht had its own repair shop, a sick bay, barbershop, schoolroom (for their daughter, Nedenia Marjorie Hutton, later known as actress Dina Merrill), electrically powered washing machine, jukebox, a unique fire detection and alarm system, leading-edge navigation equipment (including an echo sounder to indicate the depth of water beneath the keel), eight small boats (five launches for trips ashore, two lifeboats, and a sailing dinghy), enough diesel fuel (160,000 gallons) for cruising 20,000 nautical miles, and enough food (35 tons) and water (116,000 gallons) to feed all on board for a half year. Much of the food was stored in a large freeze box, a big chill box, and a separate dairy box. (The dairy box would later hold enough fresh milk to sustain some 200 men for more than two weeks.)

Marjorie Post Hutton's earlier planning work in the Brooklyn warehouse came to full fruition in the completed *Hussar* V. The shipyard's manager, Ernst Emmerich, once said of the ship's interior: "One must realize that it is a floating home in which each room reflects the lifestyle and the characteristics of the owners and their preferences in art and other cultural things."[13] Indeed, Post Hutton paid so much attention to the yacht's accoutrements—

Recently launched, *Hussar V* is floating high in the water while moored beside the Krupp shipyard in Kiel, Germany, in 1931. Notice that the yacht's deckhouse is still under construction, and the masts have not yet been stepped. (Sea Cloud Cruises GmbH)

and was so willing to pay for them—that she once laid out $10,000 just for new uniforms for the ship's crew.[14]

Hussar featured an oak-paneled dining room with an electrically operated marble fireplace, a pinewood-paneled lounge, and a smoking room for the male passengers. Paintings, objets d'art, and other decorative fixtures were liberally displayed throughout the vessel.

A spiral staircase led guests below to the bedroom cabins. Marjorie's own stateroom was furnished with cedar-lined closets containing racks for seventy-two pairs of shoes and high hanger bars to accommodate full-length fur coats. The guest staterooms were equipped with regular beds, not the usual bunks or berths found on most ships and boats, and each cabin was fitted with an electrical fireplace, carefully chosen antique furniture and personal mementos, and gold-plated water taps in the heads. The Huttons had employed a Bavarian artist to paint the bathroom floorboards to mimic

Ten walnut chairs flank a large ornate table in *Hussar*'s dining room. The two billfish mounted on the wall are said to have been caught by the Huttons' daughter, Nedenia. (Sea Cloud Cruises GmbH)

the color and structure of marble and to decorate the tiles in the heads with painted underwater scenes featuring fish and coral.

Creature comforts were not confined to the yacht's interior. Passengers could relax and catch the salt air on cushioned seating and lounge chairs back on the vessel's fantail. *Hussar* could also be conned, or driven, from this location near the stern.

Late in 1931 the virtually completed *Hussar* departed Germaniawerft for delivery to its owners. It would return to its birthplace in Germany forty-eight years later, when both the vessel and the shipyard were known by different names.

All the comforts of home await guests in their staterooms on board *Hussar* V. (Sea Cloud Cruises GmbH)

The auxiliary ship-handling position on the fantail includes an engine order telegraph (seen at left with two handles for sending port and starboard engine speed commands to the engine room), the helm for controlling the rudder and altering the vessel's direction, and a binnacle holding *Hussar*'s magnetic compass. (Sea Cloud Cruises GmbH)

The sparkling new *Hussar* slowly makes its way from the shipyard in Kiel en route to the sea and eventually Bermuda. (Sea Cloud Cruises GmbH)

Marjorie Post Hutton was so excited about her new floating palace that she had to see *Hussar* even before the yacht reached the United States. So she booked passage on the new liner SS *Monarch of Bermuda* to meet *Hussar* on that island on November 30, 1931. As she wrote in her album: "Saw ship for first time . . . She was lying in the harbor and before we could see her, we saw her great masts and yards—great kick!! She came up to all our expectations (which rarely happens)."[15]

Marjorie then spent the next ten days on *Hussar* overseeing the further installation of furnishings and arranging everything to her liking. "Loved every minute of it," she said.

The Voyages of Ed and Marjorie

Some sources report that Edward Hutton counseled his rich yachting friends not to dispose of their pricey boats during the Great Depression so they could continue to provide employment for blue-collar deckhands, riggers, mechanics, and yard workers—perhaps a nautical version of trickle-down economics. Theoretical altruism aside, clearly yachts like *Hussar* and its kin were maintained not to create jobs but to generate pleasure for their owners. And once their yacht was in hand, the power couple wasted little time in enjoying the pleasures of long-distance sailing on their sensational barque.

In January 1932, just a month after Marjorie Post Hutton first stepped on board in Bermuda, *Hussar* set out on a 11,680-mile, forty-two-day cruise in the Caribbean Sea and then on to the Pacific Ocean and back. Beginning in Bermuda, the voyage took the Huttons to Cuba, Jamaica, the Galapagos Islands—560 miles off the coast of Ecuador ("one of the best trips," according to daughter Dina Hutton[16]), across the Equator on February 11, then on to Panama, and back to Cuba and Bermuda. Barely stopping there, they set out again for Martinique, Grenada, Curacao, and finally back to Cuba and Bermuda.

Eight-year-old Dina Hutton poses with her mother along with a giant 150-year-old tortoise acquired during the Galapagos visit. The tortoise was later donated to a zoo in Hawaii. (Sea Cloud Cruises GmbH)

If *Hussar* was a ship fit for a king, it was only a matter of time until a monarch or two came aboard for some royal treatment. In 1933 King Gustav V of Sweden was a guest for a cruise from Saro, his summer residence on the coast a few miles south of Gothenburg, to the North Sea and on to London, England. That same year *Hussar* was visited in Oslo by King Haakon VII and Queen Maud of Norway. So impressed by the yacht was the Norwegian queen that she is reported to have exclaimed to Marjorie Hutton, "Why, you live like a queen!"[17]

Hussar arrived in Miami in February 1934 following a visit to the builder's shipyard in Germany. Accordingly, as it was legally reentering the United States, the owners now owed the government $95,000 in import duties, one of the highest such tabs ever accrued by a yacht. Edward Hutton's secretary, J. G. Cunningham, said at the time: "Mr. Hutton . . . in a few years expects to present the *Hussar* to the U.S. Naval Academy so that our naval officers will have the finest training ship in the world."[18] Was this statement a suggestion of Hutton's patriotism or an indication that the yacht was becoming too expensive to own and might have to be taken off his books as a donation for tax purposes? Either way, Cunningham's comment turned out to be a somewhat prescient observation, given what happened to *Hussar* a decade later. Speculation aside, in 1934 Edward Hutton formally registered *Hussar V* in the government's directory, *Merchant Vessels of the United States*, listing his home address as 250 Park Avenue in New York City.[19]

In March 1934 *Hussar* visited Tahiti and Hawaii, after which the Huttons brought their yacht to San Pedro near Los Angeles to be dry-docked for preparations for an upcoming trip north to Alaska. The proximity to Tinseltown gave Marjorie Hutton the opportunity to entertain some Hollywood notables on board. Edward Hutton (sans spouse) and his male guests then sailed up to Juneau, Alaska, on a bear-hunting trip.

Not all of *Hussar*'s travels were to exotic destinations like Tahiti and Alaska. It could also be found in "home waters" off Long Island while the Huttons entertained executives from General Foods and other wealthy friends and associates. Some of these local cruises posed certain logistical difficulties, as when the yacht was to pick up guests on the island's north shore. On those occasions, *Hussar* first had to take a roundabout track from New York City 120 miles east in the Atlantic Ocean along Long Island's south shore out to Montauk. Then, after passing the island's south fork, it reversed direction to come back another 100 or so miles west through Long Island Sound. That circuitous 220-mile run was forced on the captain because *Hus-*

sar's masts towered 200 feet above the water and were thus too high to clear the three bridges spanning the East River. A decapitated mast could ruin the whole day.

By the summer of 1935 the glorious days of Edward and Marjorie together entertaining the rich and famous were coming to an end. The power couple was having serious marital problems. They had separated, and in August they decided to divorce. On September 7, 1935, Supreme Court Justice George H. Furman granted an interlocutory decree of divorce to Marjorie Post Hutton.[20] One day later, Edward Hutton passed legal title to *Hussar* to his former wife. She subsequently expressed her new status and identity by giving *her* boat a new name: *Sea Cloud*.

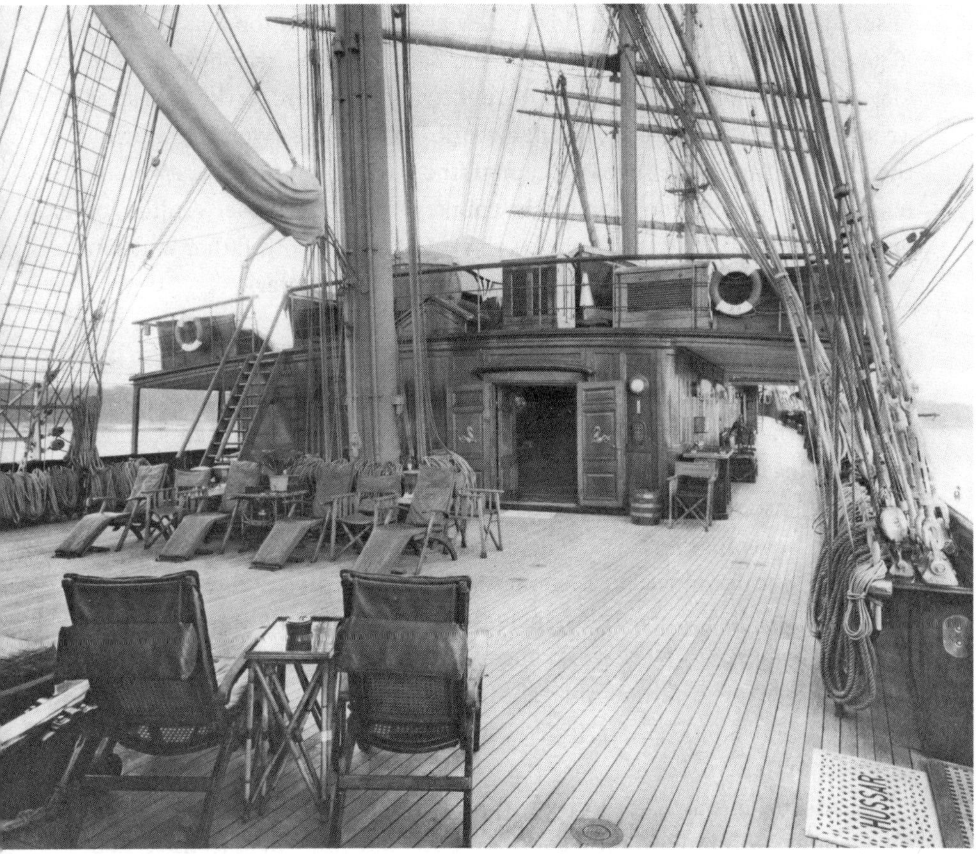

Ample lounge chairs on *Hussar*'s fantail await guests in this view looking forward along the yacht's starboard side. (Sea Cloud Cruises GmbH)

The Ambassador and *Sea Cloud*

Marjorie Post Hutton did not remain unmarried for long. She wed her third husband, Joseph Edward Davies, on December 15, 1935, just three months after her divorce from Edward Hutton.[21]

Joseph Davies was born in Watertown, Wisconsin, on November 29, 1876. He had been a successful attorney, the first chairman of the Federal Trade Commission (in 1915–16), economic advisor to President Woodrow Wilson at the Paris Peace Conference following World War I, active in Democratic politics, and a friend and ally of Franklin D. Roosevelt. Joseph Davies had met Marjorie Post at some point while the two were passengers on a liner crossing the Atlantic, and they had become close friends.

The newlyweds decided to spend their honeymoon—where else?—on a leisurely cruise on board *Sea Cloud*. They arrived in Miami on January 15, 1936, following a short hop from Nassau, Bahamas. The very next day *Sea Cloud* departed for the Dominican Republic, arriving there on the 20th after a rough transit ("bobbing around like a cork," in Marjorie's words[22]). During their stay in Santo Domingo, the capital, the Davieses attended a ceremony marking the formal adoption by the country's dictator, Rafael Trujillo, of one of his illegitimate sons—eleven-year-old Ramfis. Both father and son would play key roles in *Sea Cloud*'s history twenty years later.

Sometime after their honeymoon, Joseph asked Marjorie to lease the yacht to him for $1.00 a year (that same dollar amount will also figure in *Sea Cloud*'s future). According to Marjorie's biographer, William Wright, Joseph requested the transaction so he could tell people that *Sea Cloud* was *his* yacht.[23] (Regardless of any special "ownership" arrangement between the spouses, Marjorie Post Davies legally registered the boat in her own name as owner on November 7, 1936, listing the vessel's call sign as WCEQ.[24])

By then, she had moved to Washington, DC, a move that reflected her new husband's political connections, including his friendship with FDR, which gave Marjorie access to the world of government and to people of influence and power. But even without that, she had been doing quite well on her own accord. On April 8, 1936, Marjorie Post Davies was elected to the board of directors of General Foods.

The following month *Sea Cloud* made another visit to the Dominican Republic, this time with only Joseph Davies and some businessmen and lawyers as passengers because Marjorie was under the weather and unable to travel. Also that spring the yacht ferried a Davies daughter (he had three children from his first marriage to Mary Emlen Knight, which ended in divorce in 1935) and several of her friends to Bermuda. Neither father nor stepmother were on board.

Sea Cloud's operations solely as pleasure boat—albeit one of the largest and most luxurious of the time—were to be suspended for a few years by the US government. On November 16, 1936, the Department of State, no doubt at the instigation and approval of FDR, appointed Joseph Davies as "Ambassador Extraordinary and Plenipotentiary" to the Union of Soviet Socialist Republics. The new ambassador and his wife departed for Moscow shortly after the appointment, and he presented his credentials to Joseph Stalin's government on January 25, 1937. As *Sea Cloud* was in a shipyard undergoing some repair and refurbishment at the time, it did not catch up to its owners until a few months later.

After it had cruised up Russia's Neva River and arrived in Leningrad (present-day St. Petersburg) on July 6, 1937, the yacht became, in essence, a US diplomatic outpost as an adjunct to the US ambassador's residence in Spasso House in Moscow. High-ranking Soviet officials, including Vyacheslav Mikhailovich Molotov, Stalin's wartime minister of foreign affairs, and Maxim Maximovich Litvinov, commissar for foreign affairs and later Soviet ambassador to the United States, were among the dignitaries entertained on board.

Sea Cloud did not sit idly at the pier in Leningrad harbor. It got underway from time to time on outings along the seventy-six-mile river and beyond into the Baltic Sea to such ports as Kronstadt, Riga, and Danzig. In July 1937 *Sea Cloud* sailed to Sweden (during which voyage Marjorie Davies visited with King Gustav V for a second time) and then to Denmark and back again.

Joseph Davies later said of *Sea Cloud*'s diplomatic role: "We . . . sailed her around [Europe] entertaining diplomats, discussing matters, chinning on the afterdeck. It afforded the best kind of opportunity for getting real confidences from one's diplomatic associates."[25]

In March 1938 *Sea Cloud* changed colors—the hull was repainted all white. After losing its original black covering, the yacht stood out even more as a spectacular square-rigger. Joseph and Marjorie Davies left Moscow on May 15 for a three-week inspection tour of southern Russia, including Novorossiisk and Batum on the Black Sea as well as Rostoff on the Don. *Sea Cloud*, according to a press report, proceeded to the Black Sea ahead of them for a planned rendezvous with the couple at Odessa "to facilitate their reaching Black Sea ports and to constitute their base while they are traveling by

Marjorie and Joseph Davies on board *Sea Cloud* in 1948. (Coast Guard Historian's Office)

Dina Hutton's drawing room. She spent some time on *Sea Cloud* during its sojourn in the Soviet Union. (Sea Cloud Cruises GmbH)

land."[26] The yacht made its last cruise in Soviet waters in June with a voyage from Odessa to Istanbul, Turkey. The ambassador had wanted to take *Sea Cloud* from Monte Carlo into the Black Sea that summer, but the US Navy nixed the idea because of concerns over possible German U-boat activity.

Joseph Davies got another job the next year. On March 14, 1938, he was appointed "Envoy Extraordinary and Minister Plenipotentiary" to both Belgium and Luxembourg. He departed his post in Moscow on June 11 and presented his credentials to King Leopold III in Brussels the following month.

In his new assignment the ambassador hosted Queen Elizabeth, the mother of King Leopold, on board *Sea Cloud*. But with the threat of a European war growing daily, Joseph sent his wife and her daughter back to the United States in October 1938. Once home, Marjorie again registered *Sea*

Cloud on the official listing of US merchant vessels and gave the address of record as 815 15th Street in Washington, DC. Joseph Davies followed her back to the nation's capital when he left his ambassadorial post in Brussels on November 30, 1939 to become special assistant to Secretary of State Cordell Hull for "war emergency problems and policies." World War II had begun just three months earlier, and that global conflict would have major consequences for *Sea Cloud* and for a man named Skinner.

▪ ▪ ▪ ▪

During the decade of the 1930s, *Sea Cloud* had established itself as one of the world's premier motor-sailing vessels and luxury yachts. Although far outclassed in size and cost by the megayachts of the twenty-first century, *Sea Cloud* in its day could be considered as the gold standard for boats owned by the superrich.

In just its first nine years, the vessel

- Had been built for, and sailed by, one of the most successful and wealthy financiers in America.
- Was later owned by the heiress to a cereal fortune and probably the most affluent woman in the country.
- Served as a de facto floating annex of the US embassy in Soviet Russia during Stalin's regime.
- Sailed and motored many thousands of miles in the Atlantic and Pacific, in the Caribbean and Baltic seas, and to such distant ports as the Galapagos, Juneau, Tahiti, Leningrad, and Istanbul.
- Hosted royalty—both actual monarchs and the kings and princes of business, industry, and the arts.
- And now was about to go to war with the country that had built it.

At the same time, the young man who would later play a historic role in the nation's armed forces as *Sea Cloud*'s captain had been working as a journalist and as a minor official in the Roosevelt administration. The path he took to eventually command that vessel and then change the US sea services forever is laid down in chapter 2.

2 Young Mister Skinner

Origins and Beginnings

It was fitting and fated that the very first moments of Carlton Skinner's life began at a college. His father, Macy Millmore Skinner, was an associate professor in the German Department of Stanford University, on whose campus Carlton was born on April 8, 1913.

Macy Skinner had graduated from Harvard University at the age of twenty-three in 1894 with an AB (bachelor of arts) degree, earned an AM (master of arts) a year later, and received a PhD in Semitic languages and literature in 1897. He then studied in Germany for two years and joined the Stanford faculty in Palo Alto, California, in 1905.[1] Professor Skinner later taught German and Chinese at the University of Washington, where he was a department head, and educated students in business administration at Ling Nam University in Canton, China. He wrote in 1944 that his "profoundest pleasure has been my contacts with eager minds of young men who want to go out into the great world to implement the gospel of international intercourse and amity through the exchange of material goods and services."[2] His son, Carlton, would one day be such a person. Professor Skinner died in February 1964.

Carlton's mother, Marian Weymouth Junkins Skinner, was born in July 1880 and earned an AB degree in education from Radcliffe College in 1903 and an MA degree from Columbia University in 1923. She married Macy Skinner on September 19, 1903, and later was a professor of English and dean of women at the University of Dubuque.[3] In 1927 she founded Weylister Secretarial College in Milford, Connecticut, and during World War II was advisor to the human resources director of the Chance-Vought Aircraft Corporation in neighboring Bridgeport, Connecticut. Her second marriage was to George Wilson Beach in 1933; she died in April 1966.[4]

As the third child in a family of very bright people, young Carlton had some rather large footsteps to follow as he grew up. Not only his parents but also his siblings were impressive achievers in their academic and professional lives.

Carlton's older brother, Selby Millmore Skinner, was eight years old when Carlton was born. He earned a doctorate at the California Institute of Technology in 1933, served six years on active duty during World War II, was a research analyst for the US government, and held professorships at several universities. Selby was a member of the US Atomic Energy Commission and was expert in both physics and chemistry. As manager of corporate molecular electronics programs at Westinghouse's Defense and Space Center, he helped in the development of night-vision capabilities for US pilots during the Vietnam War. Selby Skinner died in 2002 at the age of ninety-six.[5]

The middle child was Barbara Reid Skinner, born in 1907, two years after Selby. She became private secretary to Lowell Mellett, a former journalist who was appointed by President Franklin D. Roosevelt to head the Office of Government Reports. Barbara later served as chief of archives and then acting secretary-general to the US military tribunals in Nuremberg, Germany. In 1950 she was appointed special representative to the US High Commissioner for Germany. The wife of Max Mandellaub, Barbara died in April 1953 in Frankfurt, Germany.[6]

When Carlton Skinner was just a year old, his father left the family at home to go to China as an educator for two years. Carlton's parents divorced in 1920, and his father returned to China in 1921 for another two years, taking his teenage son Selby with him.

As a consequence, Carlton lived most of his early years without a father and was shaped almost entirely by his mother's nurturing and influence. Marian Skinner, who was a native of Lawrence, Massachusetts (where her father, George Selby Junkins, served as mayor in 1896–97), moved from California to the Boston area, where she was a director of the Katherine Gibbs School during the mid-1920s.

Once back in the Bay State, she often took Carlton on visits to Marblehead, a coastal town of some 7,500 inhabitants at the time. Marblehead, sixteen miles northeast of Boston, has a strong heritage of fishing and boating. It is considered the birthplace of the US Navy and the home of numerous yacht clubs, including the Pleon Yacht Club, the oldest junior yacht club in the nation. Inevitably, young Carlton took in the salt air and nautical atmosphere of Marblehead, embraced it, and began a lifelong love affair with the sea. His bonding with the town was so strong that many decades later, long after he had lived on the West Coast and on faraway Guam, he ultimately returned to Marblehead—as a resident—very late in his life.[7] And it is possible that the future skipper of USS *Sea Cloud* acquired his first sea legs while sailing as a young man in the waters off Marblehead's rocky peninsula (Skinner had acquired his own sailboat at the age of seventeen).

With the love of boating expressed on his face, Carlton Skinner steers a small craft in foul weather. Note the navigation chart next to his right leg. Skinner would later serve as the navigator of a Coast Guard cutter in Arctic waters during World War II. (Solange P. Skinner)

Marian Skinner also fostered her youngest son's appreciation of literature and art by taking him often to the Boston Public Library—the second largest public library in the country—and to the city's Museum of Fine Arts (MFA). The library shelved millions of volumes within its walls in Copley Square, giving Carlton ready access to fascinating stories of sea adventures and naval history and to books about people, places, and events far from home. The MFA on Huntington Avenue contained hundreds of thousands of paintings, including Gilbert Stuart's famous 1796 portrait of George Washington, along with sculptures and works of art from China and Japan. Thanks to those experiences at a very early age, Carlton Skinner acquired from his mother, and then further developed, a lifelong passion for reading and art along with a devotion to learning—for himself and others.

In this undated photo, mother and son pose for the camera, probably in Milford, Connecticut. (Solange P. Skinner)

School Days

Skinner's formal education began in earnest in Tilton, New Hampshire, at Tilton School, which was founded in 1845 as a coeducational secondary school for about seventy-six boys and girls. Skinner was a student there as a teenager between 1926 and 1930. According to its mission statement, Tilton "cultivates in its students the curiosity, the skills, the knowledge and the understanding, the character and the integrity requisite for . . . personal success and service."[8]

In later life Skinner was very enthusiastic about his experiences at Tilton. He benefited from them so much that he and his wife established the Skinner Fellowship at the school to "provide financial assistance to a student or students who exhibit a consistent sense of personal integrity, loyalty, curiosity and who have demonstrated a commitment to fight injustice in all its forms,"[9] attributes that were manifested throughout Skinner's life. Moreover, the enthusiasm was mutual. In 1984 the school presented Skinner with its alumnus-of-the-year award—the Plimpton Award—for his service to the community and his outstanding contributions to society.

After graduating from Tilton in 1930, Skinner began his college studies about 180 miles down the road at Wesleyan University in Middletown, Connecticut. The school had been founded in 1831 by Methodists and Middletown residents. Despite its relationship to the Methodist church, Wesleyan offered its students a secular liberal arts program with an emphasis on social

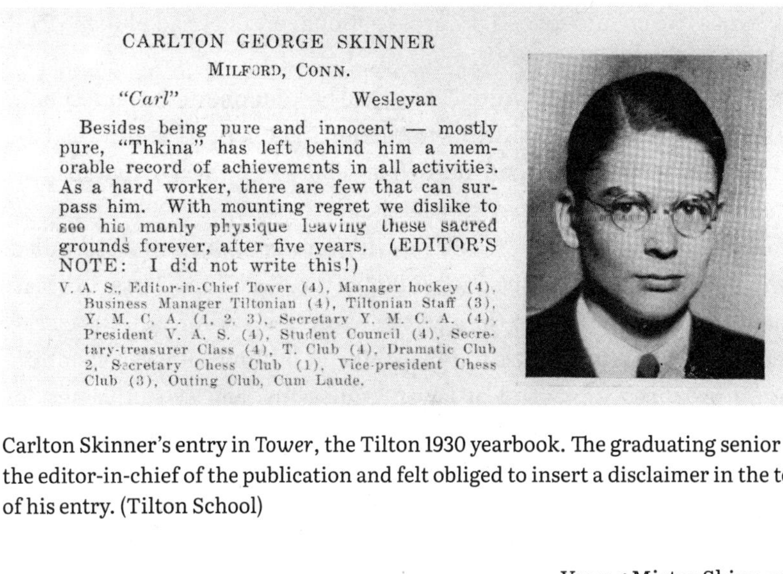

CARLTON GEORGE SKINNER

MILFORD, CONN.

"Carl" Wesleyan

Besides being pure and innocent — mostly pure, "Thkina" has left behind him a memorable record of achievements in all activities. As a hard worker, there are few that can surpass him. With mounting regret we dislike to see his manly physique leaving these sacred grounds forever, after five years. (EDITOR'S NOTE: I did not write this!)

V. A. S., Editor-in-Chief Tower (4), Manager hockey (4), Business Manager Tiltonian (4), Tiltonian Staff (3), Y. M. C. A. (1, 2, 3), Secretary Y. M. C. A. (4), President V. A. S. (4), Student Council (4), Secretary-treasurer Class (4), T. Club (4), Dramatic Club 2, Secretary Chess Club (1), Vice-president Chess Club (3), Outing Club, Cum Laude.

Carlton Skinner's entry in *Tower*, the Tilton 1930 yearbook. The graduating senior was the editor-in-chief of the publication and felt obliged to insert a disclaimer in the text of his entry. (Tilton School)

service—a natural fit for Skinner and his growing interest in political science.[10]

In 1931 Skinner opted to continue his education, not in Middletown but in Los Angeles, where he attended the University of California over the next three years. UCLA defines itself as a public research university for the "creation, dissemination, preservation and application of knowledge for the betterment of our global society," a mission that would have appealed to Skinner and reinforced what he had learned at Tilton and Wesleyan.[11] While at UCLA Skinner was a member of the Delta Upsilon fraternity, whose four founding principles are "the advancement of justice, the promotion of friendship, the development of character, and the diffusion of liberal culture."[12] Skinner completed his studies at UCLA in 1934 when he received an AB degree in finance.

Reporting from Washington

With his newly minted degree in hand, the UCLA grad embarked on the start of his professional life. He was going to be a journalist, he decided, and he would begin his career in Washington, DC, as a rookie reporter for the United Press.

Skinner was lucky to get the job. The Great Depression in the early 1930s had produced massive unemployment and financial crises. For example, some college graduates with bachelor degrees were working as elevator operators in department stores; investors had lost $74 billion; more than 5,000 banks had collapsed; and the gross national product had plunged from $104 billion to $41 billion.[13]

Skinner's first employer, United Press, had become one of the largest news wire services on the planet since its formation in 1907. At its zenith UP (later United Press International) had more than 6,000 subscribers in newspapers, magazines, and radio and television stations.

Working as a "Unipresser," as UP's wire service reporters were called, Skinner had to beat the competition (notably the Associated Press) to breaking news and quickly zip it to the agency's subscribers before anyone else.

And there was a lot of news to report. The Franklin D. Roosevelt administration produced a blizzard of laws, regulations, and executive actions right out of the gate. FDR had told his New Deal team to move quickly to try anything and everything that could get the country back on its feet. He had a mandate for change from the voters and was determined to get things done—*now*! Skinner covered for UP all of the major federal departments, as well as the Congress, in the nation's capital from 1934 to 1936. That gave him a front-row seat as both an observer and chronicler of Roosevelt's first term.

In 1936 Skinner left UP and went to work for the *Wall Street Journal*, also in Washington. His beat for the paper included the Supreme Court, which during the 1930s was hearing many cases affecting New Deal organizations and regulations, including the Agricultural Adjustment Administration, the National Recovery Administration, the National Labor Relations Act, and the Wagner Act.

Government Flack

After two years with the *Journal*, in 1938 Skinner figuratively walked across the street and joined the government he had been covering as a reporter. No longer peering in from the outside, he was now going to be on the inside looking—and reaching—out.

First stop: the US Department of Labor. This cabinet department had been established by President Woodrow Wilson in 1913, the year of Skinner's birth, "to foster, promote and develop the welfare of working people, to improve their working conditions, and to enhance their opportunities for profitable employment."[14] When Skinner came aboard in 1938 the secretary of labor was Frances Perkins, who had been appointed by FDR five years earlier as the first female cabinet member. (She held that office for twelve years, making her the longest-serving secretary of labor.)

Skinner's box on the organization chart was labeled "assistant director of information" in Labor's newly formed Wage and Hour Division, which was the enforcer of federal labor laws required by the Fair Labor Standards Act of 1938. As part of his duties, Skinner helped to inform Americans about the department's activities and programs, respond to press inquiries (some probably from former colleagues at UP and the *Wall Street Journal*) and support various other public relations activities.

In 1939 Skinner moved over to the United States Maritime Commission, created three years before by the Merchant Marine Act as an independent executive agency of the federal government.[15] The commission had several missions in the late 1930s. It was overseeing an effort to construct 500 new merchant ships over a ten-year period to replace antiquated vessels dating from World War I, administering a subsidy system, and forming a service for the training of future merchant marine officers and seamen. The first head of the commission had been Joseph P. Kennedy, John F. Kennedy's father and later US ambassador to Great Britain. His successor and the person to whom Skinner ultimately reported was retired navy rear admiral Emory S. Land. In his first assignment at the commission, and much as he did at the Labor Department, Skinner served as assistant director of information in 1939 and 1940. Later in 1940 he was bumped up to acting director of the Maritime Commission's Division of Promotion and Information, in which post he served until 1941.

From Civvies to Uniforms

Even before the United States formally entered World War II in December 1941, Carlton Skinner had been very concerned about Axis aggression in Europe and Asia. "I wished eagerly to be active in the war against fascism," he said, "active in a military service in combat or potential combat. As such, I applied for a commission in the Coast Guard Reserve as soon as it was authorized as a military reserve force."[16]

That organization had been established by the Coast Guard Reserve and Auxiliary Act of February 19, 1941. Skinner favored the Coast Guard over the navy because he knew that the navy did not send officers with eyeglasses to sea and, as his prior boating experience and personal preferences pointed him toward sea duty, the Coast Guard Reserve was his best option. Accordingly, he organized training for fellow members of the Capital Yacht Club to prepare for service in the Coast Guard. Within a few months, Skinner took the required Coast Guard examinations and was commissioned into the USCGR as a lieutenant (junior grade) on June 17, 1941. A month later he was ordered into active service and reported for duty on board USS *Northland* (WPG-49) on July 7.[17]

The Coast Guard cutter *Northland* had been built at a cost of $865,730 by the Newport News Shipbuilding and Drydock Corporation in Newport News, Virginia. It was launched on February 5, 1927, and commissioned three months later on May 7. It was 216 feet, 7 inches long, with a beam of 38 feet, 9 inches, a draft of 16 feet, 9 inches, and a maximum displacement of 2,150 tons.

Originally configured with masts and outfitted with auxiliary sails, the cutter had those removed five years before Skinner joined the ship. *Northland* was powered by one double-armature electric motor driven by two gen-

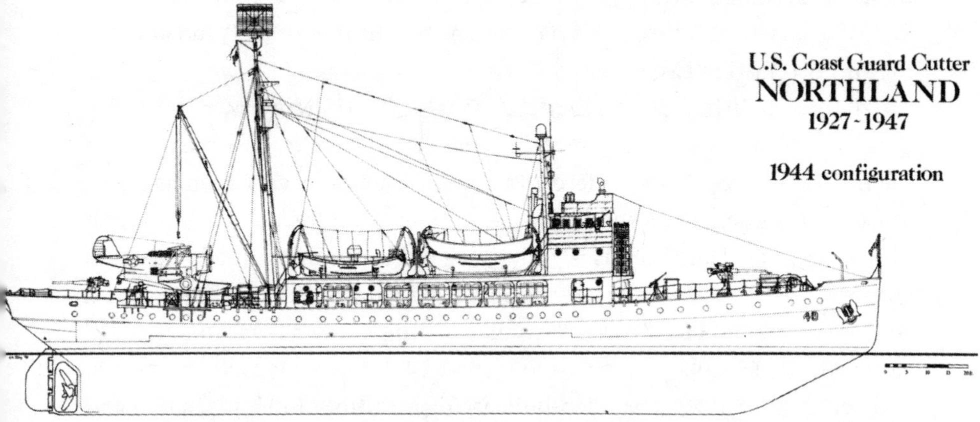

This line drawing of the cutter *Northland* shows the ship's two 3-inch guns on the bow and fantail, with its J2F-5 float plane just aft of the main mast ready to be hoisted into the water. (Coast Guard Historian's Office)

erators, which were in turn driven by two six-cylinder diesels. It was capable of a maximum speed of 11.7 knots and could cruise 12,000 miles at 10 knots and 18,000 miles at 8.2 knots.

During the 1930s, *Northland* had been based in homeports on the West Coast. As it had been built with a reinforced bow for operating in ice-filled Arctic waters, its main mission was to patrol in the Bering Sea between Alaska and Russia. Finishing up that assignment in 1938, *Northland* was decommissioned but brought back into service in June 1939 and sent to Boston to be prepared for an Antarctic expedition by Rear Admiral Richard E. Byrd of the US Navy. But events in Europe changed those plans.

On May 3, 1940, three weeks after the German army occupied Denmark, the local government of Greenland requested the protection of the United States. The Germans were already reported to have weather-reporting stations on Greenland's east coast, and they potentially threatened a cryolite mine at Ivigtut on the west coast that held a vital mineral component of aluminum. As a result, Rear Admiral Russell R. Waesche, the US Coast Guard commandant, quickly ordered some of his units and personnel to Greenland.[18]

Pulled out of the Antarctic mission, *Northland* instead entered the New York Navy Yard in Brooklyn in May 1940 to be readied for special assignments in Greenland. Along with the cutter *Duane* (WPG-33), *Northland* conducted a survey of Greenland's harbors in the summer of 1940 and another in April 1941 lasting two months.

On April 18, 1941, Admiral Ernest J. King of the US Navy, commander in chief of the Atlantic Fleet, issued his Operation Plan No. 3, which in part formed Task Force 11, and ordered it to "enter the Northeast Greenland area as early in the season as conditions permit, and . . . Prevent establishment of military, naval and air bases, or landing of European nationals except as authorized by the Governor of Greenland."[19] TF 11 was led by Cmdr. Edward Hanson ("Iceberg") Smith, USCG, and was composed of *Northland*, USCGC *North Star* (WPG-59), a ten-year-old former US Interior Department vessel, and USS *Bear* (AG-29), a wooden-hull auxiliary sailing ship built in 1874 and used by Admiral Byrd for his South Pole expedition in 1933–35.

The following month, the Northeast Greenland Patrol, in which *Northland* operated, was consolidated with the South Greenland Patrol, both now under the leadership of Smith, who designated *Northland* as his flagship for the combined unit. The seven ships performing those patrols operated some 2,000 to 3,000 miles from their homeports in seas over a mile deep—thereby nullifying the sobriquet sometimes applied to coast guardsmen as "shallow-water sailors."

Skinner began his duty on board the cutter in July 1941, initially serving as a watch officer, later as navigator (from January 1942 to December 1942), and ultimately as executive officer (from June 1942 to January 1943). In 1941 the ship's complement was approximately eighteen officers and 100 enlisted men; the commanding officer was Lt. Cmdr. Carl C. von Paulsen. *Northland* carried one Grumman J2F-5 Duck float plane and was armed with two 3-inch/50 single mounts. The Duck amphibious biplane was equipped with a centerline float or pontoon on the underside of the fuselage, with wheels that were retracted into the float, thus giving the J2F the ability to land on and take off from either water or land.[20]

As *Northland*'s navigator, Skinner would later describe the unique challenges he and the ship's quartermasters faced in safely piloting the cutter on the ten-month-long Arctic patrols:

> In the summer, there are no stars for star sights. In the winter he [the navigator] gets his morning star sights after breakfast and his evening star sights in the afternoon watch. What a wonderful opportunity for sack drill! . . . Small flies immerse themselves in the [navigating] equipment.

There are no lighthouses, buoys or radio beacons. The coastline has a deadly uniformity of variety—all peaks and fjords that look like they were turned out by machine for a Disney extravaganza.[21]

Skinner did not have accurate charts (navigational maps) to fix the ship's position and plot its course. He noted that *Northland*'s charts were labeled with this note: "This chart is from incomplete surveys and should be used with caution." As he put it, the warning meant "just that. Islands are likely to be ten miles out of place, if they are there at all. Harbors have never been surveyed. Some of them have never been used before. Then there is ice."[22]

Northland operated in waters so abundant with ice—icebergs, floebergs (a mass of hummocky floe ice resembling an iceberg), and growlers (very small chunks of floating ice that rise only about three feet out of the water)—that, in Skinner's humorous words, "you develop a fondness for *warm* Scotch and soda."[23]

Captain von Paulsen tested various techniques for breaking up ice. Sometimes he would have *Northland* ram the frozen surface in the fjords at various speeds or have the ship ride up on top of the ice so that the cutter's weight would smash it from above. He used small charges of TNT to free his vessel when it sometimes got stuck, and on at least one occasion von Paulsen ordered his crew to run from one side of the vessel to the other so as to rock the cutter and free it from the ice's grip. The results of these various tests were documented in a memorandum, which, Skinner said, was "later used by the naval architect William Francis Gibbs to design the *Wind*-class ice breakers used by the Navy and Coast Guard."[24]

Aside from the absence of reliable navigation aids and the presence of damaging ice, the cutter also had to contend with fog that often obscured the horizon. And then there were encounters with the "natives." One day a polar bear on an iceberg came aboard for an uninvited visit (and perhaps a meal) but was chased off the ship without harm to either the animal or the crew.

In early September 1941 *Northland* was informed in a message that British intelligence had discovered that Germany had deployed a trawler from Norway to establish a four-man weather station in Greenland to provide meteorological data and intelligence on Allied shipping in the Arctic Ocean. On September 12 *Northland* lookouts spotted the Norwegian sealer *Buskoe* off Greenland's east coast. The cutter sounded general quarters, came alongside *Buskoe*, and sent crewmen to board the vessel. A Coast Guard "prize crew" brought *Buskoe* into Mackenzie Bay, near Myggbukta, whereupon Captain Smith then officially seized the ship and its twenty-seven crewmembers, including one woman, for violating Greenland's territorial waters.

Skinner, using his schoolboy German (his father, Professor Skinner, would have been proud), questioned the prisoners and learned that the Germans were using a radio station about 500 miles north of Myggbukta. Captain von Paulsen ordered Skinner and Lt. Leroy McCluskey to take a landing party of twelve men ashore to capture the radio station and its operators. The Coasties—armed with six machine guns, six rifles, and the officers' two .45 pistols—set off at 0200 (2: 00 a.m.) in a motor surf boat. After they quietly sneaked up on the station and surrounded a small shack, Skinner knocked on the door and was surprised to be greeted by four very sleepy enemy combatants attired only in their long johns. Needless to say, the Germans promptly and prudently surrendered. The Coast Guard raiders discovered that radio station held transmitting equipment and cryptographic materials as well as plans for other German radio stations in the area. Before being brought back to the ship, the prisoners were put to work dismantling the station and its equipment, and its structures were burned to the ground. For this "action," *Northland*'s officers and men were authorized to fix the letter A on their American Defense Service Medals to indicate that they had "served in actual or potential belligerent contact with Axis Powers in the Atlantic Ocean between June 22 and December 7, 1941."[25]

Lt. (j.g.) Carlton Skinner was promoted to full lieutenant on June 15, 1942. Three days later *Northland* made an underwater contact on a bearing of 265 degrees at a range of 2,300 yards in the Davis Strait between the southwestern coast of Greenland and Nunavut, Canada's Baffin Island. It initiated an attack on the submerged submarine by dropping five 300-pound depth charges. Oil and bubbles were sighted on the surface, which indicated the possible damage or destruction of the U-boat. German records, however, do not indicate the loss of a submarine on that date or anywhere near that location.[26] But Skinner would get another chance to kill a U-boat two years later on *Sea Cloud*.

Skinner, a former editor and news reporter, once lightheartedly scribbled in a notebook some lines of poetry to characterize his ship's experiences off Greenland. In one entry he began:

In Davis Straits the Northland rolls
And stumbles in all the watering holes.

And all we seek is a lonely scow
A hulking, helpless old sea cow.
With a rudder full of engine juice
That never should have been let loose.[27]

Happily, this work was never submitted for the prestigious annual award of the Poetry Society of America. Had it been, its author doubtless would have been advised to stick to his day job.

In the late summer of 1942 "Iceberg" Smith was made commander of the navy's Task Force 24 (see chap. 5), and *Northland*'s captain, Carl von Paulsen, relieved him as the commander of the Greenland Patrol. The ship's executive officer, Lt. Cmdr. Francis C. Pollard, was bumped up to became the new commanding officer, and Skinner succeeded Pollard as XO.[28]

In late November 1942 *Northland* was ordered to proceed at full speed to rescue the badly injured crew of a Boeing B-17 Flying Fortress bomber that had crashed on a Greenland ice cap two weeks before. As the cutter raced to reach the airmen, the ship's Duck pilot, Lt. John A. Pritchard, suggested to Captain Pollard that he could get to the scene faster by flying his J2F-5 to the wreck site in advance of the ship's arrival. Accordingly, the Duck was hoisted in the water, and Pritchard took off to search for the survivors. He was able to locate the wreckage, land on ice four miles away, retrieve two of the three survivors, and bring them back to *Northland*. Tragically, on a second flight to the scene, Pritchard, his radioman, Benjamin A. Bottoms, and the final B-17 survivor vanished in a snowstorm on their way back to the ship and were lost.[29]

▪ ▪ ▪ ▪

The first twenty-nine years of Carlton Skinner's life had seen him evolve from being the youngest child of a largely absent father—but very caring and nurturing mother—to achieving academic success at a progressive New England prep school and two esteemed universities, then experiencing four years of intense, eyewitness-news reporting of FDR's New Deal and another four years as a public information official in two federal agencies, and finally serving as an accomplished Coast Guard officer in World War II.

By this time in his life, 1942, Skinner's personal trajectory was but months away from intersecting the course of *Sea Cloud*. The two were drawing ever closer to a fateful rendezvous. But first there was to take place on *Northland* an incident that changed Skinner's life, a catalytic and profound event that so influenced and inspired him that by the time he arrived on *Sea Cloud* in 1943, he and that ship would soon help to change the culture and policies of America's sea services and thereby make history together.

But before accounting for why and how that happened, it is useful to briefly review the role of African American and other minority men and women in the US Navy and Coast Guard in the century or more leading up to World War II—the subject of the next chapter.

3 Annals of the Black Blue Jackets

"The arc of the moral universe is long, but it bends towards justice," said Martin Luther King Jr. in Montgomery, Alabama, on March 25, 1965.

That may be—and we trust that it is—but when viewed in terms of achieving complete racial integration, full equal opportunity, and genuine justice in the nation's sea services, that arc has not bent in an even and continuous line. Not by a long shot. In the 170 years separating the American Revolution from the victory over the Axis powers in 1945, blacks and other racial minorities in the US Navy and Coast Guard experienced prejudice, discrimination, and segregation. Not always. Not everywhere. But enough—and so much so—that the arc of the moral universe took an extremely crooked and interrupted route, and a very long time, to arrive.

But to be clear, there were notable exceptions over the years to the overall pattern of inequality and racism. There were extraordinary men—white and black—who defied stereotypical profiles and accomplished great things. There were ships and stations at various points along the time line in the distant past and in the recent past where sailors performed their duties generally without regard to race. It is also true, though, that for the most part and not all that long ago—indeed right up into the early 1940s—African Americans in uniform were treated radically different from their white comrades in arms. That began to change late in World War II. Not all at once. Not uniformly. Not without missteps, backsliding, and reverses. But it did happen—and it happened in some small or large degree because of Carlton Skinner and *Sea Cloud* in 1943 and 1944.

Long before Skinner donned his dress blues and reported on board the cutter *Northland*, long before he was even born, and even scores of decades before that, black men were serving in the US Navy, the Coast Guard, and its predecessor organizations.

Eighteenth and Nineteenth Centuries

At the very beginning of US military history, blacks went to sea to fight in the Continental Navy and on board privateers during the Revolutionary War. They did so as both free men and slaves, albeit in small numbers in both cases. However, there were proportionally more blacks in the colonial navy than in the land forces during the war.[1]

Similarly, black sailors fought against the Royal Navy—for the second time—during the War of 1812 and engaged in many of the sea battles of that conflict. A number of African American seamen served with Commodore Oliver Hazard Perry in the September 10, 1813, Battle of Lake Erie. Commodore Isaac Chauncey, who commanded US naval forces on Lake Ontario, reported that "I have nearly 50 blacks on board this ship [*General Pike*] and many of them are among my best men . . . Attentive and obedient, and as far as I can judge, are excellent seamen."[2]

This should not be a surprise. After all, during the eighteenth and early nineteenth centuries black seamen manned merchant vessels and worked as fishermen and whalers, providing many of them with the experience, knowledge, and skills to perform ably as sailors on US warships.

During the Civil War (1861–65) approximately 30,000 blacks served in the Union Navy, constituting about 10 to 20 percent of each ship's crew. As a notable example, one of the heroes of that conflict, Robert Smalls, a black slave, hijacked a Confederate transport ship, CSS *Planter*, on May 13, 1862, sailed it from Charleston harbor, and turned it over to federal forces blockading the port. Smalls, who had been a de facto pilot on *Planter*, eventually was given command of the vessel in 1863. Eight African Americans were awarded the Medal of Honor during the Civil War.

The US Coast Guard as such did not have blacks among its personnel in the eighteenth and nineteenth centuries simply because the uniformed service with that identity was not formed until 1915. However, African Americans served in or were employed by some of the Coast Guard's predecessor organizations.

A case in point is the US Revenue Cutter Service, which owed its beginning to the nation's first secretary of the treasury, Alexander Hamilton, who proposed a sea service to assist in the enforcement of tariffs and the confisca-

Officers and men of USS *Hunchback* sometime in 1864–1865 while the ship was operating in the James River of Virginia. Along with the banjo player in the foreground, about 20 percent of the vessel's 99-man complement appear to be African Americans. A former New York side-wheeler ferryboat acquired by the navy on December 10, 1861, USS *Hunchback* operated in North Carolina and Virginia, captured three Confederate vessels in 1862, and was decommissioned and sold in 1865. Photograph by Matthew Brady. (Naval History and Heritage Command)

tion of contraband. Acquisition of the first ten revenue cutters was approved by Congress in 1790. By early in the nineteenth century it was not unusual for officers on board revenue cutters to use black slaves both as regular seamen and as cooks and stewards. But on November 1, 1843, a regulation was issued that prohibited any slave "from ever being entered for the Service, or to form a complement of any vessel of the Revenue Marine of the United States."[3] Nevertheless, and as one of those notable exceptions to the rule, Michael A. Healy, the only black to have been commissioned in any of the

Coast Guard forerunner organizations, served as the commanding officer of the cutter *Bear* between 1887 and 1895. Healy retired from the Revenue Cutter Service in 1903 as its third highest-ranked officer, and almost a hundred years later the US Coast Guard named a new icebreaker in his honor.[4]

The US Lighthouse Service—established in 1789 and joined the Coast Guard in 1939—employed blacks at least as far back as 1718 when a slave worked at the Boston Lighthouse. Blacks served aboard the first lightships but were restricted to working as cooks because of an 1835 regulation excluding African Americans from other roles (and not for the last time). In addition, there are some limited documented instances ashore in which white lighthouse keepers had black assistants, including those at Simons Island Light and Cape Florida Light in 1836 and the New Point Comfort Lighthouse in Virginia in 1852.

The US Life-Saving Service, another predecessor of the Coast Guard, was formed in 1878 and became part of the Coast Guard when it was established in 1915. That service had a number of black members—boat-smart fishermen and oystermen who had worked along the mid-Atlantic coastline and as such were very experienced in handling small craft in rough surf and sea conditions. These men performed the same duties as their white counterparts: patrolling the beaches, launching the station's lifeboat, repairing equipment, and cleaning the station—and, importantly, rescuing mariners in distress.

Blacks also served on board naval warships and auxiliary vessels during the Spanish-American War (1898–1900). One of those men, Gunner's Mate 1st Class John Christopher Jordan, is reported to have fired the first shot from the cruiser *Olympia* (C-6) at the Battle of Manila Bay on May 1, 1898. And that shot, of course, was in response to Commodore George Dewey's famous order to the cruiser's captain: "You may fire when ready, Gridley."[5] John Jordan had enlisted in the navy on June 17, 1877, and advanced over the years to eventually be rated as a chief gunners mate—the highest rank attainable by a noncommissioned officer at the time. Jordan retired from the navy on December 1, 1916, after thirty years of service. On that occasion the secretary of the navy wrote to Jordan, saying: "You were a valuable man in the upbuilding of the Navy and while the department is glad to know that you will now enjoy the benefits of the retirement law, yet it regrets very much to see you retire from active life in the Navy."[6]

In contrast to what took place in the early twentieth century, blacks served in a generally integrated navy during most of the late nineteenth cen-

Sailors and a chief gunner's mate stand in one of the torpedo rooms of the armored cruiser USS *Maine* (ACR-1) in the late-1890s. The ship exploded and sank in Havana Harbor on February 15, 1898, with the loss of three-quarters of the crew, presumably including some of the men pictured here. The ship's destruction influenced the US decision to go to war against Spain later that year. (Naval History and Heritage Command)

tury, constituting between 20 and 30 percent of the enlisted personnel.[7] And for many of the decades after the War of 1812, African Americans remained a relatively important source of manpower in the navy. But as time passed, the numbers of blacks declined, and by the early 1900s they were not playing a significant role in the sea services. As will be seen below, it was not until World War II that black sailors joined the navy in large numbers to participate in general service.[8]

Early Twentieth Century

After 1900 the number of African American navymen dropped dramatically, reflecting the Jim Crowism that was manifest in civil society. What few blacks were in uniform on navy ships were generally relegated to food-service tasks in the galley and on the mess decks or were assigned to shoveling coal into the ships' boilers. But even the manpower needed for that latter occupation declined as the navy shifted from coal to oil fuel for making steam.

During the US involvement in World War I (1917–18), there were just 6,750 blacks in the navy, a mere 1.2 percent of its enlisted personnel. This extremely low number included twenty-four female reservists (dubbed yeomanettes).[9] Of the 11,000 men who were commissioned as officers during the war, not one of them was a black.[10] Some of the black enlisted men had been chief petty officers, like John Jordan, who had risen in the enlisted ranks to become senior NCOs before racial restrictions were imposed in the 1920s; and a few black petty officers (e.g., gunner's mates, torpedomen, and machinist's mates) remained in uniform into the 1930s. But on the other hand, most blacks were employed as messmen (the equivalent of busboys) and stewards (akin to servants for officers).

Regulations issued in 1922 shut the door to black enlistment. And when the navy resumed recruiting a year later, it enlisted Filipinos rather than blacks as stewards. However, in the early 1930s the navy again allowed blacks to serve as stewards, and the black population in that specialized branch rose from 441 in 1932 to 4,007 in June 1940 (about 2 percent of the overall total of 170,000 navy personnel).[11] Generally, however, "black participation in the Navy remained severely restricted during the rest of the interwar period."[12] And, significantly, that participation was largely confined to service in the Steward Branch—external to the navy's general service ranks. (Stewards wore distinctive uniforms and insignia, staffed the officers' mess and wardroom, and maintained the officers' berthing areas on board ship. Picture, if you will, the footmen in *Downton Abby*).

As for the Coast Guard, even though it had a tradition of enlisting blacks in the nineteenth century, "unlike the Navy, [it] had always severely restricted Negroes both in terms of numbers enlisted and jobs assigned."[13] Thus, in the thirteen interwar years prior to the Japanese attack on Pearl Harbor, the number of blacks serving in the Coast Guard shrank. Despite that overall decline, there were some standout black coast guardsmen. In

Three messmen on board the submarine tender USS *Bushnell* (AS-2) take a break from their duties during World War I. The ship had been commissioned in 1915, was manned by approximately 150 officers and enlisted personnel, and provided support to submarines at Queenstown, Ireland, during the war. (Naval History and Heritage Command)

1928, for example, Boatswain's Mate 1st Class Clarence L. Samuels, an Afro-Caribbean who had enlisted eight years before, was given command of AB-15, a sixty-seven-foot harbor patrol cutter based in Savannah (see chapter 5). That post made him, according to Coast Guard historian William H. Thiesen, "the first minority enlisted man to command an official U.S. ship of any kind. Samuels predated the Navy's first African-American ship captain by almost 35 years."[14]

World War II Changes Things—But Not Everything

At the time that the United States declared war on Japan, Germany, and Italy in December 1941, black personnel made up 2.4 percent (5,026 men) of the navy's overall strength. (As a comparison, at the same time, blacks constituted approximately 10 percent of the civilian population.) They were still largely blocked from regular general service positions, although there were some very few exceptions to this exclusionary practice. As the Bureau of Naval Personnel reported in 1947, "When World War II opened there were on active duty in the Navy, in other than the messman branch, [just] six rated Negroes of the regular Navy, 23 rated men who had returned from retirement to service in the regular Navy and 14 rated men in the Fleet Reserve."[15] In other words, virtually none at all.

Notwithstanding the immediate need for large numbers of men to join the wartime navy, the service's uniformed leadership resisted efforts to add significant numbers of blacks to its ranks. As Morris J. MacGregor Jr. put it in his scholarly study of racial integration in the armed forces: "Generally, these men [the navy's top brass] were ardent military traditionalists, and despite the progressive attitude of the Secretary's [Secretary of the Navy Frank Knox] highest civilian advisors, changes in the racial policy of the Navy were to be glacially slow."[16]

Even before the United States entered the war, Secretary Knox advised President Roosevelt on June 18, 1941, that the navy could not accept black men in general service "because men live in such intimacy aboard ship that we simply can't enlist Negroes above the rank of messman."[17] The next month Knox appointed a committee of navy and Marine Corps personnel officers to examine the question of black general service and report its findings to him. In January 1942, a month after the attack on Pearl Harbor, that committee found that no changes in existing black assignment policy were necessary, although a minority report of the committee did recommend that a limited number of blacks be enlisted for general service on small boats and craft supporting naval shipyards and shore stations.

FDR was not pleased with this report, and on January 15, 1942, he asked Knox to take another look at the issue, saying that he believed there must be something "colored enlistees could do in addition to the rating of messmen"; that there had be a triangulated alternative to an absolute restriction to the Messman Branch on the one hand and total integration of blacks in general service on the other.

Finally, on April 7, 1942, the navy announced that 277 black volunteers a week would be accepted for enlistment for general service *in the reserve components* [emphasis added] of the US Navy, Marine Corps, and Coast Guard. "All ratings in those three branches of the Naval Service will be opened to them," the announcement stated, "and recruiting is to be begun as soon as a suitable training station is established."[18] A key aspect of the announcement stipulated the types of roles the black sailors would fill: "Duty in District craft [i.e., boats assigned to local administrative regions within United States] of various kind, in maritime activities around shore establishments, in Navy yards, and in the Navy's new construction crews and companies which will be employed in developing bases outside the United States." In other words, the recruited black enlistees *would not* be serving on board the hundreds of ships in the "regular" navy's fleet. In addition, the actual enlistments would have to wait for the construction of "suitable" (i.e., segregated) facilities. The navy established a goal of 14,000 blacks to be enlisted for general service in the first year.

Yet in assessing the qualifications and occupational backgrounds of blacks who would be enlisting, the navy had determined that "an armed force which will fight the most effectively and efficiently evolves only when men are doing the things for which their background and experience best fit them."[19] That is a most reasonable proposition (and it is highly relevant to Carlton Skinner's thinking and actions in 1943 and 1944), and here is what the navy determined:

> There are Negroes who have had training and experience in practically all civilian occupations. Of the 534 different occupations listed in the Census of 1940, all but four were practiced by some Negroes. A survey of all armed forces inductees over a ten-month period listed 428 specific occupational specialties acquired by enlisted men in civilian life. Approximately 85 percent of the 428 skills, trades and professions had been practiced or learned by Negro inductees, although in some the numbers were small. The scarcity of Negroes with skills in occupations of critical importance in the Naval Establishment requires that no qualified individuals be overlooked and that the development of needed skills through training be emphasized.[20]

Nevertheless, black sailors were heavily restricted from participating in the occupational ratings for which they were qualified and were to be trained in segregated facilities.

Two weeks after the navy's April announcement, Secretary Knox approved a plan that incoming blacks would be trained at Camp Berry (later renamed Camp Robert Smalls, the Civil War hero) at an isolated section of the Great Lakes Training Center adjacent to Lake Michigan and about forty miles north of Chicago.

Black enlistments began on June 1, 1942, and the volunteers began arriving at Great Lakes later that month to form classes of 277 men. Concurrently the navy enlisted an unrestricted number of blacks for service as laborers in its Construction Battalions (Seabees) and as messmen. After eight weeks of recruit training, about 31 percent of the black recruits had been qualified for Class A Schools (for training in such occupational specialties as radioman, electrician's mate, and cook). During the first weeks of open enlistment, only 1,261 blacks volunteered for general service, and 58 percent of them were rejected for physical and other causes. MacGregor concludes that this low turnout was because of the navy's "reputation as the exclusive preserve of white America."[21]

Meanwhile, the Coast Guard planned to enlist approximately 500 blacks for general service, 300 of whom would be trained for duty on small vessels and 200 for nonsegregated shore duty in six coastal cities. In advance of the actual enlistments, the Coast Guard's commandant, R. Adm. Russell R. Waesche, specified which of its vessels, mostly buoy tenders and patrol boats, would have black crews (supervised by white petty officers, i.e., NCOs).

In March 1942 the Coast Guard received the first 150 blacks who had volunteered to serve. They were trained in all-black companies—concurrently with similar all-white recruit units—at the Coast Guard's Manhattan Beach Training Station on the southern tip of Brooklyn, New York. The boots received four weeks of training in basic seamanship and small-boat handling. Although the classes themselves were integrated, the barracks and mess halls were segregated. Graduates of the boot camp were initially sent to assignments in "traditional minority shipboard positions" (e.g., food service), although some blacks qualified for specialized follow-on training in such ratings as yeomen, radiomen, electricians, carpenters, pharmacist mates, coxswains, and boatswain's mates.

By May 1942 the Coast Guard had made all of its enlisted rates open and available to minority recruits. The next month Congress enacted a law that enabled the Coast Guard to create a "temporary reserve" force of volunteers to supplement the service's active-duty personnel. This provision enabled some blacks to acquire various enlisted rates in the "temporary reserve" organization.[22] By August 1942 some 300 blacks had been recruited, trained, and sent to general service billets, but at the same time, the Coast Guard continued to recruit hundreds of blacks for the separate Steward Branch.

Both the US Navy and Coast Guard recruiting programs came to a hard stop at the end of the year because on December 5, 1942, President Roosevelt ordered an end to volunteer enlistments of all men aged eighteen to thirty-eight. The new Selective Service would be responsible for drafting men in that age group beginning in February 1943. The navy defined its first draftee requirements on a racial basis: it specified the separate number of white and black men needed for the navy, Coast Guard, and Marine Corps, and it looked to acquire 1,200 blacks each month for general service and another 1,500 African Americans to serve as stewards and messmen. In other words, the navy would now be drafting men on the basis of race. It subsequently increased the number of blacks it needed to 5,000 in April and 7,350 for each month from May to December 1943.

In 1943 the navy asked the Selective Service for 116,000 black draftees. It received only 77,854 (compared to 672,437 whites), up 240 percent over the black enlistment rate in the prior year.

By February 1943 the navy's muster lists carried 26,909 blacks (still only about 2 percent of the overall manpower), including 6,662 in general service, 2,020 in the Seabees, and 19,227 (or two-thirds of the total) in the Steward Branch. The Coast Guard drafted relatively few men, inducting only 15,296 during the war, of whom merely 1,667 (10 percent) were black. On average, 137 African Americans and 1,000 whites were inducted into the Coast Guard each month in 1943—and not many more than 5,000 blacks in total served in the Coast Guard in World War II. In this case, though, the small number of blacks in general service—less than 1 percent of the total enlisted manpower—made racial integration relatively more acceptable to whites if only because it was generally inconspicuous. Still the evidence suggests that "the majority of black stewards, about 63 percent of all the Negroes in the Coast Guard, continued to function as servants throughout the war."[23]

▪ ▪ ▪ ▪

In reviewing the history of African Americans in the sea services, we can make two key observations.

First, it appears that there was more racial integration and equality in the navy of the 1800s (ironically in an era of black slavery)—especially during the Civil War—than there was in the early twentieth century (more than fifty years after the Emancipation Proclamation[24]).

And, second, even as the nation was massively scaling up from a peacetime navy of 790 active ships to an ultimate wartime level of 6,768 vessels, which therefore required hundreds of thousands of additional officers and sailors to man those new ships, the drag and dregs of racial prejudice all but closed off a key source of manpower.[25] Amazingly, at the very time democracy and the nation's existence itself was at risk, the legacy of nineteenth-century Jim Crow constrained navy and Coast Guard recruitment of blacks—even with a progressive commander in chief in the White House. And as for the blacks who nevertheless did join those services, that same legacy, that same prejudice and discrimination, more often than not assigned them to menial occupations and denied them the opportunity to enhance their skills and contribute their abilities to the war effort to the maximum extent and in the best way possible.

This malady and misfeasance was manifest during the same period—1941–43—in which Carlton Skinner was serving on the cutter *Northland* in Greenland. It is the backdrop to Skinner's actions on that ship and, more importantly, later on *Sea Cloud*. It explains why his individual initiatives and his collective achievements in 1943 and 1944 were so historically significant. Those actions and achievements will be described in chapter 5. In addition, chapter 5 will examine some of the other wartime events that affected African Americans in the US Navy and Coast Guard.

But before that account we need to step back aboard *Sea Cloud* in the first days of World War II to see it transformed from a luxury yacht owned by a former ambassador and his wealthy wife into a nondescript utility vessel in Uncle Sam's navy.

4 *Sea Cloud* Goes to War

It was a time of both war and peace. In 1941 Japan invaded Thailand, the Malay Peninsula, and the Burma Road; the German Luftwaffe was bombing London and other cities in Britain; the Wehrmacht stormed into the Soviet Union; and the Kriegsmarine was conducting submarine warfare in the Atlantic. In October the submarine U-568 torpedoed and damaged the destroyer USS *Kearny* (DD-432), killing eleven sailors—the first US military casualties of World War II—and the U-552 torpedoed and sank the destroyer USS *Reuben James* (DD-245), killing more than 100 navymen.

In March President Franklin Roosevelt signed the Lend-Lease Act to provide aid to US allies; declared in May an unlimited state of national emergency; in June ordered the freezing of German and Italian assets in the United States, the seizure of their vessels in US ports, and the closing of German consulates; in August signed the Atlantic Charter with Winston Churchill; and in November placed the US Coast Guard under the direction of the US Navy.

On the other hand, many elements of life in the United States continued pretty much as they had. You could still buy a hot dog for five cents, go to the movies for twenty cents (to see such films as *Citizen Kane* and *Sergeant York*), and buy a dinner for forty cents. Americans with limited spending money could listen at no cost on the radio to such song hits as "The Anniversary Waltz," "I Don't Want to Set the World on Fire," and "The White Cliffs of Dover," while many baseball fans could tune in that summer to cheer for or root against Joe DiMaggio, who set a major league record in 1941 when he hit safely in fifty-six consecutive games.[1]

Carlton Skinner, who began the year at the Maritime Commission in Washington, was now serving as a watch officer on board the Coast Guard cutter *Northland* in the Arctic Ocean, and Joseph Davies was working in the nation's capital as a special assistant to Secretary of State Cordell Hull.

In the spring of 1941 Joseph and Marjorie asked Cox & Stevens—the marine architects who had designed Edward Hutton's *Hussar* V over a decade before—to survey their yacht *Sea Cloud* and assess the vessel's value, a proactive step usually taken by owners who were considering selling their boats. The estimate they received may have shocked the couple. Excluding its pricey furnishings, *Sea Cloud* was valued at just $275,000—about a quarter of what Hutton had spent to build it and obviously far less than the cost of a comparable vessel in 1941. And 1941 was not exactly a propitious time to be offering a luxury yacht for sale. Indeed, Marjorie was advised by Daniel H. Cox on June 6, 1941, that "the only possibility of selling a yacht of [*Sea Cloud's*] type under these conditions is to some government (and particularly the American Government) for a military purpose of some character, or possibly, if a customer could be found, effecting a sale for some commercial purpose."[2] As it happens, a "military purpose" was already at hand.

In 1940 the US Navy and Coast Guard had begun buying civilian motor yachts and converting them for use in the Inshore Patrol, which was to provide local defense in coastal waters and supplement regular army, navy, and Coast Guard aircraft and ships.[3] This concept was broadened into the Coastal Picket Patrol (sometimes referred to as the "Hooligan Navy"), a civilian fleet of sailing yachts, motorboats, converted fishing vessels, and small freighters that were to intercept and investigate vessels approaching the East and Gulf Coasts of the United States during the war.[4] (Eventually, the smaller yachts and boats that had been acquired for the Coastal Picket Patrol in 1940–42 were phased out. In January 1943 Adm. Ernest J. King, the navy's senior officer, cut the picket force by 35 percent, as eighty-three-foot Coast Guard cutters were arriving in enough numbers to replace the civilian craft. While a few of the larger yachts were retained, the "Hooligan Navy" went out of business on October 1, 1943.[5])

On January 23, 1941, the secretary of the navy established the Auxiliary Vessels Board to "Coordinate the Demands for Additional Large [civilian] Ships to Convert into Naval Auxiliaries."[6]

Later that year Joseph Davies took Cox's advice and offered *Sea Cloud* to the navy for use in the "current emergency." President Roosevelt initially opposed the move because he did not want to see what would happen to his friend's beautiful yacht when it was converted into a utilitarian naval auxiliary. Nevertheless, on December 4, 1941—three days before the Pearl Harbor attack—the Auxiliary Vessels Board considered and assessed the practicality of acquiring *Sea Cloud* for the navy. It determined that the yacht could be used ("repurposed" in today's lingo) either as a weather ship or training vessel for the Coast Guard or as a patrol gunboat for the navy and thus recommended that it be brought into the service.[7] The board stipulated that the owners were to remove the yacht's furnishings (furniture, art work, paneling and rugs, etc.) and that the navy in turn would take off all sails, masts, and related materials, store them, and then return them along with the ship to the owners upon completion of its service. Finally, the board left it to the navy to determine the specific use to which *Sea Cloud* would be put.

Accordingly, the navy bareboat-chartered *Sea Cloud* (official number 232881) on January 2, 1942, at the token rate of $1.00 per year. The duration of the charter would run from the effective date of the vessel's delivery to the government and last until the date "the President declares as the end of the national emergency." Under the initial terms of the charter, if *Sea Cloud* were to become a total loss, the owners would be compensated with $600,000—more than twice the yacht's value as estimated by Cox & Stevens six months earlier.[8]

The yacht's acquisition by the navy was reported in one major publication as follows:

> The Navy Department has leased for a dollar a year the *Sea Cloud*, a powered four-masted brigantine clipper owned by Joseph E. Davies, former Ambassador to Russia. It will be returned to its owner after the war. The *Sea Cloud* is being converted for Coast Guard duty. The vessel, built in 1931 at Kiel, is of 2,323 gross tons, is 281 feet long and has engines which develop 3,600 horsepower.[9]

A photo accompanying the press report showed the vessel's main deck and superstructure completely covered in canvas from stem to stern, with only the top of the funnel visible.

Sea Cloud was not the only yacht joining the nation's sea services. Two months after it was acquired, a total of twenty-three private vessels, ranging in length from 36 feet to 316 feet (*Sea Cloud*), had been converted for wartime service according to the Maritime Commission. Of this group, thirteen yachts were in the navy, seven (including *Sea Cloud*) were serving in the Coast Guard, and three were sent to the US Maritime Service.[10] Some of these ships were assigned to antisubmarine duty, others worked as patrol craft, three were used as training ships, and one or two (including *Sea Cloud*) were deployed as weather ships. These twenty-three vessels, according to a press report, "are valued at several millions of dollars and their donors have made it possible for the Navy and the Coast Guard to convert cutters, previously employed in coastal work, to gunboats to join the combat forces."[11]

From Princess to Plebeian

On January 2, 1942, the assistant commandant of the Coast Guard, V. Adm. Lloyd T. Chalker, directed the commander of the Coast Guard's base in Charleston, South Carolina, to cooperate with *Sea Cloud*'s master in transferring it from Winyah Bay in Georgetown, South Carolina, to the Coast Guard's Curtis Bay shipyard in southern Baltimore, Maryland. Two Coast Guard warrant or chief warrant officers and an unspecified number of enlisted men were detailed for temporary duty to assist *Sea Cloud*'s master on the voyage up to Baltimore.[12] *Sea Cloud* began the relatively short cruise north on January 8, 1942, arriving at the shipyard on January 11.

Yard workers began the yacht's transformation almost immediately. They removed three of the masts and bowsprit, along with its golden eagle figurehead and luxurious furnishings, which were taken ashore and put in storage. *Sea Cloud*'s beautiful white hull lost its brilliant luster as painters applied an overcoat of dull gray.

According to the Coast Guard's history of the ship, *Sea Cloud* was equipped with some offensive and defensive fighting capability during the conversion. It was fitted with heavy armor plating, two 3-inch/50 guns (one forward near the bow and the other aft near the fantail), eight 20 mm guns for use against aircraft, one Mark 10 hedgehog projector (for firing contact-fused projectiles over the bow at submerged submarines), two racks for rolling depth charges (of which the ship carried forty-four) off the stern down onto submarines, and four K-guns for firing depth charges off the sides of the ship. Carlton Skinner later noted that *Sea Cloud*'s armament consisted of four twin-mount 40 mm and eight 20 mm guns, the two 3-inch/50s, plus the hedgehog mount and K-guns. He also wrote that the yacht's main mast had been retained in the conversion, and a small deck house had been installed aft for use in inflating helium weather balloons employed in gathering meteorological data.[13]

Sea Cloud kept its four original Krupp 800 hp diesel engines and twin screws, capable of propelling the ship at 14 knots; as its future captain put it, "with the hull form of a clipper ship, the *Sea Cloud* was an effective and comfortable ship for weather patrol."[14]

The interior of the ship was reconfigured to provide berthing for its complement of 160 enlisted men, thirteen chief petty officers, one warrant officer, and twenty-one commissioned officers—all coast guardsmen. Skinner once recalled that even months after the conversion, the officers' quarters still reeked of the perfume that had been applied in the 1930s to the yacht's wallpaper in the guest cabins. Although that old paper had been removed from the bulkheads at Curtis Bay, the unique fragrance that remained behind in each stateroom was said to be so pungent that it permeated the Coast Guard officer's uniforms. Said Skinner: "It was so strong that at night on deck you could identify the officer next to you by his smell even if you couldn't see his face."[15]

Sea Cloud's electronics suite included three radars (an ET 80198-2-22MC, ET 8010C 375–500 KC, and ET 8012B 2100–3000 KC), a sonar for detecting and tracking submarines, a range recorder, a Submarine Signal fathometer for measuring depth, and upgraded radio communications gear.

On February 2, 1942, the navy's chief of naval operations formally assigned *Sea Cloud* to the Coast Guard for commissioning, operation, and maintenance, effective January 6, 1942. On March 17, the navy designated Boston as the ship's permanent homeport, with repairs and reconditioning to be completed by April 1. In all, the four-month conversion of *Sea Cloud* from yacht to weather ship cost the government $318,101.[16]

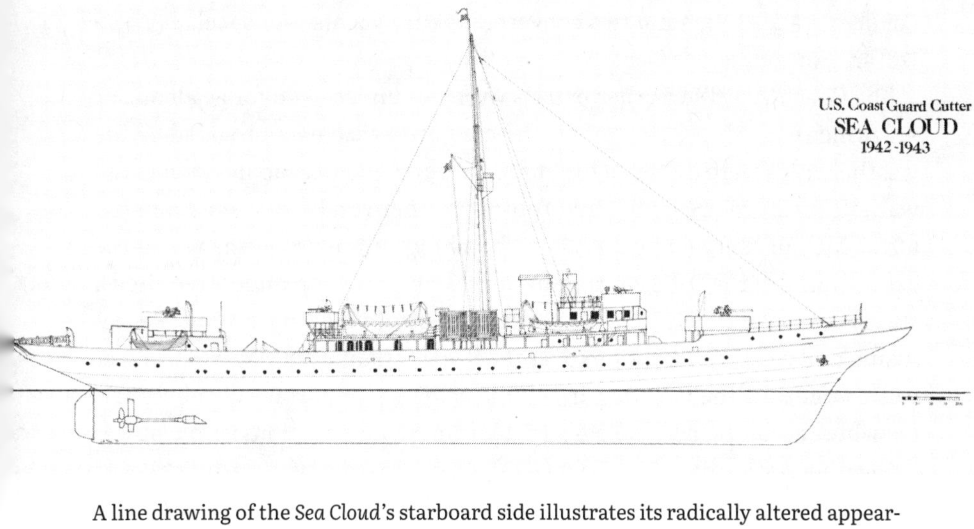

A line drawing of the *Sea Cloud*'s starboard side illustrates its radically altered appearance following the 1942 conversion at Curtis Bay. (Coast Guard Historian's Office)

With its port side moored to the pier at Curtis Bay, *Sea Cloud* was formally commissioned as a Coast Guard cutter (WPG-284) on the afternoon of April 4, 1942 (for its specifications, see appendix B). Lt. Cmdr. G. N. Bernier, USCG, the ship's captain, six officers, and 116 enlisted men officially reported on board for duty (see appendix C for a list of the ship's personnel). Later that month the cutter motored up to Boston, its new homeport, to begin its role as a unit in the navy's Task Force 24.

Whither the Weather Ships

In January 1940 President Roosevelt ordered the formation of the Atlantic Weather Observation Service, which was to employ Coast Guard cutters of the Secretary or Treasury class and observers from the US Weather Bureau. After the Coast Guard was placed under the navy on November 1, 1941, its weather ships became part of the navy's Atlantic Fleet and under the operational control of the District Coast Guard Officer, First Naval District, in Boston.

Once the United States entered the war in December, the Secretary-class cutters—including *Bibb* (WPG-31), *Duane* (WPG-33), *Alexander Hamilton* (WPG- 34), and *Spencer* (WPG-36), were pulled from weather patrol duty and redeployed to handle antisubmarine missions.[17] Their replacements included two navy Q-ships—USS *Big Horn* (IX-207) and USS *Asterion* (AK-100),[18] some Coast Guard buoy tenders—*Evergreen* (WAGL-295), *Sorrel* (WAGL-296), and *Conifer* (WAGL-301),[19] and two converted luxury yachts—*Nourmahal* (WPG-122) and, of course, *Sea Cloud*.[20]

The Coast Guard's weather patrols were not undertaken for academic or scientific research per se. Rather, the meteorological data provided by the weather ships were intended for immediate and practical application to the war effort. Since prevailing and future weather conditions could and did affect such military actions as Allied bombing runs over Germany and the exact timing of the D-Day assault in Normandy, US war planners required a steady stream of timely weather forecasts to devise their operations. Recognizing that weather conditions over the North Atlantic one day would affect western Europe the next day, it became critically important to collect and distribute accurate meteorological data from remote locations far out at sea.

Weather station duty for *Sea Cloud* required it to patrol within fifty miles of a fixed position in the Atlantic for a period of between twenty-one and thirty days, after which it would be relieved by another weather ship. Initially there were four weather stations: one off Bermuda, another between Newfoundland and Greenland, a third between Greenland and Iceland (waters that Skinner knew well from his time as *Northland*'s navigator), and the fourth off the coast of France. While on patrol, the weather ship was to file reports compiled by the four to six meteorologists on board every four hours by radio to the navy's weather center in Arlington, Virginia. Following completion of each patrol, *Sea Cloud* would return to Boston for reprovisioning and any necessary repairs. As Skinner would later point out, the ship's German engines had become a maintenance concern because the builder was now behind enemy lines and replacement parts, mechanical drawings, and service manuals were no longer available to the ship's engineering personnel in Boston.

Two months after it was commissioned, *Sea Cloud* demonstrated for the first time that it could accomplish more than merely reporting weather conditions. On June 16, in true Coast Guard fashion, it rescued eight crewmen from the Portuguese fishing schooner *Maria da Gloria*, which had sunk off the Grand Banks of Newfoundland. The schooner's sole survivors (out of a crew of forty-four) had been adrift in a lifeboat for ten days when *Sea Cloud* pulled them from the sea.[21]

Sea Cloud's patrols that spring and summer were conducted in Weather Patrol Station No. 2 at approximately 52°N, 42°30' W (i.e., south of Greenland and east of Newfoundland). Over the next few months it subsequently relieved the cutters *Monomoy* (WAG-275), *Manasquan* (WAG-273), and *Manhassett* (WAG-276) in their patrols.[22] On July 20 it was directed to cover Weather Station No. 1 between August 3 and August 24 "due to the failure to complete conversion of *Manhassett* [from a miscellaneous auxiliary to a weather station vessel] on schedule," and *Sea Cloud* was instructed to transfer its weather equipment to *Manhassett* in Boston at the completion of that patrol.[23]

This merry-go-round succession of duties—out of Boston to relieve a weather ship, patrol on station, relief by another weather ship, return to Boston—continued through the remainder of 1942 and into 1943. For example, during the autumn of 1942 *Sea Cloud* operated in Weather Patrol Station No. 1 from October 26 to November 16, returned to Station No. 1 on February 8, 1943, to relieve *Manhassett*, and then was subsequently relieved by *Manhassett* on March 1. Four days later *Sea Cloud* returned to Boston,

Sea Cloud underway on October 22, 1942, six months after its conversion into a Coast Guard weather ship. (Coast Guard Historian's Office)

mooring at Constitution Wharf at 0840 (8:40 a.m.). The next day the ship entered the Bethlehem Atlantic Works shipyard (owned by Bethlehem Steel Corporation) in East Boston, Massachusetts, for a two-week availability. It went back out on patrol in March and April 1943, relieving *Manasquan* as a weather ship, and was in turn replaced by *Manhasset* on April 19.

That month *Sea Cloud* had a change in "ownership." The navy had earlier asked the Coast Guard for administrative control of the converted yachts *Nourmahal* and *Sea Cloud*, and the two vessels were duly transferred to the navy. USS *Sea Cloud* was officially commissioned as a naval vessel on April 9—although still manned by an all–Coast Guard crew—and redesignated as the navy's IX-99.[24]

Sea Cloud then spent late April through mid-May back at the Atlantic Works shipyard, and after fueling on May 19 went out to sea to replace *Manasquan* on May 23. The latter vessel relieved *Sea Cloud* on June 13, and it was back in Boston—either moored at Constitution Wharf or at Atlantic Works—from late June to early July, throughout August into early September, and through October 1943. In between those times, it patrolled in Weather Station No. 2.

On November 18, 1943, with *Sea Cloud* then moored at Constitution Wharf, a thirty-year-old Coast Guard lieutenant walked up its brow, saluted its colors, and stepped onto the quarterdeck. Certainly, there was nothing particularly remarkable about that; it was absolutely routine. But unbeknownst to the officer of the deck who greeted the arriving young lieutenant, and unrecognized at the time by the weather ship's officers and men, with this arrival the winds of transformative change were about to blow.

▪ ▪ ▪ ▪

All during *Sea Cloud*'s conversion into a Coast Guard weather ship in 1942, its early patrols in the Atlantic in 1942 and 1943, and then its transfer into the navy, Carlton Skinner was serving on the cutter *Northland* while dodging icebergs and capturing German agents in Greenland. And as we will next see in chapter 5, an event on that cutter, followed by a few brief stops along the way afterward, would lead Skinner to report on board USS *Sea Cloud*, where he would soon help to change the policies, practices, and culture of the nation's sea services.

5 Skinner Takes Command

There occurs in the lives of almost everyone a single event that at the time seems innocuous, mundane, or random but turns out later to have had life-altering consequences. As a hypothetical illustration, the so-called butterfly effect in chaos theory postulates that if one butterfly in New Mexico flaps its wings at just the right moment in time and in just the right place in space, that singular action can touch off a series of connected and cascading meteorological events that ultimately will cause a typhoon in Asia.[1]

The Henry Case

For Carlton Skinner, his life-altering "butterfly" event took place in 1942 while he was serving as executive officer (XO) of the Coast Guard cutter *Northland* in the waters off Greenland. On naval ships, the XO is the vessel's second in command and he or she functions as a combination assistant captain, chief operating officer, and chief human resources officer.

One of the crewmen on the cutter, Oliver T. Henry, was an African American whose job as a steward was to serve the ship's officers. But Henry also happened to be an excellent machinist and, in the words of Skinner, "a genius with diesel motors." The young black man spent his off-duty hours poking around down in the engine room and studying textbooks and manuals about engines. One day Henry told the XO that he wanted to leave the Steward Branch and wished to be tested and rated as a motor machinist's mate 3rd class—a petty officer—so that he could work full time in the engineering department. Skinner then consulted the engineering officer about Henry and was told that *Northland*'s chief machinist's mates (senior NCOs) were favorably impressed with Henry's knowledge and abilities. So Skinner had Henry tested and, based on the results, he then submitted a formal recommendation to Coast Guard headquarters that the steward be rated as a motor machinist's mate. But the enlisted personnel division at headquarters did not agree and rejected Skinner's recommendation on the grounds that Henry was "a Negro and Negroes were only accepted in the Steward's Branch."[2] Skinner said later: "This irritated me, it infuriated me."[3] Could that have been the sound of a butterfly's wings just beginning to flutter?

Rather than quietly accepting the rejection and putting Henry's case aside—which most of his peers would have done—Skinner had Henry reexamined and then fired an appeal back up the chain of command. The XO believed that the headquarters decision was, in his words, "both unfair and inefficient, and therefore undesirable for a military service."[4] And on this second try headquarters reversed itself, and Henry's request to be rated and transferred to the engineering department was approved. That victory for Skinner and Henry turned out to be good not only for them but for the Coast Guard as well. By allowing Oliver Henry to leave the Steward Branch, the Coast Guard and the ships on which he served benefited from his superior mechanical talents for many years. As a result of his sustained performance, Henry earned several promotions during his career and eventually retired as a chief warrant officer.

The Henry case prompted Skinner to think long and hard about the efficient use of manpower—*all* manpower—in wartime. As he put it in a 1970 interview:

> That Negroes can only serve at sea as officer servants . . . would eventually cause racial trouble in the United States for this reason: that the stewards and steward's mates of the seagoing units of the Coast Guard and Navy make up only three to four percent of the total complement of a ship. The Negro group was roughly 11 percent of the [US] population. With seamen for the Coast Guard and Navy coming from the draft, over a period of several years, the other eight percent who could not go to sea would be given shore duty and the percentage of Negroes ashore in safe jobs would rise very rapidly. And I felt the white sailors coming home from dangerous duty could very well resent this and there could be race riots in the sea ports.[5]

This was not a farfetched analysis. Skinner remembered the tension and animosity felt by navymen on sea duty and army troops serving overseas toward military-age men who remained in the United States during World

War I, and he recalled that there had been race riots during and after that conflict.[6]

Another element in Skinner's thinking was that by excluding blacks from general service ratings aboard ship, the US Navy and Coast Guard were making inefficient use of available manpower. Such racially based exclusions forced African Americans who already had the requisite knowledge or skills for various shipboard specialties to instead be segregated, restricted, and underutilized as mess attendants and officers' servants. In effect, some of the best men available to perform a specific general service job could not be assigned to those jobs. Such a race-based policy was not only foolish; it was unjust.

Those thoughts and ideas were percolating in Lieutenant Skinner's head—and the figurative butterfly's wings were flapping faster and harder—during his second patrol to Greenland in the spring of 1943. That's when he received orders detaching him from *Northland* to become the commanding officer of a Coast Guard crew that was training to man a new navy tank landing ship (LST). But either just before he took up that assignment or at some point during it, Skinner was detailed to help prepare for the commissioning of a most unlikely "warship."

Sixteen Days on *Gresham*

The Coast Guard cutter *Gresham* was an antique veteran of the former Revenue Cutter Service, the US Navy, and the Coast Guard. It had been built in Cleveland, Ohio, for service as a revenue cutter on the Great Lakes. Commissioned on May 30, 1897, *Gresham* was initially homeported in Milwaukee. When the Spanish-American War began, the Revenue Cutter Service was brought into the navy, and the vessel was ordered to deploy to the Atlantic Coast. Unfortunately, its 205-foot hull was too long to fit in the locks on the St. Lawrence Seaway, and the cutter had to be cut in half and ferried through the locks in two pieces. *Gresham* later served in the Atlantic and performed patrol and escort duty during World War I. With the conclusion of hostilities, the navy returned the cutter to the Coast Guard on August 28, 1919.

In 1935, when *Gresham* was nearly forty years old, it was sold by the Coast Guard to be dismantled. But faced with increased wartime requirements for additional naval ships—practically any ships—the Coast Guard reacquired the old cutter from the scrappers before it was cut up, and it was sent to the General Ship Repair Company in Baltimore to be fitted out as an escort vessel for coastal convoys. Still equipped with its obsolete nineteenth-century bow torpedo tube (but now welded shut), the cutter was readied for war with four 3-inch guns (dating to 1918), a single 1-pounder and two 6-pounders, three .50-caliber guns, two 3-inch/50 guns, twenty 20 mm/80 single-barrel guns, two K-guns, two stern depth charge racks, and two hedgehog mounts (of 1943 vintage). The old cutter was to be manned by nine officers and sixty-three enlisted personnel.

And it was aboard this creaky veteran that Carlton Skinner assumed the duties of executive officer on March 20, 1943.[7] Just three days later, the cutter *Gresham* was recommissioned in the Coast Guard and designated as WPG-85. Apparently, and for good reason, Skinner was not impressed with this ship. He once described it, quite fairly, as a "Spanish-American period war vessel resurrected from the boneyard."[8] Which is just as well because only sixteen days after he became XO, Skinner was released from *Gresham* to be readied for command of an LST.

Prospective Skipper of a Large Slow Target

During World War II hundreds of Coast Guard personnel at various times operated 77 of the US Navy's 1,041 LSTs.[9] Dubbed "Large Slow Targets" by many sailors, LSTs were unique 328-foot amphibious vessels that ran right up onto an enemy-held beach to unload through large bow doors their cargoes of tanks and other vehicles, troops, and supplies. LSTs typically were operated by about ten officers and 104 enlisted personnel.

Available Coast Guard records are not clear about when Skinner actually began his assignment as the skipper of an LST crew in training.[10] Those records are equally unclear as to where, in fact, Skinner commanded the LST crew. (It is likely, though, that he and his men took a ten-week course provided by the Amphibious Training Squadron at Camp Bradford in Little Creek, Virginia.[11]) And the available records do not specify which LST Skinner was slated to command.[12]

But what we do know is that at some point during his LST training in the spring of 1943, Skinner visited the Coast Guard's Public Relations Office in Washington, DC, to propose that a cameraman be assigned to his LST when it eventually deployed to the Pacific Theater. He suggested that during his time at sea he would write some articles and photo captions to complement the cameraman's film footage and photography, all of which could be distributed to media outlets to publicize the Coast Guard's role in the war against Japan. Skinner's proposal had a solid basis because he had already proven himself as a competent reporter, public relations practitioner, and published writer (of an article on arctic navigation).[13]

Skinner Steps Ashore

Evidently, Skinner's PR pitch succeeded but not as he had envisioned. Rather than obtaining a Coast Guard cameraman to be detailed to his ship during its operations in the Pacific, Skinner's suggestion resulted in orders detaching him from sea duty and reassigning him as the executive officer of the Coast Guard's Public Relations Office. Someone in the chain of command must have thought that Skinner could be more valuable in the war effort by applying his talents as journalist and public information officer than by serving as the skipper of an LST.

Family Matters

The new job at Coast Guard headquarters wasn't the only change in Carlton Skinner's life in 1943. On May 1 of that year, the thirty-year-old Coast Guard lieutenant married Ens. Jeanne Rowe, USNR, at the home of her sister in Dayton, Ohio. The bride had been born on April 1, 1917, was a graduate of the University of Nebraska, and was selected for the first Women's Auxiliary Volunteer Emergency Service (WAVES) training class at Northampton, Massachusetts. After receiving her commission, Ensign Rowe was assigned to the Pictorial Section of the navy's Office of Public Relations and later, as a lieutenant (junior grade), to the service's PR shop in New York City.[14]

The two officers had three children during their marriage: Franz Carlton Skinner, born on April 5, 1945; Andrea Weymouth Skinner, born on April 12, 1948; and Barbara McDuffee Skinner, born on September 4, 1957. The Skinners separated in 1966 and were divorced soon thereafter. Jeanne Rowe Skinner died on April 19, 1988, in Palo Alto, California, at the age of seventy-one.[15]

The Proposed Experiment

By now Skinner's thinking about the efficient use of available manpower and racial integration had evolved to the point where he wanted to present his ideas to the Coast Guard's highest command. He did not formulate his proposal on a rationale of civil rights or social justice. Instead, "it was for me a program for increased military effectiveness," he said.[16]

At the outset he realized that African Americans could not be accepted into general service billets simply by some edict from headquarters. For one thing, many blacks lacked the same skills and experience of most whites because they had been held back and undereducated in the South and elsewhere. For another, there would be considerable resistance by traditionalists and bigots who would argue that African Americans could not perform as well as whites in general service jobs aboard ship.

Skinner believed that the solution would not be to designate a ship to be entirely manned by blacks. Since new and inexperienced sailors learn from other veteran sailors, a better approach would be to have a ship manned by a racially mixed crew, a truly integrated ship, "black and white at all levels, officers, petty officers and seamen." That way, qualified and experienced enlisted men and officers could pass along their knowledge to the newer personnel and together demonstrate that a racially integrated ship would be as effective as an all-white vessel. Skinner also believed that the commanding officer of what he regarded as "the experimental ship" had to be "sympathetic to the idea, want it to work, and be willing to give it the special care necessary to make it work."[17] Hmmm. Who could that be?

In addition, Skinner wanted the experimental ship to be assigned to regular missions and tasks. It had to be a regular unit of the fleet and not a special case "on privileged duty for purposes of show." He reasoned that, first, if other ships regarded the experimental ship as a kind of "handle with care" package, their all-white crews would be hostile to the integrated ship and its personnel. Secondly, he was concerned that white and black men assigned to the experimental ship might feel entitled or special and therefore might slack off in their performance. And, lastly, Skinner felt that if higher commands viewed the experimental ship as unique and atypical, they would tend to dismiss it as an aberration unworthy of acceptance and support.

There were other aspects to Skinner's proposal. He wanted the bulk of the training of the general ratings to be performed at sea. He wanted the selection, testing, and advancement of the black seamen into the petty officer ranks to be controlled aboard the experimental ship. In addition: No special favors in assignment of the ship to duty, in the rotation of crew, or in anything else, even movies. This was not to be a "show" ship. Second, no spotlight of publicity. If the newspapers and cameramen were wandering around the ship when it was in port, there would be problems in discipline.[18]

Skinner put all these ideas and thinking into a four-page memorandum that he wanted to send to the commandant of the Coast Guard—its top officer—R. Adm. Russell R. Waesche.[19] The subject line read: "Utilization of Negro Personnel for Military Efficiency." Following procedure, Skinner first submitted the memo to his boss, Capt. Ellis Reed-Hill, the chief of public relations, in June 1943.[20] Either because Reed-Hill disagreed with the content or because he did not want to lose Skinner to the experimental ship, he deep-sixed the memo.

Undeterred, Skinner had a yeoman retype it, and this time over the place for Reed-Hill's signature, he added the notation: "Forwarded, Disapproved." Skinner then walked into Reed-Hill's office with the amended paperwork, dated June 25, along with a copy of Coast Guard regulations requiring senior officers to forward reports up the line with an indication of their views, one way or the other. And after that he hand-carried the disapproved memo, now dated July 3, 1943, to Cmdr. Willard Smith, the admiral's aide, and asked him to forward it to his principal.

Skinner later said that Admiral Waesche was "a remarkable man and a remarkable officer. My direct contact with him was very limited . . . I believe him to represent the finest type of U.S. military or naval officer. Calm, cool, intelligent and intellectual, forceful, thoughtful of his officers and men, and demanding the highest performance."[21]

In any event, the admiral undoubtedly agreed with Skinner's proposed experiment because in November 1943 he received orders to report to USS *Sea Cloud* (IX-99) as its executive officer. There was no specific reference to Skinner's memo or its contents; it was, as far as Skinner was concerned, a routine personnel transfer.[22] After all, based on his experience on the cutter *Northland*, he was a qualified seagoing watch officer, navigator, and XO—and more than ready for the new job. "So I asked no questions, took my leave of the Public Relations Officer, packed my trunk and reported aboard the *Sea Cloud* at Constitution Wharf, Boston, where it was then based."[23] Skinner's new commanding officer, USS *Sea Cloud*'s second captain, was Lt. Cmdr. W. E. Schweizer, USCG.

On Board *Sea Cloud*

It is somewhat odd that Skinner was not officially or directly advised at the time that the commandant had approved his proposal or ordered him to implement it. So it was only by reading some indirect signs that Skinner was able to conclude that the experiment had been actually green-lighted.

But before that could happen, Lieutenant Skinner went back to sea. About ten days after he joined *Sea Cloud* on November 18, the ship departed Boston for a weather patrol in Station No. 4 off Bermuda. He says that he was assigned the midwatch (i.e., 0000–0400 or midnight to 4:00 a.m.) for thirty consecutive days. That seems unusual for two reasons: (a) Skinner was a senior lieutenant with considerable at-sea experience, and typically less experienced officers stand the midwatch; and (b) naval personnel are usually assigned to specific watch periods on a rotating basis. Thus, to catch the same undesirable watch period for one straight month would be highly irregular, if not punitive. Skinner concluded from this that "the captain was not so happy with my assignment [to *Sea Cloud*]."[24]

Regardless of any unhappiness Schweizer may have felt about his new officer, the Coast Guard had other views because on December 22, 1943 Skinner was promoted to lieutenant commander.

After *Sea Cloud* completed its patrol and was still at sea on its return run to Boston, the ship received a message ordering Schweizer to be detached and replaced by Skinner upon arrival back in port. This development was probably interpreted by Skinner as a strong indication that his experiment was a "go" in that he would now have his own ship in which to implement it.

Accordingly, the change of command took place on January 26, 1944, and the new captain had to prepare *Sea Cloud* for its next weather patrol and the first under his command.[25] At 0900 (9:00 a.m.) on his second day as skipper, Skinner took *Sea Cloud* over to the navy's fuel pier in Boston to top off. Supplies were brought on board, some officers and sailors departed for their next assignments, and some new personnel arrived to replace them.

Significantly, as it turns out, among the new arrivals was a draft of twenty African American apprentice seamen who had been sent to the ship by the Coast Guard Receiving Station at the old Hotel Brunswick three days before *Sea Cloud* was to depart on patrol.[26] In exchange for the new seamen, the ship detached an equal number of white sailors. Nicholas Rossi, one of the departing sailors, later said: "It was a complete shock to see them coming.

Lt. Cmdr. Carlton Skinner and captain of USS *Sea Cloud* (Coast Guard Historian's Office)

We'd never, ever seen a black crew before and didn't know how they'd make out."[27] Those new crewmen were still another indication to Skinner that he had the blessing from above to enact his plan. He attributes this development at least in part to the Task Force 24 commander, R. Adm. Edward H. "Iceberg" Smith, USCG, who "was very friendly and had already arrived at somewhat similar conclusions [regarding racial integration on naval vessels] and begun replacing the deck force with . . . black seamen, fresh from boot camp."[28] Skinner later wrote: "It was clear to me that I was being assigned to carry out what I had proposed. The method [i.e., no formal announcement] was probably the best in that it called the least attention to the program. In fact, it was responsive to my recommendation that there be no special attention or publicity."[29]

No special arrangements were made for the new men or any of the subsequent black sailors. They were berthed among the white crew, and the best racks went to the men of both races based on their seniority. There were instances in which veteran black petty officers and seamen received better berthing than nonrated white sailors. And there was one case in which a black chief commissary steward was accepted into the chief's mess—considerably better accommodations than those enjoyed by white petty officers and seamen.

The new crewmen were assigned watches and duties exactly the same as those of their white predecessors. As soon as they had accumulated sufficient on-the-job training, they were considered for promotion to seaman 1st class and then to coxswain or petty officer. Skinner later received two black officers from the Coast Guard Reserve Officer Training program (see below), and they, too, were assigned to the same duties as white boot ensigns—initially as junior watch officers, and eventually, after they were fully qualified watch officers, they were moved into more senior assignments.

Over the course of the year in which Skinner commanded *Sea Cloud*, the crew was composed in varying percentages by up to a maximum of 65 percent blacks, and the wardroom had between two to four African Americans along with about a dozen white officers.[30] He noted in a memoir that when the proportion of blacks in the total crew of 175 reached about 50 percent, "I suspended the special recruitment in order to keep a reasonable number

African American seamen in *Sea Cloud*'s deck force pose for a photograph by Lt. (j.g.) Joseph Jenkins. (Coast Guard Historian's Office)

The captain (second from right) discusses the function of the ship's after-steering equipment with some of his men. (Coast Guard Historian's Office)

of long service men and to avoid the possibility that due to past discrimination," some blacks "might try to dominate or be arrogant. In summary, it worked well."[31]

Ship's Company

As it happens, Skinner and *Sea Cloud* were rewarded with—and the experiment benefited from—some exceptional African American personnel.

Jacob Lawrence

Even before he joined the ship, Jacob Lawrence was a star. Born on September 17, 1917, in Atlantic City, New Jersey, Lawrence had already become a renowned artist by the time he turned twenty-four. Some of his first significant works—such as the famous "Migration of the American Negro" series—were produced in the 1930s.

He was drafted into the Coast Guard in October 1943 and immediately experienced the sting of uniformed racial discrimination. Lawrence was assigned as a steward's mate, the lot of most blacks in the Coast Guard. Fortunately, once on board *Sea Cloud*, he found an enlightened commanding officer who not only recognized and supported his artistic talent but helped him to eventually obtain a petty officer's rating of public relations specialist 3rd class.[32] Skinner authorized ship's funds to be used for the purchase of art supplies and arranged for Lawrence to work half days as a steward but then spend the other half painting.[33]

The seventeen paintings Lawrence produced on *Sea Cloud* show members of the racially mixed white and black crew performing their daily activities. "I was a correspondent," he said, "and all I saw were servicemen on board, period. I brought back images of what *servicemen* do."[34]

Lawrence had a good reputation on *Sea Cloud*. He was considered very congenial and was dedicated to his duties. Robert Hammond, a shipmate, recalled that Lawrence "was just one of the crew. But he would go to the engine room, go to the bridge, or be on deck with his sketch pad, drawing every day."[35]

Jacob Lawrence in his "night job" as the ship's artist. Photograph by Lt. (j.g.) Joseph Jenkins. (Coast Guard Historian's Office)

Lawrence records on a sketch pad members of *Sea Cloud*'s crew as they go about the wartime business of manning and operating the former yacht in 1944. (Coast Guard Historian's Office)

Following his assignment on *Sea Cloud*, Lawrence next served as one of the Coast Guard's first combat artists on board USS *General* W. P. *Richardson* (AP-118), ironically, a segregated troop transport.[36] He was honorably discharged in December 1945.

Eight of Lawrence's *Sea Cloud* paintings were displayed at the Museum of Modern Art in New York in October and November 1944. But those works were never returned to the Coast Guard and, along with another eight paintings illustrating coast guardsmen on duty, have been lost.[37] Lawrence's fourteen-painting series "War," depicting his wartime experiences, is now part of the permanent collection at the Whitney Museum of American Art in New York City.[38] During his twenty-six months in uniform, Lawrence produced more than fifty paintings, including one of his skipper, Carlton Skinner, which today is in the collection of the National Museum of American Art in Washington, DC.

Lawrence shows some army personnel his painting *Embarkation*, which portrays a tightly packed group of soldiers in a landing craft. (Coast Guard Historian's Office)

Lawrence's painting of his captain pictures Skinner and *Sea Cloud* against a background of naval vessels at night. (Solange P. Skinner)

Lawrence later said of his time on *Sea Cloud*, "It was the best democracy I've ever known." He could not point to even one significant incident of racial prejudice in the eight months he spent on the ship. "I think everyone was really relieved that integration had finally come. Segregation was such a burden to everyone, really. We were like a family on that ship."[39] (See the epilogue for information on Lawrence's later life.)

Robert Earl ("Rocky") Hammond

Rocky Hammond enlisted in the Coast Guard in September 1942 and went through boot camp in a segregated unit (Company 24) at the Manhattan Beach Training Station in Brooklyn. After graduation he was assigned to a black beach patrol and search-and-rescue crew at the Salisbury Beach Station in Massachusetts.[40]

In January 1944, while working as a steward at the Boston receiving station, Hammond heard that the Coast Guard was looking for twenty volunteers for an unspecified assignment. He raised his hand, packed his sea bag, and found himself and the other African American volunteers on a pier to which USS *Sea Cloud* was moored. A chief warrant officer cautioned the men to ready themselves for possible problems they could encounter from the ship's all-white crew. As Hammond later remembered it: "We were told that we were going to be called by every racial epithet that we knew, and at absolutely no time were we allowed to retaliate."[41] Initially the new men were indeed subjected to some name-calling by some white crewmen, but over time the African Americans earned the respect of their shipmates, if for no other reason than that they suffered and persevered equally from the mind-numbing cold, stormy seas, and less than appealing food.

In a 2007 interview Hammond praised the ship's captain. "Mr. Skinner was a very nice man and a very fair man. We were given an opportunity to strike [be trained] for any rate we wanted to."[42]

After striking for boatswain's mate, Hammond then was assigned to the troop transport USS *General George M. Randall* (AP-115).[43] He went on to command two Coast Guard patrol boats, the ninety-five-foot Cape-class WPB-95315 and the sixty-four-foot WPB-64308, and was the first officer in charge (the equivalent of captain) of the sixty-five-foot small harbor tug *Hawser* (WYTL-65610), based in Bayonne, New Jersey.[44] Hammond rose through the ranks to master chief boatswain's mate—the highest rank for an enlisted man—and retired from the service in September 1963 after a twenty-one-year career.[45] (See the epilogue for information on Hammond's later life.)

Joseph Charles Jenkins

Born in 1914, a year after Carlton Skinner, Jenkins earned a bachelor's degree in civil engineering at the University of Michigan in 1937, was a graduate student at Michigan State and the University of Michigan, and received a business administration degree through an extension program. Jenkins was an accomplished highway designer before the war, and he supervised the construction of the Detroit Crosstown Super Highway and the Willow Run Industrial Expressway.

He enlisted in the Coast Guard on June 15, 1942, and was originally rated as a boatswain's mate 1st class and then promoted to chief boatswain's mate within a month. He began his service as a recruiter in the Detroit area and then applied for the Officer Candidate School at the US Coast Guard Academy. Jenkins graduated as the first African American ensign in the Coast Guard Reserve in April 1943, almost a full year before any blacks were commissioned in the navy.[46]

After he was on board USS *Sea Cloud*, Jenkins was promoted to lieutenant (junior grade) and then qualified as the ship's navigator. Near the end of the war, he served under Skinner's command on board the Tacoma-class patrol frigate USS *Hoquiam* (PF-5) (see chapter 6). Jenkins was separated from active duty in the Coast Guard on November 2, 1945.[47]

Clarence Lorenzo Samuels

Born and raised in Panama, Samuels enlisted in the Coast Guard in 1920 as a seaman 2nd class on board the cutter *Earp* while it was visiting the Canal Zone.[48] Promoted rapidly through the enlisted ranks, he was given command of the Savannah-based forty-two-foot harbor patrol cutter AB-15 in July 1928. Perhaps because of his mixed Afro-Hispanic ethnicity, Samuels avoided the usual practice of assigning blacks to food service billets; he was able to serve in general duty roles and was promoted to chief quartermaster in 1929—the first minority to reach the highest NCO level in the Coast Guard. During the 1930s, he had a number of shore duty postings.[49]

Samuels was one of the first two blacks to become a Coast Guard warrant officer. He was commissioned as a lieutenant (junior grade) and assigned to USS *Sea Cloud* as its damage control officer. He served on it for a year and then became the first minority in the twentieth century to command a

Coast Guard vessel in wartime—first as captain of Lightship No. 115 on July 29, 1944, and later commanding officer of Lightship No. 91 on May 18, 1945.[50] Three months after that, on August 2, he was named CO of the Coast Guard buoy tender *Sweetgum* (WAGL-309), based in Miami.[51]

As the Coast Guard demobilized at war's end, Samuels was returned to the enlisted rate of chief boatswain's mate. He was given command of the Manzanita-class buoy tender *Tulip* (WAGL-249), which operated in the Philippines, and he retired there in 1947 after twenty-seven years of service.[52]

Harvey Clarence Russell

Like Carlton Skinner, Russell was the son of a college professor. He earned a degree at Kentucky State University and, like Jenkins, did graduate work at the University of Michigan. He enlisted in the Coast Guard as an apprentice seaman in December 1942 and became a coxswain in the spring of 1943. As he had previously been a high school teacher, the service assigned him to be a signalman instructor at its Advanced Seamanship School at the Manhattan Beach Training Station in Brooklyn.[53]

In September 1943 Russell attended the Reserve Officer Training Course nine months after Jenkins. With his training completed in February 1944, new ensign Russell joined Samuels and Jenkins on *Sea Cloud*, where he served as its training officer. He and Jenkins became friends, and the two officers were both later assigned to USS *Hoquiam* (PF-5), Carlton Skinner's second command (see chapter 6). Russell went on to serve as executive officer on a cutter in the Philippines and then assumed command of the racially integrated army fuel vessel TY-45 shortly after the war. (See the epilogue for information on Russell's later life.)

Reflections of a Captain

In 1983, forty years after he first came aboard *Sea Cloud* as a lieutenant and once again walking the decks of his former ship, Carlton Skinner reminisced about his wartime days as its captain. He told a group of passengers on the yacht that "any commanding officer becomes intimately familiar with the ship that he commands. An almost mystical relationship develops between the captain and the ship. . . . I can't say that he adores his ship, but he has a deep emotional relationship to it. Certainly, the *Sea Cloud*, which was my first command, was immensely important to me and emotionally important to me." Skinner spoke of his intimate knowledge of the ship—checking the

Striking an officer-like pose in their dress blues on *Sea Cloud* are (from left) Lt. (j.g.) Clarence Samuels, Ens. Harvey Russell, and Lt. (j.g.) Joseph Jenkins. (Coast Guard Historian's Office)

ship's bottom while it sat in dry dock, crawling around the engine spaces, peering in the carpenter's locker. "If something happened on the ship, as commanding officer, I had an almost instant realization of where it happened and what happened."[54]

One aspect of the ship that was not emotionally important but was certainly close to Skinner was the captain's sea cabin. Located on the bridge deck just abaft the bridge, the small sea cabin is used by the skipper for catching a few z's at night while his ship is underway, positioning him close to the bridge should he be needed in an emergency. Since *Sea Cloud* had been built in Germany and its first master was a small-statured Norwegian, the bunk in the sea cabin was just six feet long from head to toe. Skinner, being six feet three inches in height, could not squeeze into the bunk, so he ended up spending his at-sea nights "sleeping in a blanket on the transom or settee next to the desk" in the sea cabin.[55] In this case, at least, rank did not have its privileges.

▪ ▪ ▪ ▪

By the spring of 1944 Carlton Skinner's experiment was well underway. That first flapping of the butterfly's wings on *Northland* the year before had produced first a growing breeze and then a building tropical gale that would soon churn the waves of the naval establishment.

Chapter 6 will chronicle the further course of the experiment on *Sea Cloud*, the subsequent events in Skinner's and *Sea Cloud*'s Coast Guard service, and finally the significant wartime developments in the struggle for racial equality in the US Navy and Coast Guard.

6 Skinner's Barrier-Busting Experiment

As Carlton Skinner assumed command of USS *Sea Cloud* on January 26, 1944, World War II was far from over. After four years of bloody conflict, the tide was turning in favor of the Allies. In the past six months they had invaded Italy, landed in Bougainville and the Gilbert Islands, and taken Tarawa and Makin. But in the next six months the Allies would have to invade the Marshall Islands, Normandy, the Marianas, and southern France; all told, there would still be another year beyond that of heavy fighting in Europe, Asia, and in two oceans. That meant that Skinner had about eighteen months to fully implement and evaluate his unique experiment in racial integration at sea.

Training Days

The new captain viewed training as an essential requisite and foundation of his integration experiment. If new African American sailors were to be able to fill the roles usually performed by his ship's veteran white seamen and petty officers, they first had to be trained in those duties by the more experienced crewmen. That is why Skinner said: "I was particularly fortunate in the length of experience of the [white] petty officers and chief petty officers, many of whom had been in the Coast Guard for 15, 18 and 25 years. As a result, the body of experience of the petty officers on the *Sea Cloud* was probably superior to that of many ships at sea."[1]

Skinner also believed it essential that the men under his command be thoroughly trained—and retrained—to ensure that they were fully capable of "fighting the ship"—that is, able to use its weaponry efficiently and effectively both to defend themselves or to attack an enemy vessel. Even though

Sea Cloud was a mere weather ship and not a lucrative target, it was still at risk from German submarines or warships in the dangerous waters of the North Atlantic. Tragic evidence of this threat was the destruction of the cutter *Muskeget* (WAG-48), which was sunk with the loss of all 121 of its officers and crew while patrolling in Weather Station No. 2 on or about September 9, 1942.

As a unit in the navy's Task Force 24, *Sea Cloud* already had to meet a number of standard training requirements. On top of those, the Coast Guard also required a certain number of specialized drills. So for the officers and crew on the weather ship, every day found them taking part in various abandon-

(Top) *Sea Cloud* crewmen train at their general-quarters stations while Skinner, seen at lower right, and two other officers observe. The device in the enclosed platform at the top of the photograph is a rangefinder used to determine the distance to a target for the ship's 3-inch guns. Below the rangefinder in front of the sailor with binoculars is a 24-inch searchlight. Behind him and facing the camera is a signal lamp (blinker light) used for sending signals in Morse code. (Coast Guard Historian's Office)

(Bottom) A *Sea Cloud* sailor practices on one of the ship's eight 20 mm guns. (Coast Guard Historian's Office)

ship, man-overboard, damage-control, and general-quarters (battle stations) "evolutions" (i.e., activities or drills).[2]

Even when *Sea Cloud* was back in port after a weather patrol, training and education continued ashore. Officers and sonarmen were detailed off the ship to participate in antisubmarine tracking drills, gun crews took antiaircraft training in Rhode Island, and various petty officers and strikers went ashore for schooling in their specialty ratings.

Skinner explained that the "training was exactly that of any other Coast Guard unit operating in the Navy. I may have watched more closely than if I had not felt responsibility for the experiment. But I was convinced that it would work only if it were routine."[3] In other words, he wanted no special handling for the black sailors; if the experiment was to succeed, they had to be trained identically to everyone else.

Tests, Trials, Triumphs, Cumshaw, Midnight Reqs

Skinner's trailblazing experiment faced a number of challenges as it played out both at sea and ashore during the first ten months of 1944. There was, of course, some initial resentment, resistance, and expressions of racism by some whites directed toward the new black apprentice seamen. But over time, as all of the men were treated equally and suffered equally in performing their duties under very difficult conditions, resentment was replaced by acceptance, resistance was replaced by cooperation, and racism was left on the beach.

Intraracial Conflict

Not all the racial tension in the early months of the experiment was between white and black personnel. Some of the friction, which occasionally led to fighting, was between African Americans from the North and others from the southern states. These disturbances ended after Skinner appointed an African American—Boatswain's Mate 1st Class Paul L. Perkins—as the ship's master-at-arms (i.e., top cop), who, by using various subtle and unsubtle means of persuasion, quieted the discord.[4]

Intraracial Polarity

There were occasions when some of the African American enlisted men serving in a division led by a white officer indicated that they preferred to deal only with a black officer. And the reverse was sometimes the case, with some white enlisted men wanting to be led only by a white officer. Skinner put a stop to that because he knew that if this propensity was left unchecked, it would undermine the authority of all officers—black and white alike—and create a shipboard community aligned along racial lines.

But while the effort to bridge the racial divide was successful aboard his ship, Skinner found that he was unable to change the crew's attitudes ashore. He noticed that when liberty was called at the end of the working day (i.e., when men not in the duty section were free to leave the ship), his white sailors departed together to socialize only among themselves and his black sailors also stayed together. There was very little or no mingling of the races off the ship, even though there was general harmony, professional collaboration, and good will between them aboard ship.

Thanks but No Thanks

By the summer of 1944 some Coast Guard commands in the United States had learned through unofficial (grapevine) means that *Sea Cloud* was taking African Americans into its crew as replacements for departing white personnel. Consequently, those organizations began to transfer their black sailors with disciplinary problems to the ship. Once Skinner detected this practice, he realized that too many of these castoffs could corrupt his experiment.

So the captain met with Wilfred N. Derby, the senior Coast Guard officer in the First Naval District (encompassing most of New England), to explain the problem. Commodore (later Vice Admiral) Derby agreed that *Sea Cloud* should not become a kind of garbage dump for rejects and problem children, and he ordered his personnel officer to put a stop to the transfers and to work with Skinner if he "received a problem assignment" that he felt was "bad for the ship."[5]

Cumshaw for the Yardbirds

Some of the civilian workers in the Charlestown Navy Yard demonstrated that they did not want to work on a naval ship manned in part by black seamen and officers. The shipyard workers—called "yardbirds" by many sailors—either refused outright to come on board or failed to perform assigned work orders when they did show up. Skinner solved this problem by employing the time-honored navy practice of cumshaw: providing an item or service to someone in exchange for the provision of an item or service by that person. Some people might term this bartering; others might classify it as bribery.

In any event, Skinner knew that the civilians in Boston were experiencing shortages of coffee, butter, and sugar. So from time to time he had his chief commissary steward put together a cumshaw package of those items from *Sea Cloud*'s supplies to be handed off to the yard quarterman or leading man (i.e., the head civilian honcho) and voilà, as if by magic, yard personnel would then appear on board to accomplish the necessary tasks.[6]

Midnight Requisition

On another occasion, when *Sea Cloud* was moored at the South Boston Naval Annex, Skinner became concerned by the approach of what turned out to be the Great Atlantic Hurricane of September 1944. Wanting to ensure that his vessel was more than adequately secured to the pier, the captain dispatched his African American chief boatswain's mate to the yard to borrow a spool of wire with which to quadruple the ship's mooring lines on the dock. The chief came back to the ship empty-handed, telling Skinner, in what was obviously a case of racial discrimination, that the yardbirds had refused to give him any wire cable, claiming that there was none to be had.

Skinner queried the chief, asking if he had seen unused cable spools lying around the yard. Yes, sir, replied the chief. Well, the captain suggested, perhaps it might be possible for one of those spools to somehow get over to us in the dark of night. And lo and behold, sometime after sunset the needed wire arrived via what navymen call a "midnight requisition." The cable was then played out and rigged to reinforce the existing mooring lines, and *Sea Cloud* rode out the storm without any damage. Afterward, the borrowed wire was placed back on the spool and was returned to its place in the yard.[7] As Shakespeare would have put it: all's well that ends well.

Four Men Walk into a Bar

One day when *Sea Cloud* was back in Boston, the captain thought it was time to nudge along the integration of his black officers into the navy's shore-based establishment. And what better place to do it than the Charlestown Navy Yard Officers' Club, where off-duty officers gathered to eat, drink, and swap sea stories.

Having to overcome their initial reluctance, Skinner encouraged three of his African American junior officers to accompany him one evening to the all-white "O" Club. As the quartet walked in, every head at the club's fifty-foot bar cranked around to check out the unusual, perhaps unprecedented, arrival of three black Coast Guard officers. The *Sea Cloud* men ignored the stares, went quietly to a table, sat down, ordered a drink, downed it casually, ordered a second, finished it, and again quietly got up and departed. Happily, no unpleasant business occurred.

Skinner repeated this "drill" over the next three evenings with the same result. On the fifth night, he told his officers to go to the "O" Club, but this time without him. They did. Again there was no unpleasantness. The test was successful. As the captain later recalled: "I, of course, have no way of knowing whether there would have been any incident if they had gone in [initially] by themselves without me present but in any case . . . the Charlestown Navy Yard officers' club was [now effectively] integrated."[8]

The Voyages of USS *Sea Cloud*

Lt. Cmdr. Carlton Skinner took his ship to sea for the first time as captain at the beginning of February 1944. *Sea Cloud* relieved the cutter *Conifer* (WAGL-301) on the fifth day of the month and performed its weather patrol mission until February 26 within 100 square miles of 52°N, 44°30' W (i.e., in a box approximately 745 miles south of Greenland and 620 miles east of Newfoundland). After it was relieved on station, the ship headed back to Boston, arriving there on March 4.

Sea Cloud next underwent a one-week availability at the Bethlehem Atlantic Works shipyard in East Boston, and set out again on March 11 to patrol in Weather Station No. 1, centered at 34° N, 55° W (i.e., approximately 560 miles east of Bermuda), beginning on March 14 and ending on April 4.

On March 23, 1944, all of the Atlantic Ocean weather patrol vessels were assigned to the commander in chief of the US Atlantic Fleet (Adm. Ernest J. King), with operational control exercised by the commander of Task Force 24 (R. Adm. Edward H. "Iceberg" Smith) and administrative control assigned to the commander of the Atlantic Fleet's destroyer force (R. Adm. O. M. Read). Skinner was advised in a secret message that same day that effective April 1 the responsibility for maintenance and operation of the weather patrol had been assigned to Admiral King and that *Sea Cloud* was now part of the Atlantic Fleet.[9] At the end of the month Admiral Smith directed Skinner to continue to base his ship in Boston and to maintain the patrol schedule already established by Commodore Derby. But those instructions were soon to change.

On April 1 the weather stations in the North Atlantic were reorganized into eight areas under the control of Task Force 24 at the US Naval Station

Blacky, a supernumerary and mascot of *Sea Cloud*'s crew, relaxes while the ship patrols at sea. The "potted plant" predates Captain Morgan's palm tree in *Mister Roberts* by two years. (Coast Guard Historian's Office)

in Argentia, Newfoundland.[10] This organizational realignment, too, would shortly affect *Sea Cloud*'s upcoming operations and crew.

Three days later the cutter *Sorrel* (WAGL-296) relieved *Sea Cloud*, allowing it to depart Weather Station No. 1 and set course for Boston. While homebound on April 5 in the general vicinity of 39°27' N, 62°30' W (approximately 775 miles east of New Jersey and 310 miles south of Nova Scotia), the ship's radar detected a small surface vessel almost dead ahead and 3,000 yards distant. Skinner brought the ship to general quarters, but *Sea Cloud* lost the contact about ten minutes later. The target had been moving at about 10 knots, heading north, and was considered to be a submarine. *Sea Cloud* dropped a string of "ash cans" (depth charges) in the immediate area and then came about and dropped a second string, but unfortunately all attempts to reacquire the contact over the next six hours failed. Skinner informed Task Force 24 of the encounter and resumed his transit back to Boston.

Triggered at least in part by Skinner's report, two units of Destroyer Division 32 under the command of Cmdr. C. L. Melson began hunting German submarines in the area. On June 11 one of the hunters—USS *Champlin* (DD-601), a Benson-class destroyer—picked up an underwater sonar contact at 1542 (3:42 p.m.).[11] It was joined by USS *Huse* (DE-145), an Edsall-class destroyer escort, and the two ships dropped depth charges and fired hedgehogs on the submerged sub.[12] Finally, after more than an hour of bombardment from above, the U-856 surfaced to do battle with the attackers. During the exchange of gunfire and a ramming by *Champlin*, Cmdr. J. J. Schaffer, *Champlin*'s captain, was mortally wounded—the only US fatality of the battle. U-856 lost the fight and sank at 1714 (5:14 p.m.), while two other US destroyers managed to rescue twenty-eight German survivors of the *Champlin*'s attack.[13]

Carlton Skinner believed that *Sea Cloud* had shared in the destruction of U-856. He told a group of guests on board his former ship in 1983 that "in later naval publications we have been credited with an assist in that submarine attack."[14] In any event, whether a direct, indirect, or incidental partner in the U-856 kill, USS *Sea Cloud* arrived back in Boston on April 7. Over the next two weeks the ship conducted upkeep, repair, and maintenance activities and went about preparing for the next patrol.

On April 20 USS *Sea Cloud* got underway and headed for Weather Station No. 2 to relieve USS *Zircon* (PY-16) five days later.[15] It in turn was relieved by the cutter *Sorrel* on May 16. But while still at sea Skinner received a message from Task Force 24 telling him that *Sea Cloud*'s homeport had been changed to Argentia and that he was to head there rather than to Boston. This change in basing was necessary because Argentia was closer than Boston to three of the principal weather stations and would require less transit time for the weather ships between patrols. Nevertheless, Skinner recalled years later that this order led to "the disappointment of many of the crewmen whose families lived in Boston," more than 900 miles from Newfoundland.[16] "Disappointment" might be a classic understatement.

With the new orders in hand, *Sea Cloud* then duly motored up to Argentia, arriving there on May 20, 1944. Skinner was already familiar with the port, having visited it several times during his *Northland* service. This knowledge came in handy when *Sea Cloud* neared the harbor and was met by a navy pilot who was to guide the ship safely to its assigned pier. When it came time to hand the conn over to the pilot, he demurred and said to Skinner: "I think you know the ship better than I do, why don't you dock her?" Although the proposal was quite unusual, Skinner agreed but discovered on his approach to the pier that he had only 315 feet of space available in which to squeeze his 316-foot ship, with a vessel already moored both immediately ahead and astern of that slot. Captain Skinner gave the benefit of the doubt to the port commander who had assigned the space, figuring that he had used *Sea Cloud*'s length between perpendiculars rather than its overall length in determining where it could be moored.[17] In any event, Skinner managed to get *Sea Cloud* tied up with no damage to either his ship or his two new neighbors.

USS *Sea Cloud* departed Argentia on May 30 to relieve USS *Zircon* for patrol in Weather Station No. 3—an area of 100 square miles centered at 43° N, 37° W (about halfway between Newfoundland and Europe and approximately 400 miles off the coast of France)—beginning June 2.[18] During the morning watch that day, Skinner and his lookouts observed over the horizon a very large body of warships heading east. "The ocean was literally covered with ships," he recalled.[19] Knowing that the Allies were soon to invade France, Skinner and his crew began to think—and hope—that perhaps they might be diverted to join the naval armada and get to participate in the D-Day landings.

On June 10 USS *Croatan* (CVE-25), a 465-foot Bogue-class escort carrier with about twenty-four aircraft on board, was steaming in the Atlantic near *Sea Cloud*'s position.[20] The carrier and its antisubmarine hunter-killer team (Task Group 22.5 under the command of Capt. J. P. W. Vest) had been informed that a German U-boat was operating in the vicinity of the Azores.[21] On June 11 *Sea Cloud* received orders from a navy TBF Avenger torpedo bomber flying from *Croatan* to change its course to 035 degrees (northeast). Skinner did so and pushed his ship to "all ahead full." At 1655 (4:55 p.m.) *Sea Cloud* sighted *Croatan* and its consorts, including the destroyer escorts USS *Frost* (DE-144), USS *Inch* (DE-146), and USS *Huse* (DE-145).[22]

Sea Cloud moored starboard side to the pier in Argentia in the summer of 1944. (Coast Guard Historian's Office)

At 1748 (5:48 p.m.) *Sea Cloud* was directed to report to *Croatan* and four minutes later was ordered to take station astern of the carrier. It was all *Sea Cloud* could do to squeeze out even 14 knots from its Krupp engines while the carrier was capable of 17 knots. Nevertheless, the weather ship was somehow able to keep up but at 2001 (8:01 p.m.), *Croatan* ordered *Sea Cloud* to break off from its escorting task and instead to proceed to a position at 40°12' W to investigate a life raft that had been spotted by one of its aircraft. *Sea Cloud* arrived at the location at 0318 (3:18 a.m.) on June 12 and began the search. After nearly thirty hours of fruitless searching, *Sea Cloud* broke off the hunt at 0918 (9:18 a.m.) on June 13 and returned to its assigned weather station. Thus, Operation Overlord—the Allied invasion of Normandy—went on without *Sea Cloud*.

As *Sea Cloud* was off looking for the life raft and possible survivors, *Croatan*'s destroyer escort hunter-killers had been maintaining intermittent sonar contact with a submarine, dropping depth charges and firing hedgehogs at the submerged boat, and waiting for an opportunity to catch the sub up on the surface as it recharged its batteries. Finally, not long after *Sea Cloud* had left the carrier on the search mission, USS *Frost* picked up the sub on its radar. *Frost* and *Inch* opened fire with their five-inch guns, and after a wild chase on the surface, the target disappeared from the radar. Minutes later, the DEs found a number of German sailors in the water and on yellow rubber rafts, and at 2210 (10:10 p.m.) a large underwater explosion was heard. It marked the death of the U-490, a "milk cow" submarine designed to provide fuel and provisions to other U-boats. Despite the loss of the boat, sixty Germans, including U-490's captain, were pulled out of the ocean and saved. Here again *Sea Cloud* had been an indirect or incidental participant in the destruction of a German submarine.

Sea Cloud was relieved in Weather Station No. 3 on June 21 by *Sorrel* and shaped a course for the return to Argentia, arriving at its new base three days later. Skinner maintained the crew's training regimen in Argentia that he had practiced in Boston. On June 27, for example, Ens. Harvey Russell, one of the black officers, took a group of twenty men off the ship for training at the base's fire-fighting school, while nine officers and six enlisted men returned to *Sea Cloud* from antisubmarine warfare school.

After two weeks in port for repairs and maintenance, Skinner got *Sea Cloud* underway on July 8 and proceeded to Weather Station No. 4, centered at 55° N, 44°30' W (south of Greenland and east of Newfoundland), where it relieved *Zircon*. It remained on that patrol until August 2, when it was itself

Capt. Carlton Skinner (right) and his executive officer, Lt. Cmdr. Wallace B. Bishop, pose for photographer Ens. Joseph Jenkins while at sea in the North Atlantic. Besides serving as XO, Bishop was also the ship's unofficial cartoonist-in-residence. (Coast Guard Historian's Office)

relieved by *Sorrel*, after which it undertook a search for possible survivors of a downed aircraft.

The Ending of the Beginning

While *Sea Cloud* was still out at sea on patrol on July 29, the navy's commander in chief, Adm. Ernest J. King, advised the commander in chief of the Atlantic Fleet (CINCLANT), Adm. Royal E. Ingersoll, that he was seeking the ship's early release from active duty and inquired when that could happen. Two days later Ingersoll told Rear Admiral Smith, commander of Task Force 24 (CTF 24), that *Sea Cloud* was to proceed to Boston "for further disposition" on or about August 8. At 1208 (12:08 p.m.) on August 2, CTF 24 ordered the ship to "report to Comm One [commandant of the First Naval District headquartered in Boston] for disposition upon arrival." On August 5 the chief of naval operations advised the commandant of the Boston Navy Yard that *Sea Cloud* had been assigned an availability in his yard "for docking, bottom painting and urgent underwater repairs," that the ship's underwater equipment should be removed during the docking period, and that the ship should be docked on August 15.[23] Following orders, *Sea Cloud* arrived in Boston on August 7 as its naval career was drawing to a close.

One might wonder why the navy wanted to dispose of *Sea Cloud* just twenty-eight months after being brought into the service and with the war not yet won. Well, in the first place, by mid-1944 the navy was acquiring a vast number of purpose-built warships of various types and classes. The fleet had grown from 790 hulls at the start of the war to about 6,000 ships. Thus, there was no further need for nonstandard, oddball vessels such as converted yachts and trawlers. Secondly, *Sea Cloud* was proving difficult to repair and maintain because of its one-off propulsion plant and the lack of spare parts. In short, the navy now had a sufficient inventory of highly capable ships ready to take its place in the war.

The navy's Office of Public Relations issued a statement that "with the improved submarine situation off the Atlantic coast and in the Caribbean the Navy was returning to their owners or former owners several hundred pleasure craft and fishing vessels taken for coastal patrol activities. The return of these craft would relieve the Navy of the expense of their operation and allow the assignment of men to other activities."[24] In reporting this news the *New York Times* informed its readers that *Sea Cloud* specifically would be returned to Joseph Davies about November 1 and that the "terms of an agreement, releasing the Navy from its obligation to restore the vessel to its former condition, are 'under negotiation.'"[25]

When *Sea Cloud* tied up at the Charlestown Navy Yard on August 7, Skinner was informed that his ship was going to receive a Board of Inspection and Survey (INSURV) inspection prior to its decommissioning. Such inspections are extremely complex, comprehensive, and thorough and are performed to carefully evaluate the material condition of a ship and its equipment and machinery as well as to determine what actions might be required to correct any deficiencies and problems.

Skinner thought it unusual for a ship in wartime to receive an INSURV inspection since it meant in a sense disabling the vessel prior to and during the examination. But then he soon realized "that the ship was to be returned to the civilian owner, Ambassador and Mrs. Davies, and the Navy was concerned that the Ambassador, being a friend of President Roosevelt, it was very important to the Navy that the ship be in the best possible condition when it was returned."[26]

Skinner consulted with his engineering officer and determined that it was going to be very difficult to properly prepare *Sea Cloud* for an INSURV. To do so, Skinner borrowed twenty machinist's mates from the Boston receiving station (the same source from which his first African American seamen had come the year before), canceled all leave for the crew, and limited liberty to just the six hours before midnight.

Skinner (second from right) and three of his officers discuss the work to be performed on *Sea Cloud* at the Atlantic Works shipyard. (Coast Guard Historian's Office)

On August 31 Commodore Derby, the senior Coast Guard officer in the First Naval District, directed the commanding officer of the Chelsea, Massachusetts, Coast Guard base that any and all of *Sea Cloud*'s equipment, spare parts, and related materials that had been stored at his facility be invoiced and delivered to the ship during its availability at the Bethlehem Atlantic Works shipyard.

Sea Cloud entered the Atlantic Works shipyard in East Boston in September for two months of decommissioning work. Among the jobs to be performed were these:

- Reconnecting the vessel's holding tanks. *Sea Cloud*'s builder-installed holding tanks (which stored the human waste produced in the heads) had been disconnected by the navy (actually *Sea Cloud*'s own personnel) so that the crew's waste could be discharged directly overboard. That arrangement had to be restored to its antebellum status. In addition, the interior of the holding tanks had to be cleaned and covered with a preservative. The ship's crew and not shipyard workers handled this unpleasant task.

- The 316-foot hull had to be repainted. The navy's gray paint had to first be chipped off down to bare metal by men sitting on planks and scaffolding hanging over the sides. Here again, instead of using yard workers for the job, the navy employed *Sea Cloud* personnel to do it.

While all this was going on, William R. Wood, the representative of Joseph Davies, along with people from Cox & Stevens and Gibbs & Cox, visited *Sea*

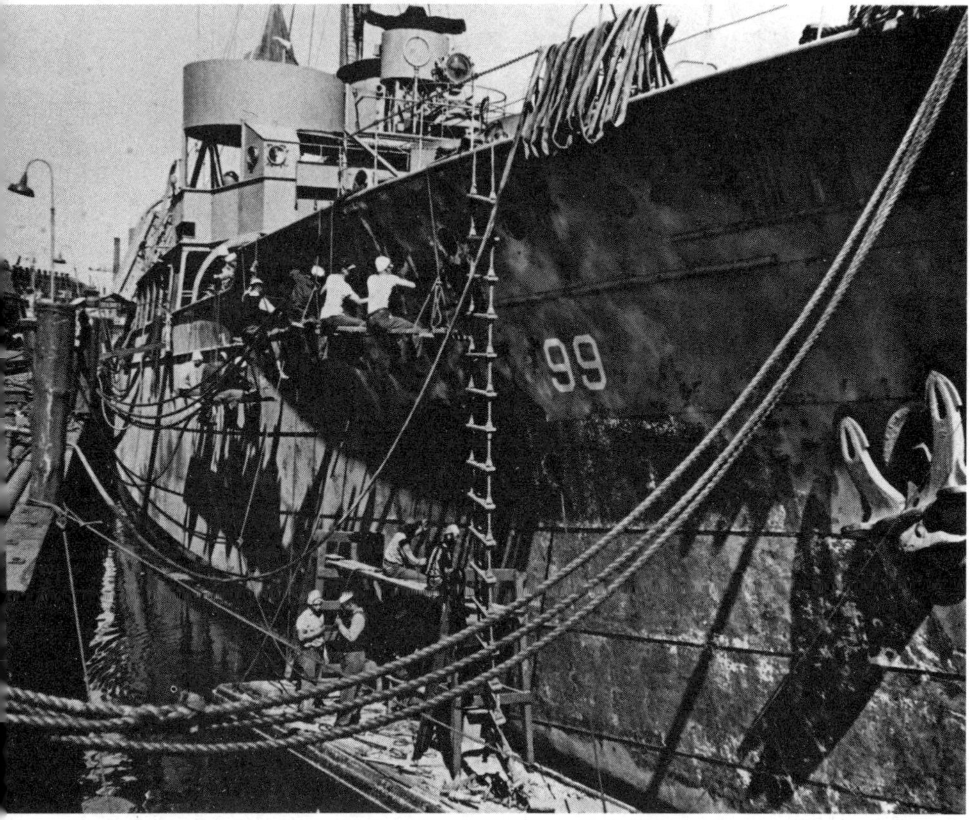

Crewmen on scaffolding chip away *Sea Cloud*'s wartime paint from the starboard hull. (Coast Guard Historian's Office)

This view of the chipping work on the 316-foot port hull provides some perspective on the overall scope of the project. (Coast Guard Historian's Office)

Two crewmen suspended just below the hull perform the difficult task of removing the old paint. (Coast Guard Historian's Office)

Cloud from time to time to check on the progress of the yacht's restoration and to ensure that the work conformed to the original requirements and standards met by the vessel during its construction and fitting out in Germany.

On October 27 the chief of naval operations advised the commandant of the First Naval District that the Board of Inspection and Survey would inspect *Sea Cloud* on November 3 "to determine present material condition of the vessel" and that the commandant was authorized to place the ship out of commission the day after the inspection. In the meantime,

> the crew should continue to clean ship. All strictly Navy and Coast Guard equipment which may be placed to future Navy use will be removed except

Sea Cloud's spare tire? A nine-foot, six-inch manganese bronze propeller sitting on the ship's main deck at the Atlantic Works shipyard is a vivid illustration of one of the many parts needed to move a 3,000-ton vessel through the water. (Coast Guard Historian's Office)

> the equipment spares and stores received with the vessel or the equivalent replacements. Vessel will be delivered to owner or his authorized agent on or about 4 November. A complete inventory of equipment spares and stores will be furnished the owner or his authorized agent at the time of delivery and a proper receipt for the vessel and equipment spares and stores in accordance with the above inventory obtained.[27]

Two days later *Sea Cloud* sent a classified message estimating that the earliest possible inspection date would be November 7 and that since five to seven days would be required to reassemble all of the machinery that had been opened for the inspection, the earliest possible decommissioning date should be set for November 12.[28]

The inspection was conducted by an admiral, two captains, three commanders, some lower-ranking officers, and a yeoman. Skinner personally escorted the admiral from one end of *Sea Cloud* to the other and into every nook and cranny. At one point during the tour the admiral said to Skinner: "I noticed that you have a bath tub [a holdover from its yachting days] in your quarters. Will you have your steward draw me a cold bath? I would like to take a cold bath. Notify me when lunch is ready."[29] So while the admiral cooled himself in Skinner's bathtub, the rest of the inspection went on, and by the middle of the afternoon, the admiral and his team had departed. Whether the bath had anything to do it will never be known but, in any event, *Sea Cloud* passed the inspection in fine shape. As Skinner sardonically put it: "The Navy treated us exactly like any other ship . . . that was being returned to the civilian owner who was a friend of the President of the United States."[30]

After the board formally completed its inspection of *Sea Cloud* on November 4, it informed the navy's Bureau of Ships in a classified message of the following:

> As far as can be determined by material inspection alongside dock vessel is considered in a seaworthy condition for return to the owner and it is the Board's opinion that $175,000 represents an equitable sum to be paid to the owner upon return of the vessel, which sum is also considered to be less than the cost to the owner of restoring the vessel to its former condition as a yacht.[31]

Skinner himself pegged the cost to the navy for the work performed by the shipyard at $750,000. He estimated the cost of the work performed by his own crew at another $750,000. And he said that the navy paid Joseph Davies $750,000 for such items as replacement of the masts, sails, and rigging and restoration of various surfaces that had been cut or deformed (for the installation of gun mounts, for example) when the yacht was converted to a weather ship.[32] He also observed: "I suspect that all that still did not fully compensate Ambassador and Mrs. Davies and if we look at the probable cost of the replacement of the *Sea Cloud* today [1983], I would suspect that the original cost in Kiel, Germany of less than $1,000,000 is now in the neighborhood of $40 to $50 million."[33]

On Friday, November 4, 1944, USS *Sea Cloud* (IX-99) was moored with its starboard side to Pier 2 at the Atlantic Works shipyard. The 10:10 a.m. entry in the ship's log book reads as follows: "Lt. Cmdr. Carlton Skinner USCGR was officially relieved of his command by Cmdr. J. Stone, USNR, and the ship was officially decommissioned and turned over to the owner's repre-

Looking almost as good as new, *Sea Cloud* nears the end of its restoration at the Atlantic Works shipyard. (Coast Guard Historian's Office)

sentative Mr. William R. Wood."[34] Wood accepted the ship and signed a receipt for the transfer five minutes later.

The officers and men of *Sea Cloud* were detached from further duty on the ship and most of them were granted ten days of leave, to be followed by

Back where it belongs. The yacht's original golden eagle figurehead has been reinstalled on *Sea Cloud*. (Coast Guard Historian's Office)

During the decommissioning event Skinner (right), his XO, Lt. Cmdr. Wallace B. Bishop (left), and the crew enjoy a humorous comment in the final hour all of these men will be together. (Coast Guard Historian's Office)

reporting to the Coast Guard Receiving Station at 320 Boylston Street (Hotel Brunswick) for assignment for further duty. (See appendix C for a listing of the ship's crew.)

In Skinner's case, he was directed to report to the commanding officer of the US Naval Training Center in Miami for instruction at the NTC's Command School.

Sea Cloud's name was struck from the official list of naval vessels on November 13, 1944, and with that stroke of the pen, its naval service was formally, fully, and forever over.

Evaluating the Experiment

Carlton Skinner considered his racial integration project on board *Sea Cloud* as a success. As he told the President's Committee on Equality of Treatment and Opportunity in the Armed Forces in 1949, his ship met and performed all of its duties and assignments well. It had received an extensive inspection by a team from the navy's Atlantic Fleet, and compared with other ships under the aegis of Commander of Destroyers, Atlantic Fleet, *Sea Cloud* had been rated excellent or very good in every department.[35] In addition, the ship had passed its thorough Board of Survey and Inspection examination prior to decommissioning.

He told an interviewer in 1970 that there had been no incident of racial trouble on the ship and that he was "very proud of the fact it [*Sea Cloud*] was a functioning seagoing unit."[36] Skinner summed it up this way:

> The experiment in racial integration aboard a naval ship worked as I had believed it would. It was no more difficult than I expected. It made me tense at times and I am sure made my Negro officers tense at times, but it worked. . . . Upon reflection I have wondered if I should not have evangelized for my theories, put on a campaign for their general adoption. I did not, first because I was too busy as commanding officer making them work, and second, because of my basic belief that this kind of thing should happen naturally and should not be in the spotlight.[37]

But he did tell at least two people about the experiment. The first was Erwin Canham, editor of the *Christian Science Monitor* in Boston. Skinner had known Canham from his time as a reporter in Washington and invited him for lunch on board *Sea Cloud*.[38] Skinner discussed the project with Canham, showed him around the ship, and introduced him to some of the crew. But Canham "showed no interest of any sort in the project and never wrote about it."[39]

The second person was Eugene S. Duffield, who had been a colleague of Skinner's at the *Wall Street Journal* in 1936–38.[40] In 1944 Duffield was serving as a civilian assistant to the secretary of the navy, James V. Forrestal. Just before Skinner began his training in Miami, he spoke with Duffield in Washington and gave him a complete briefing on the experiment, together with his thoughts on how it could be replicated and employed in the war effort. Duffield, Skinner says, promised to pass that information along to SecNav.[41] This conversation may have been one of the most important in Skinner's life and in the navy's handling of its African American personnel during the war. As we shall see, just a few months after the discussion with Duffield, Secretary Forrestal set in motion the first initiative to get black sailors assigned to general service on board the navy's ships—something that Skinner had already achieved on *Sea Cloud* the year before.

North to Alaska

In January and February of 1945 Carlton Skinner attended an eight-week command training course at the NTC in Miami, and it was there that he most likely enjoyed some of the balmiest weather he had experienced at any point of his Coast Guard service. Those many months on *Northland* off Greenland and then the year on *Sea Cloud* in the North Atlantic, and even stays in port in Argentia and Boston (in the winter), must have deeply chilled his bones. But the semitropical warmth in South Florida would quickly fade into Skinner's rearview mirror as he left Miami for his next and final duty station as commanding officer of USS *Hoquiam* (PF-5) on patrol in the Alaskan Sea Frontier.

Hoquiam was a Tacoma-class patrol frigate that was commissioned on May 8, 1944. Just under 304 feet long and displacing 2,230 tons, it was manned by 190 officers and enlisted men, one of seventy-six navy PFs operated by the Coast Guard (see appendix B for specifications). As a unit in Escort Division 27, *Hoquiam* patrolled and escorted convoys along the Alaskan coast, visiting Adak in the Aleutians in early December and Attu in late December 1944 and early January 1945.

Along with two black officers from his former command—Joseph Jenkins and Harvey Russell—and about thirty enlisted *Sea Cloud* sailors, Skinner was flown up to Adak in March. He relieved Lt. Joseph G. Bastow Jr. as commanding officer on March 8, 1945, and continued on *Hoquiam* the experiment he had begun on *Sea Cloud* the year before. This time he had a good head start since at the outset about 20 percent of both the wardroom and of the crew were veterans of the earlier project.

Over the spring and summer months additional African American enlisted men were assigned to the ship and ultimately made up about 40 percent of the crew. The PF performed convoy escort missions in the Aleutians practically right up to the eve of V-J Day. Skinner later told the President's Committee on Equality of Treatment and Opportunity in the Armed Forces that *Hoquiam* had experienced no major problems and had met all of its operational requirements. With respect to the experiment, he said that "there

USS *Hoquiam* underway near Cold Bay, Alaska, in 1945. (Coast Guard Historian's Office)

was no segregation by compartments, departments or messes, and white and colored sailors were assigned the duties of their rates."[42] In another account, Skinner noted that "the ship functioned well—in fact, better than under my predecessor."[43]

When President Roosevelt died on April 12, *Hoquiam* was moored in a narrow fjord on Adak Island, along with two aviation gasoline tankers, two or three patrol craft, and a few small yard craft.[44] Skinner decided to exercise his responsibilities and prerogatives as the senior officer in that "flotilla" to convene a memorial service honoring the late president. He had all of the various crews mustered on the dock at 0800 (8:00 a.m.) and, using the *Hoquiam*'s 1MC public address system, read a few paragraphs from FDR's speeches and a verse from the Bible, followed by taps sounded on a bugle. Skinner was proud of this commemoration, which he suspected would be frowned upon by the politically conservative senior officers at the nearby district headquarters. As he put it, "I had my own private and personal funeral service for President Roosevelt, strictly in accordance with Navy regulations, as [determined by] the Senior Officer Present Afloat in that remote area [i.e., himself]."[45]

In mid-1945 Carlton Skinner faced another integration challenge. This time it was not centered on race but instead on the merging of two different nationalities, languages, and cultures. In June 1945 *Hoquiam* was designated to be transferred to the Soviet Union under the terms of a Lend-Lease agreement so that the ship could be used by the Russians in the planned invasion of Japan. To accomplish this, *Hoquiam* first had to be modified to accommodate the new Russian crew, and, second, that crew had to be quickly trained in the operation of the frigate. Accordingly, *Hoquiam* steamed down to Seattle for performance of the necessary shipyard work and then cruised 1,500 miles back up to Cold Bay, Alaska, where a three-month training program was conducted.

During the ensuing weeks some 200 Russian sailors arrived on board to replace the ship's US crew and learn the fundamentals of navigation, seamanship, gunnery, and operation of the propulsion machinery as practiced by the US Navy. Skinner had retained command of the frigate even after the Russians were on board, and he also had the assistance of Jenkins and Russell, as well as three of his enlisted personnel, as he readied the Soviets to take over. The captain rated the Russians as excellent gunners but "poor navigators and lousy seamen."[46]

Despite the questionable navigation and seamanship, USS *Hoquiam* was indeed decommissioned and transferred to the Soviet navy on August 16, 1945, and renamed EK-14 by the Russians. At the same time, Skinner officially relinquished command of the ship. As Japan had already surrendered two days before the transfer, *Hoquiam* (or EK-14) was never used by the Russians as intended. It nevertheless remained in Soviet service for four years but was returned to US possession on November 1, 1949, and turned over in Yokosuka, Japan. So it finally did get to Japan after all.[47]

With the war now over after six years of global conflict, the services of Lt. Cmdr. Carlton Skinner, USCGR, were no longer needed by his country. Accordingly, he was "released to inactive duty under honorable condition" in Alameda, California, on October 3, 1945. After three years and two months of sea service during World War II, he was now unemployed.

▪ ▪ ▪ ▪

In considering the events on *Sea Cloud* and *Hoquiam*, the question some would fairly ask is: was Skinner's bold experiment really unique and unprecedented? And the answer to that would have to be: in some respects no, not entirely, as there were a few other instances in the early twentieth century in which African American or other minority sailors manned naval vessels.

Sea Cloud Approximations

After World War I the navy used a segregated crew of Filipinos on one ship and an all-Samoan crew on a second vessel. But the service's Bureau of Navigation, which was then responsible for personnel matters, was dissatisfied with those experiments and concluded as a consequence that a black-crewed ship would prove to be no better.[48]

At about that same time, the Coast Guard cutter *Yocona* operated out of Vicksburg, Mississippi, in 1919–25 with an enlisted crew of black nonrated seamen supervised by white petty officers and officers.[49] Although the Coast Guard does not regard this case as an experiment in racial integration per se, according to a service historian, *Yocona* may be considered as the "20th century's first desegregated federal vessel."[50]

Later, in 1944, while Skinner was commanding a *fully integrated* crew on *Sea Cloud*, the navy assigned 196 African Americans to serve on board USS *Mason* (DE-529), an Evarts-class destroyer escort that was commissioned on March 20, 1944.[51] It should be noted that in this case the blacks were led by forty-four white officers and petty officers (NCOs), although the black seamen were to eventually fill all of the enlisted billets once they were fully trained and qualified.[52] On October 18, 1944, while escorting a convoy, *Mason* encountered heavy weather in the North Atlantic that caused severe structural damage and threatened the vessel's seaworthiness. Fortunately, the ship's largely black crew was able to make emergency repairs and continue their escort mission. In an overdue recognition of their accomplishment, President Bill Clinton in 1994 awarded commendations to the sixty-seven surviving *Mason* crewmen.[53]

In addition to the USS *Mason* test case, in 1944 the Bureau of Naval Personnel—which had succeeded the Bureau of Navigation—assigned fifty-three African American seamen along with fourteen white officers and petty officers to man USS PC-1264, a PC-461-class submarine chaser that was commissioned on April 25, 1944.[54]

A navy publication reported in the following year that "the manning of a DE and a PC with predominantly Negro crews has been entirely satisfactory. Both ships are now successfully performing escort duties."[55] Nevertheless, the navy did not rush to embrace the concept of assigning significant numbers of African Americans to its ships. Despite what the service regarded as the success of the *Mason* and PC-1264 experiments, only four additional patrol craft with segregated crews joined the fleet before the Japanese surrender.[56]

Skinner knew about these two tests but held to his view that naval ships should have racially mixed crews and not be manned almost entirely by blacks or exclusively by one race or another (e.g., *Mason* and PC-1264). In a somewhat forceful June 10, 1945, memorandum to the Coast Guard commandant, Skinner wrote that "an all-Negro Coast Guard crew is inefficient, impractical and undesirable." In two-and-half tightly-written pages he argued that such a practice would be inefficient "because it sets up an arbitrary and unnecessary standard for assignment to duty and advancement," that it would be impractical because it "violates the basic Coast Guard principle that all personnel in any rank or rate are trained and available for any job set up for that rank or rate," and that it would be undesirable because it "creates racial friction and is destructive of morale, both of white and Negro personnel." Written while he was commanding USS *Hoquiam* in Alaska, Skinner referred to the recently announced navy policy of manning its auxiliary vessels with up to 10 percent of the crew made up of African Americans. "This policy appears to be the best solution for attaining efficient utilization of Negroes in the Coast Guard." He concluded his memo to Admiral Waesche by recommending that "no all-Negro crew be established in the Coast Guard" and that "a ten percent limit on assignment of general service Negro personnel be set up as Coast Guard policy."[57]

The Door Opens Another Inch or Two

Aside from these two limited (compared with *Sea Cloud*) trials, the navy in 1944 ever so slowly and incrementally began to broaden the employment of African Americans in its seagoing vessels. New Secretary of the Navy James V. Forrestal advised President Roosevelt on May 20 of that year that blacks would now be assigned to large auxiliary ships and that their numbers would not exceed 10 percent of the ships' complement.[58] And then, if there were no problems, Forrestal planned to detail small numbers of African Americans to other types of ships "as necessity dictates." FDR agreed with this approach.[59] Thus, on August 9, 1944, Fleet Adm. Ernest J. King, the navy's top officer, informed the commanding officers of twenty-five large fleet auxiliary ships that blacks would shortly be sent to them but in numbers no greater than 10 percent of their total manpower.

To help reinforce this policy, Fleet Adm. Chester W. Nimitz, the commander in chief of the Pacific Fleet, advised the commanding officer of one amphibious cargo ship (AKA) that there would be less racial trouble aboard naval vessels if blacks were housed among other members of the crew rather than be isolated in segregated berthing. "When we say we want integration," he told the captain, "we mean *integration*."[60] Eventually, the African Americans were placed in general service billets on navy auxiliary vessels, and their captains later reported that racial integration had worked on their ships.[61] As Morris MacGregor puts it in his comprehensive study of the subject: "Thus integration grew out of both idealism and realism"—which was certainly the case in Carlton Skinner's 1943 proposal and its subsequent successful results on *Sea Cloud*.[62] In fact, as we have seen, Eugene S. Duffield, one of Forrestal's assistants, had been briefed by *Sea Cloud*'s skipper on his experiences in achieving the most efficient use of manpower—black and white—and senior naval officials had studied a report on Skinner's experiment.[63]

A Momentous Sequence of Events

So let us now connect some dots. First dot: Carlton Skinner encounters a clear case of official racism when Coast Guard headquarters denies one of his *Northland* sailors the opportunity to change occupations and advance in rank simply because he is black. Skinner succeeds in his fight to reverse that race-based decision. Second dot: Skinner recommends to the head of the Coast Guard that one of its cutters be used as a test bed to evaluate the effectiveness of a fully racially integrated ship. His proposal is approved, and Skinner is put in command of that ship—*Sea Cloud*. Third dot: *Sea Cloud*, with an integrated crew, meets all US Navy and Coast Guard administrative, material, and operational requirements and performs well in the Battle of the Atlantic. Fourth dot: Skinner informs an assistant to Secretary Forrestal about the *Sea Cloud* experiment. Fifth dot: Five months later, Forrestal directs that blacks should now be allowed to fill general service billets on some—albeit not all—naval ships. What conclusion does one draw from this sequence of events? Any connection of those dots leads to the reasonable conclusion that Carlton Skinner, with his pragmatic idealism as applied and practiced on board USS *Sea Cloud*, opened doors, broke down barriers, and helped lead the way to the eventual full integration of the US Navy. Put in other words, that first figurative flutter of the butterfly's wings on *Northland* in 1942 produced a hurricane howling through the halls of the Pentagon that eventually changed national policy.

Baby Steps

This is not to say that it was Skinner's actions in 1944 alone that integrated the US Navy and Coast Guard. In that year both services took some additional small steps toward achieving equal opportunity for their minority members.

For example, on January 1, 1944, the first sixteen black officer candidates reported to the navy's Great Lakes Training Center for (segregated) training leading to a commission. The following month twelve of those African American enlisted sailors were commissioned as navy ensigns, and a thirteenth was promoted to warrant officer. These so-called "Golden Thirteen" constituted the first group of black sailors to complete officer training in the navy, thereby leading the way for future such commissionings, and by the end of the war sixty-four African Americans had become naval officers.[64]

In another example, President Roosevelt instructed the navy on October 19, 1944, to begin taking black women into the Women Accepted for Volunteer Emergency Service (WAVES) organization. By July 1945 the navy had trained seventy-two African American WAVES in a fully integrated and routine manner.[65] The first two black women to be commissioned as naval officers were Frances Eliza Wills, a social worker, and Harriet Ida Pickens, a public health administrator. Upon graduation on December 26, 1944, they and the seventy-two black enlisted WAVES were the only African Americans serving alongside the navy's 86,000 WAVES.[66]

Meanwhile, in the autumn of 1944 the Coast Guard recruited five black women for the US Coast Guard Women's Reserve (SPARS). That very small number is partially a result of SPARS ending all of its recruiting efforts, except to replace departed personnel, on November 23, 1944.[67]

By August 1945, 965 blacks wore the uniforms of Coast Guard petty officers and warrant officers, often in the general services. Many of these warrant officers worked at shore stations and served as instructors at the Manhattan Beach training facility, while many black petty officers could be found serving in mostly white crews and as personnel in shore installations.[68]

In the end, though, blacks never constituted even 3 percent of the Coast Guard's wartime personnel strength, significantly less than in the other armed services and in comparison with their representation in the overall US population. Again, that small percentage is explained in part by the Coast Guard stopping all inductions in early 1944 whereas the other services continued to draft men and women into their ranks.

In the navy, on the other hand, there were in uniform at war's end some 164,942 enlisted African Americans (or 5.37 percent of the total personnel)—more than twice as many as in 1941. But as it turned out, the integration of the navy's officer ranks, the WAVES, and Nurse Corps had encompassed very few black men and women. By mid-1945 there were just thirty-six male and two female African American officers in the navy, including twenty-three line officers, three in the Supply Corps, two in the Dental Corps, three in the Medical Corps, two in the Civil Engineer Corps, and two chaplains.[69] And even though black enlisted men had entered some sixty-seven ratings and specialties by V-J Day, all too many of them—68,000, or 40 percent—were serving as stewards. "Here again," MacGregor concludes, "integrated service affected only a small portion of the Navy's black recruits during World War II."[70]

▪ ▪ ▪ ▪

The navy's return of *Sea Cloud* to Joseph and Marjorie Davies in November 1944 and Carlton Skinner's departure from the Coast Guard in October 1945 put the ship and the man on diverging courses. For the ship, there would be a six-year period of notoriety in the Dominican Republic, then almost a decade of physical decline and litigation, followed by restoration and renaissance. For the man, there would be some twenty years of government service, first in Washington and later as a statesman in the South Pacific, and then a successful career in business. Interestingly, the ship and the man were reunited on three occasions after they had gone their separate ways. When and how will be explained later—in chapter 7, covering *Sea Cloud*'s postwar decline and rebirth, and in chapter 8, chronicling Skinner's years as a governor and executive.

7 *Sea Cloud*'s Metamorphosis

Depending on how you count, SY *Sea Cloud* has had at least as many lives as the proverbial cat. During its first fourteen years it had three existences: initially as Edward Hutton's *Hussar*, the world's largest privately owned yacht at that time; then, secondly, it was Marjorie Post's *Sea Cloud* (see chapter 1); and in its third life the barque was stripped of its masts and luxurious appointments, armed with guns and antisubmarine weapons, and converted into an utilitarian naval ship (designated as WPG-284 and later as IX-99) during World War II (see chapters 4, 5, and 6).

After service in the Battle of the Atlantic and during the fifty years between 1944 and 1994, *Sea Cloud* assumed various other roles and identities: beginning with the restoration by her civilian owners to prewar splendor; then sailing as *Angelita*, the presidential yacht of a Caribbean dictator and love boat for his son; then, after that, languishing as *Patria*, the unwanted property of the Dominican government; followed next by a renaming as *Antarna* and repurposing as an ersatz schoolhouse; then six years of rot and deterioration in a Panamanian backwater; and, ultimately, salvation by German businessmen who returned the square-rigger to its original magnificence and role as the *Sea Cloud* of today.

In this chapter we'll review that half century of adventures and morphs, twists and turns, and near-deaths and resurrections. (Chapter 9 will cover *Sea Cloud*'s most recent history and current operations.) Let's start by examining the yacht's fourth life—the decade immediately following USS *Sea Cloud*'s homecoming from the war and its years in the service of Marjorie and Joseph Davies.

Marjorie's Baby

Although the navy had spent two months and expended at least $1 million to return *Sea Cloud* to its prewar condition, the restoration had not been fully completed when the vessel was formally given back to its owners on November 4, 1944. It was still missing its masts, sails, and rigging, and none of the former cabin furniture, furnishings, and artwork had been reinstalled. Marjorie Davies was not pleased with what she had reacquired.

Nevertheless, *Sea Cloud* reverted to its antebellum role as a luxury sailing yacht, making its first pleasure cruise after the war on July 4, 1946, with Joe and Marjorie, seven of their friends, ten officers, and a crew of sixty-two on board, They voyaged from Alexandria, Virginia, south to the waters off Florida and Cuba. But still not happy, Marjorie bemoaned the absence of the vessel's masts and sails: "As soon as we can find 55,000 square feet of canvas and eight miles of manilla rope, *Sea Cloud* will be restored. The stuff is still rationed or not available."[1]

Yet, even without those masts and sails, the yacht still looked beautiful, especially in contrast to its navalized configuration during the war. Regardless, in 1946 *Sea Cloud* was sent to the Bethlehem Shipbuilding Corporation's Sparrows Point shipyard in Baltimore for further reconditioning work.[2] Interestingly, this facility was just a few miles across the Patapsco River from the Coast Guard's Curtis Bay shipyard, where the vessel had been converted into a weather ship just four years before.

During the yard availability, air conditioning equipment and a new generator system were installed and furniture and draperies were returned on board.[3] As they were in the 1930s, the owners' master staterooms were made to appear as in a comfortable home ashore, featuring French period furniture and bathrooms with marble and gold-plated fixtures. The World War II naval berthing spaces that had accommodated 160 enlisted men were totally redone and replaced by six staterooms, each with its own head, for the use of eight guests. The staterooms were also well furnished and offered their occupants the comforts of an electric fireplace and a tile bath. With its hand-hewn oak beams and walnut furnishings, *Sea Cloud*'s dining room resembled the interior of a sailing vessel of the 1800s. Rare painted seascapes decorated the bulkheads. The yacht's salon featured a library and a marble fireplace. And to provide the best in cuisine, grooming, and medical care to the owners and their guests, *Sea Cloud* was equipped with two galleys, a barbershop, and a well-outfitted sick bay.

Sea Cloud underway around 1946 as a typical—albeit very large—motor yacht. The next year it would reacquire the masts and sails that Marjorie Davies badly wanted to return the vessel to its prewar splendor. (Courtesy of Hillwood Estate, Museum & Gardens, Archives and Special Collections)

In terms of marine engineering and navigation, the vessel was superbly equipped. Its postwar hardware inventory included a gyroscope, fathometer, direction finder, radar, aerometer, fire detection system, telephone, auxiliary electric power generators, machine tools, electric sail hoists, and seawater evaporators for making fresh water. The refrigerators could preserve 35 tons (that's 70,000 pounds!) of frozen foods. *Sea Cloud*'s storage tanks held 116,000 gallons of fresh water, 186,000 gallons of fuel oil, and 4,200 gallons of lubricating oil.

During the yard availability at Sparrow's Point, *Sea Cloud*'s four masts were stepped on the yacht. In all, the four masts carried a spread of 34,000 square feet of sail. In addition, *Sea Cloud* could now deploy its own miniflotilla of eighteen boats and small craft, including the thirty-two-foot owner's launch, a thirty-two-foot fishing boat, a twenty-six-foot speedboat, a twenty-six-foot crew's launch, a twenty-six-foot motor whaleboat, two thirty-foot lifeboats (each capable of carrying fifty-two people), a twenty-foot dinghy, a thirteen-foot rowboat, and nine rafts. (By contrast, Edward Hutton's *Hussar* had carried eight boats.) It took a complement of seventy-two people to operate and maintain the ship and serve its owners and their guests.

Emerging from the yard early in 1947, *Sea Cloud* now looked much as it had in the 1930s. It was a combination of a seagoing yacht and a modern transatlantic passenger liner. Indeed, in the early postwar years Lloyds Registry of Shipping equated it to a commercial maritime vessel of the same size and draft and gave *Sea Cloud* a top rating of 100-A-1. The yacht also met the requirements of the International Convention for Safety of Life at Sea (SOLAS), the worldwide maritime treaty requiring signatory nations to ensure that ships flagged by them met minimum safety standards in construction, equipment, and operation.

Sea Cloud departed Baltimore on or about April 7 and sailed south to Florida to prepare for a long pleasure cruise. Marjorie Post's biographer quotes her reaction when she first saw her yacht after its restoration: "*Sea Cloud* in full sail came over the horizon as we watched from the eighth floor of Whitehall [a hotel in Palm Beach, Florida]. It's the first time Joe and I have seen her made out in full sail and not been on board. What a picture she is! We watched, excited and fascinated, until she was out of sight beyond the Breakers. Joe said, 'Well, dear, there goes your baby.'"[4]

In the spring of 1947 *Sea Cloud* undertook a two-week shakedown cruise to the Bahamas, which included a cocktail party on board for a staggering 150 guests—almost as many people as the entire complement of Coast Guard officers and men who had served on the vessel during World War II.

Over the next three years the yacht performed often and well in its continuing role as "Marjorie's Baby." For example, there was a visit to Bermuda in the summer of 1947; an onboard lunch for Mamie Eisenhower in Alexandria, Virginia; a series of cruises and soirees off Glen Cove, Long Island; a visit aboard by Andrei Gromyko, at the time the Soviet Union's representative at the United Nations; a dance party for Marjorie's daughter, Dina Merrill, and 400 of her friends; and port calls in Newport, Rhode Island, and coastal Maine for parties and dinners.[5]

Marjorie's biographer, William Wright, noted: "During the at-sea portion of those *Sea Cloud* days, there were always guests. Family and friends were picked up here and dropped off there—with the same logistical precision that marked all of Marjorie's operations. . . . Gliding around the bright seas of the Caribbean or South Atlantic, guests would be treated to free-form days of rare luxury."[6]

As in prior years, royalty was hosted on the yacht. In March and April 1948 the former King Edward VIII of the United Kingdom, then the Duke of

Windsor, and his wife were guests of Joseph and Marjorie for a cruise from Florida to the Bahamas and Cuba.[7]

On another voyage that same spring, Rafael Trujillo, the president of the Dominican Republic, had dinner on board *Sea Cloud*. The next day Trujillo presented Marjorie Davies with the Juan Pablo Duarte Order of Merit medal.[8] Seven years after that dinner, Trujillo would radically change the yacht's course and future.

For whatever reason, all of this cruising, partying, and hosting was not enough to satisfy Joseph Davies. Although never much of yachtsman who loved his boat, the former ambassador nevertheless wanted some formal recognition or award by the US government for *Sea Cloud*'s service to the nation during World War II. He contacted Carlton Skinner, its wartime skipper, who was then director of information for the US Department of the Interior, and asked for his assistance in securing some form of appreciation from the navy. As Skinner later recounted, he had to undertake a "lengthy and complicated negotiation, which resulted in an agreement to issue a certificate to the ship and to authorize it to carry five chevrons to be painted on its stack, one chevron for every six months of naval service."[9]

A presentation ceremony was arranged to take place in Annapolis, Maryland, on May 22, 1948, while *Sea Cloud* was in transit from Long Island Sound to Florida. Secretary of the Navy John L. Sullivan and R. Adm. James L. Holloway Jr., the superintendent of the Naval Academy, as well as Skinner, attended the event.[10] The distinguished guests were treated to a formal dinner on board the yacht the evening before the ceremony. It might be fairly argued that Marjorie Post Davies ran a tight ship. As an example and in accordance with her strict rules, cocktails were served promptly at 6:30 p.m.—with only one drink provided to each guest; late comers were to receive none—followed by a meal served exactly thirty minutes later. The next day, presumably precisely on time, Joseph and Marjorie and the VIPs gathered on deck for the presentation of a special navy certificate and a Naval Reserve Yacht Owners Distinguishing Pennant.[11]

Immediately after the ceremony *Sea Cloud* got underway using its engines for propulsion, but once sufficiently away from its anchorage, the crew went aloft and unfurled the sails, and so it then cruised powered by the wind in Chesapeake Bay over the next three to four hours. After that brief excursion, the sails were then furled and the yacht returned to its Annapolis anchorage propelled solely by its diesels.[12]

Dignitaries attending the 1948 presentation (from left to right): Secretary John Sullivan; R. Adm. James Holloway in service dress khaki; Lt. Cmdr. Carlton Skinner in service dress blues; Marjorie Post Davies, with the navy's certificate in hand; and Joseph Davies in his customized yachting attire. At the far right is believed to be Capt. (later R. Adm.) John B. Heffernan, director of naval history, in service dress khaki, along with various *Sea Cloud* officers (including its captain, next to Heffernan) in their dress blues. (Coast Guard Historian's Office)

UNITED STATES NAVY

This certifies that

Honorable Joseph E. Davies

made available to the United States Navy the

Sea Cloud

which served honorably in World War II as the

U.S.S. Sea Cloud (IX-99)

and in virtue thereof, is authorized to fly the Naval Reserve Yacht Owners Distinguishing Pennant on any craft he may own or sail under charter

James L. Holloway Jr. — COMMANDANT ___ NAVAL DISTRICT

John L. Sullivan — SECRETARY OF THE NAVY

DATED 22 May 1948

No. 51-G

The navy's certificate authorizing Davies to fly the Naval Reserve Yacht Owners Distinguishing Pennant, signed by Secretary Sullivan and Rear Admiral Holloway. (Sea Cloud Cruises GmbH)

The tempo of *Sea Cloud*'s operations slowed significantly following the visit to Annapolis. During the period from mid-1948 through 1950 the yacht was relatively inactive and in port for extended periods. Its complement had been reduced from about seventy-two to about thirty personnel. Those who were laid off were told that their unemployment would be temporary and that they would be called back to the ship when it was time to begin preparing for another voyage. The owners needed to keep the laid-off crewmen "on standby" because seamen capable of manning a square-rigged sailing vessel were not readily available in the late 1940s. Similarly, the owners retained *Sea Cloud*'s officers, mates, and most experienced crewmen on board and on the payroll during the laid-up periods to serve as a continuing nucleus staff and to ready the ship in port for the next cruise.

In February 1949 *Sea Cloud* was fitted with a set of new sails. Weighing some 13,000 pounds, the sails, which were made in Gothenburg, Sweden,

Sea Cloud crewmen tend the sails while the yacht is underway, presumably near Annapolis in May 1948. (Coast Guard Historian's Office)

had required 4,318 man-hours to produce.[13] That summer, one of the ship's topmasts was splintered by a lightning strike. A replacement sixty-foot Oregon pine topmast was turned to size in Boston, Massachusetts—*Sea Cloud*'s homeport during the war—and in a tricky three-hour job installed at the Merrill-Stevens shipyard in Jacksonville, Florida.[14]

Joe and Marjorie Davies went to sea for the last time on *Sea Cloud* during a cruise in the Caribbean between August and November 1950. After that, the yacht was no longer used for sailing, entertainment, or housing by either the former ambassador or his wife; it was proving to be just too expensive, even for wealthy owners, to operate and maintain.

Consider what a sharp-eyed accountant would have told Marjorie at the time. It had cost $1,225,000 initially just to build *Sea Cloud*. From 1946 through 1950, another $3,145,188 had been spent to rehabilitate the yacht after its naval service and for ongoing operations and maintenance broken out as follows: $1,144,431 in 1946; $980,333 in 1947; $455,214 in 1948; $218,964 in 1949; and $346,246 in 1950. (In 1951 those expenses were $73,047—approximately $720,800 in today's dollars. The book value of the furnishings at the end of 1951 was $267,528.)[15] One estimate is that Marjorie had spent between $5 million and $7 million on furnishings, maintenance, and refurbishing exclusive of the operating costs of personnel salaries, fuel, insurance, port fees, and the like.[16] And her accountant would have also pointed out that in addition to *Sea Cloud*, the lady maintained a number of other expensive residences and properties: the 207-acre Camp Topridge with sixty-eight buildings in New York's Adirondack Mountains; Mar-a-Lago, a 126-room, 110,000-square-foot house and estate in Palm Beach, Florida (now owned by Donald Trump); and Hillwood, a mansion and thirteen acres of formal gardens in Washington, DC, all of which also required significant outlays from her resources to staff and keep up.

So it comes as no surprise that near the end of the 1950 cruise to the Caribbean, Marjorie summoned her chief marine engineer, Clyde B. Ault, to Washington to discuss *Sea Cloud*'s future. It is often humorously said that the two happiest days for boat owners is the day they buy their first boat and the day they sell their last. Marjorie had been very happy in 1931 when she and Edward Hutton acquired *Sea Cloud* (née *Hussar*) but now, twenty years later, she was looking for her second happiest day. After considering all of her considerable current and future personal expenses, the projected utilization of the vessel, and the various subjective pros and cons of retaining the yacht, Marjorie decided to sell her baby.

She therefore instructed Ault to have *Sea Cloud* permanently moored in Jacksonville upon her return from the Caribbean, to dismiss all of the crew members except for four men who would provide security for the vessel, and to prepare for removing the owners' personal belongings and furniture. These instructions were implemented beginning in January 1951 and completed four months later.

During January a number of paintings were taken off the vessel, and in March and April some 250 items of personal property, including ten cases of silverware, were removed from staterooms, guest cabins, the smoking room, living room, dining room, passageways, wine cellar, and steward's pantry. Also during January Ault laid off about half of the crew, including the captain, second mate, third engineer, refrigerating engineer, able-bodied seamen, and most of the stewards. The survivors were assigned to various decommissioning tasks; by mid-February there were only ten crewmen left, and by May, just four.

Decommissioning and deactivating *Sea Cloud* was not a matter of merely turning off the lights and shutting down the engine room. Ault's decommissioning checklist would have included the following tasks:

- Closing off all of the ship's living spaces except for the two that were used by the four-man security detail.
- Taking down the rigging, sails, and upper yardarms.
- Securing on the forecastle 30,000 square feet of the new sails and nine miles of rope.
- Covering the yacht's deck houses with canvas for protection from weather.
- Spraying the remaining mirrors, art, and furniture with a protective solution and covering them with French cloth for protection against Florida's humidity.
- Laundering the vessel's linens and stowing them in sealed packages.
- Dismantling the stoves in the two galleys and greasing cooking utensils and securing them in lockers.
- Disassembling, galvanizing, and storing the refrigerators.
- Covering the upper and lower decks with canvas.
- Emptying and sealing the air conditioning units.

- Decommissioning the motorboats and launches and treating their engines with fogging oil to protect them during a long period of inactivity.
- Taking deck furniture ashore.
- Taking down radio antennas and radar equipment.
- Disconnecting the ship's screws.
- Blowing out, cleaning, and sealing the pumps and boiler. (The main generators were left operational in order to turn the propeller shafts biweekly for maintenance.)

Most of *Sea Cloud*'s 186,000 gallons of fuel oil was removed and sold for $5,273 while a small amount was retained to run the auxiliary engines from time to time to prevent their deterioration. Electrical equipment plates and switches that would be subjected to the climate's moisture and humidity were removed. Impressively, all of these tasks were accomplished in just four months.[17]

Marjorie visited *Sea Cloud* in March 1951, when she arranged for the disposition of personal property, and then stepped on board for the last time in 1953, when she issued final instructions about removing some of the remaining pictures and furniture in the owners' stateroom and guest cabins.

As the decommissioning process was nearing completion, she requested an estimate of what it would cost to replicate a yacht comparable to *Sea Cloud*. With that number in mind she offered her baby for sale in 1951 at an asking price of $1.2 million in a furnished condition or $1 million unfurnished (approximately $11.8 million and $9.8 million, respectively, today). Over the next four years a number of marine brokers were involved in finding a buyer, including John H. Wells, Perry-Cox & Stevens, Victor B. Bendix, Inc., and Sparkman & Stevens, all four firms in New York; John G. Alden, Inc., in Boston and New York; George Michaud Company in Los Angeles; Mary Van Zandt-Williamson in Fort Worth; and Philip L. Rhoades and W. A. White Jr. The primary interface between the owners and the brokers was William R. Wood, Marjorie's business manager (who had represented Joseph Davies when USS *Sea Cloud* was decommissioned and returned by the navy in 1944).

In March 1951 John H. Wells brought an offer of $450,000 from a man who knew the yacht very well, having been a frequent guest (some say *the most frequent* guest) on board—Generalissimo Rafael Trujillo. That offer was declined because of the constraining legal requirements affecting yacht sales to noncitizens. In September another notable figure, Aristotle Onassis—

the Greek shipping tycoon and later husband of the widowed Jacqueline Kennedy—made a conditional offer of $1 million via Perry-Cox Stevens. This time, Marjorie deemed the offer to be satisfactory (even though Onassis was not a US citizen). Onassis had *Sea Cloud* inspected in November 1951, and then he and a marine surveyor inspected it in February 1952. But ultimately Onassis did not purchase the barque.

Between 1952 and 1954 Wood exchanged numerous letters and messages with several people and governments in furtherance of a sale. Among the men and entities who had indicated an interest in acquiring *Sea Cloud* were Fulgencio Batista, then president of Cuba (overthrown by Fidel Castro in 1959); Faisal bin Abdulaziz Al Saud, the crown prince of Saudi Arabia (who became king in 1964); Axel L. Wenner-Gran, a Swedish businessman residing in the Bahamas; and representatives of the governments of Iran, Portugal, and Argentina.[18]

By 1955 the owners had already spent $200,524 for the yacht's preservation and maintenance, including wages, insurance, fuel, pilotage, and towing. (As it was necessary to perform various preservation work beyond the capabilities of the four-man crew, such as painting the metal hull and bottom to prevent saltwater corrosion, *Sea Cloud*—lacking self-propulsion—had to be towed by tugboats into and from dry docks from time to time.)

Prompted by this continuing expense, the owner in 1953 reduced the asking price to $1 million furnished and $800,000 unfurnished. When still unsold early in 1955, the asking price for *Sea Cloud* was again reduced to $600,000 unfurnished. This was at a time when Marjorie's marriage to Joseph Davies was coming undone, finally ending in divorce in March 1955. That summer, and still without any takers for her yacht, Marjorie cut the price in August to $500,000 partially furnished.

This time, someone did buy the barque. Many published sources state that the purchaser was frequent guest and the Davieses' friend, Trujillo. Some even suggest that the transaction was a kind of barter the yacht in exchange for a new Vickers Viscount turboprop aircraft.[19] Nevertheless, legal documents filed with the US Tax Court in 1961 stipulated that *Sea Cloud* was sold by Marjorie on August 15, 1955, to George W. Gibbs Jr., the president of Gibbs Corporation, for $500,000.[20] According to that filing, Gibbs provided Marjorie Davies with a deposit of $25,000, closed the sale by the end of the month, and quickly sold the yacht to Trujillo for $550,000. Still, a spokesman for Trujillo told the Associated Press on October 6, 1955, that the generalissimo had purchased *Sea Cloud* for $500,000.[21]

One might reasonably infer from this transaction that Gibbs had served as a kind of cutout—a trusted intermediary or middleman—to facilitate the transfer of ownership from Marjorie Post to Rafael Trujillo. It is unlikely we'll ever know for sure, as none of the principals are alive today. In any event, in October 1955 *Sea Cloud* was no longer the property of its longtime mistress. Marjorie's baby had set sail to start still another life, this time as the "presidential yacht" of the Dominican Republic.

She's No Angel

During his lifetime Rafael Leonidas Trujillo Molina was referred to by several titles and nicknames. He had been "El Presidente" (president of the Dominican Republic from 1930 to 1938 and from 1942 to 1952), "Generalissimo" (General), "El Jefe" ("The Chief" or "The Boss"), "El Benefactor" ("The Benefactor of the Nation"), "Chapitas" ("Bottle Caps"—for the many medals he wore), and "El Chivo" ("The Goat"). Trujillo has also been called, and not without basis, "strongman," "dictator," and "murderer."

When it came time in 1955 for Trujillo himself to bestow a name, he decided to call his newly acquired yacht *Angelita* (Spanish for "little angel"), in honor of his youngest daughter, María de los Ángeles del Sagrado Corazón de Jesús Trujillo Martínez (who was known as Angelita). Given that *angelita* denotes a diminutive being of exemplary conduct or virtue, and considering the sordid activities that would later occur on the yacht, that name is easily one of the most ironic appellations ever given to an oceangoing vessel, especially one with *Sea Cloud*'s pedigree, reputation, and history.

As an early indication of how the new image of *Angelita* would differ from that of the blue chip *Sea Cloud*, Trujillo added a twelve-person Latin-music band to the regular crew of seventy-three seamen (who were periodically rotated on and off the ship for security reasons).

Following delivery to its new owner in Santo Domingo (then known as Ciudad Trujillo), *Angelita* suffered an engine casualty on its first sea trial, a short five-mile trip to La Caleta. That mechanical problem forced the ship to generally operate relatively close to its homeport on short cruises until new engines could be installed. Nevertheless, *Angelita* did manage a voyage of more than 800 miles to Miami in December 1957.

Over the next few years, Rafael Trujillo used *Angelita* infrequently. However, his son, General Leonidas Trujillo Martinez (known as Ramfis Trujillo), treated the yacht as his own personal playground and love boat. Ramfis often hosted boisterous party cruises on board, which were so loud that they attracted considerable attention from people on shore.

In February 1958 Ramfis entertained Zsa Zsa Gabor, the Hungarian American actress and socialite, on *Angelita* while the yacht was tied up in New Orleans for Mardi Gras. Two months later Rafael Trujillo sent his playboy son to California to study law, an odd choice considering the son's bon vivant proclivities. Ramfis took advantage of that opportunity by employing *Angelita* both for lodging in the Golden State and as a venue for enjoying the intimate company of motion picture starlets. For example, Gabor and Kim Novak attended a June 21 reception on board while the yacht was anchored in Los Angeles Harbor. The next day, according to an Associated Press report, Ramfis had *Angelita* moved thirty-five miles north to Santa Monica—and closer to Hollywood—presumably to facilitate visits by young actresses.[22] In its coverage of Trujillo's visit the *Los Angeles Times* referred to *Angelita* as a "floating fun house." One wonders what Marjorie would have said about that.

The parties and "meetings" with other starlets went on into early July. All these activities culminated mid-month when *Angelita* crewmen happened to notice news photographers and bystanders staring and laughing at the yacht. The focus of their amusement were the words "Zsa Zsa Slept Here," which someone had painted in two-foot-high letters just above the waterline on the ship's starboard quarter (outboard of the pier). Outrageous! The crew quickly launched a dinghy, and two unlucky sailors got the job of painting over the offending notice.[23]

In late July *Angelita* cruised south to San Diego, and on July 27 Ramfis was vacationing on board in Acapulco, Mexico. But now his nautical entertaining was about to end. The next month Rafael Trujillo summoned his son and his yacht back home. One assumes that the public notoriety accorded Ramfis for his antics on *Angelita* proved to be too much, even for the father, who was certainly no paragon of virtue.

Angelita returned to Ciudad Trujillo in early August while still another wild party was winding down on the yacht. One source reports that when the senior Trujillo stepped aboard to meet his newly arrived son, he was shocked to find Ramfis and his friends too incapacitated to even stand up to greet El Jefe.[24]

Even with all this scandal *Angelita* retained a certain claim to prominence and legitimacy in the public record. It was, after all, still one of the world's premier pleasure boats. According to the 1959 *Lloyd's Register of American*

Yachts, *Angelita* was the third-biggest such vessel listed in that compendium.[25]

Between March and July 1959 the yacht acquired four new eight-cylinder, 1,500 hp diesel engines built by the Enterprise Engine & Foundry Company. Replacing *Hussar*'s original Krupp diesels, the new engines were installed at a shipyard in Alabama during a $1.38 million overhaul. At the same time, the yard replaced the ship's gearboxes and air conditioning system.

Rafael Trujillo's ownership of *Angelita* and his thirty-one-year dictatorial regime came to a sudden, violent end during the evening of May 30, 1961. While riding in a chauffeured blue 1957 Chevrolet Bel Air to an intimate rendezvous in San Cristobal, El Jefe was ambushed by a small group of assassins, who killed him in a fusillade of more than two dozen machine-gun bullets. Ramfis, who had been in Paris at the time, flew back to Santo Domingo two days later and assumed the posts of commander of the Dominican armed forces and the country's secretary of state (ostensibly serving under the figurehead president, Joaquin Balaguer). The younger Trujillo then hunted down the assassins and the plotters, along with other opponents of the regime, and had them executed, some by his own hand. His father's body was interned—temporarily, as it turned out—in a crypt at a chapel in San Cristobal.

The record shows that Ramfis's reign was considerably shorter than his father's. On November 14, 1961, less than six months after ascending to power, he resigned as commander of the armed forces. Four days later Ramfis fled the Dominican Republic on board *Angelita*, intending to head for Cannes, France. On board the yacht were not only Ramfis Trujillo but also some family members, including his brother Hector Negro, along with bank notes and other financial instruments, reportedly worth some $4 million to $5 million, and a casket containing the remains of Rafael Trujillo!

The son had had his father's coffin removed from the San Cristobal chapel and stowed in the yacht's smoking room.[26] Ramfis left *Angelita* in Martinique and flew from there directly to Paris. Meanwhile, *Angelita* sailed on toward France, but by the time it reached the Canary Islands, the Dominican government ordered the yacht to return. The government's interest in recovering the yacht had more to do with the treasure that was supposedly on board than the value of the vessel itself. Press reports at the time stated that there were rumors that *Angelita* was carrying "millions of dollars in gold smuggled out of the country."[27]

On November 29, 1961, after almost two weeks at sea, *Angelita* returned to the Las Calderas naval base. Trujillo's body and the recovered loot were removed, and the next day President Balaguer sent the dictator's corpse to Paris in a chartered Pan Am DC-7. It was interned—for the second and last time—on December 3 in a cemetery in the French capital.

Meanwhile, having disposed of the deceased dictator, the government of the Dominican Republic now had to decide what to do with his yacht.

Take My Yacht . . . Please!

Now that *Angelita* had been reacquired as both a de jure and de facto asset of the Dominican Republic and renamed *Patria* ("Fatherland"), the question facing the government was: what use, if any, did the navy have for a thirty-year-old four-masted sailing vessel? And the simple answer was: none.

For one thing, the navy of the Dominican Republic was already relatively well equipped with ships. In the early 1960s its fleet consisted of two ex-British destroyers (*Duarte* and *Sanchez*), two former Tacoma-class frigates, another frigate and five corvettes from Canada, five patrol vessels (former US submarine chasers and US Coast Guard cutters), a medium landing ship (LSM), two utility landing craft, two fleet oilers, and a handful of Coast Guard vessels, tenders, launches, and tugs.[28]

Secondly, the country did not need another presidential yacht; it already had one. The former frigate *Presidente Trujillo* (F-101) had been renamed *Mella* and converted for the personal use of the chief of state by expanding the deckhouse on the main deck to provide additional accommodations for VIP passengers.[29]

Thirdly, the ex-*Angelita*, now *Patria*, would be too expensive to own and operate. United Press International reported in 1963 that it needed a crew of at least 80 hands (other reports say that Trujillo had used as many as 120 personnel on board) from a navy with only about 3,300 officers and men; and that its operation and maintenance would have cost about $1,000 each day (not including the crew's pay). If the ship needed a new set of sails, that would cost the navy around $30,000, and if the hull needed to be painted, that would have required $3,000 for the paint alone.[30]

Thus in the spring of 1962 the former Trujillo family houseboat was put up for sale. The initial asking price recommended by a naval board of officers was $2.5 million. The board regarded that sum as a bargain.[31] After all, the ship's relatively new engines had only 800 hours of use to date. Still, the overall material condition of *Patria* was declining from inactivity and inadequate maintenance. By the next year, the minimum price had been reduced by 20 percent. A sign posted on the ship's starboard side read: "For sale, this 316-foot yacht. Luxurious interior appointments. Minimum offer $2 million. For additional information, please contact the national government."[32] The Colombian navy (Armada Nacional de la República de Colombia, or ARC), which was looking to acquire a large sailing ship for training, checked out *Patria* in 1966 as a possible candidate but opted instead to buy a new three-masted barque built especially for the ARC in Spain.[33] An Associated Press reporter described the unwanted former Trujillo yacht that year: "Tan, sleek and proud, the powerful *Patria* today lies amid the oily rubble of a Dominican Navy yard, like a faded, bejeweled dowager gone slumming."[34] Eventually, with no takers, the asking price was slashed to $800,000.[35]

Antarna's Trials and Tribulations

In 1965 Clifford E. Barbour Jr. formed Operation Sea Cruise, Inc. (OSC) in Panama for the purpose of acquiring ownership of, repairing, and operating *Patria* as a luxury cruise ship.[36] Barbour, who was the sole owner of OSC, then purchased the yacht in 1967 at a reported purchase price of $725,000.[37] Once in the hands of a new owner, the former *Sea Cloud* received its fifth name: *Antarna* (referring to Antares, the brightest star in the Scorpio constellation).

Shortly after Barbour acquired *Antarna*, it was sent to Naples, Italy, for a badly needed overhaul. It was repainted, and repairs were made to the woodwork, electrical system, and pipes. The interior was rehabilitated and enhanced with new furnishings. And the yacht came back to the United States in 1968.

It made one voyage for Operation Sea Cruise but then ran into the first in a series of legal and financial difficulties. The US Customs Service sought an $80,000 payment of import duties from OSC, which the corporation and Barbour initially were unwilling and unable to pay. Barbour had used his own personal funds to purchase *Antarna*, and unlike Marjorie Post, he was not a person of vast wealth. In fact, the refurbishment of the yacht in Italy was accomplished by way of payments by Barbour through purported personal loans to OSC, in effect borrowing from Barbour to pay Barbour to pay the Italians.[38] Without the import duties payment, customs officials impounded *Antarna* in Miami, leaving Barbour essentially out of business and OSC without a source of income.

As a consequence, *Antarna* reverted back to its previous condition when it was the unwanted and neglected *Patria* in the Dominican Republic. Over the next year and a half *Antarna*'s physical condition again deteriorated, the engine room took on water, the electrical system and generators were damaged, and the bowsprit was smashed by a passing freighter.

While *Antarna* and Barbour were suffering in Miami, Stephanie Gallagher and her husband Charles formed the Oceanics Schools in 1970 as a nonprofit entity to offer high school and college students a semester (sixteen weeks) of work, study, and travel on board large square-rigged sailing ships on voyages to Europe, West Africa, and South America. The sixty or so students (fifty boys and ten girls) would pay a tuition of $7,000 for the experience, although many had scholarships that reduced that cost.[39]

Needing a big sailing vessel for their school, the Gallaghers learned that *Antarna* was in effect under federal lock-and-key in Florida and arranged with Barbour's representative, John Blue, in 1971 to charter *Antarna* at no cost for one year in exchange for paying off all of OSC's debts and making the vessel operational.[40]

That wasn't going to be easy. *Antarna* had become virtually encased in barnacles and marine growth. It had that broken bowsprit, a flooded engine room, a list to port, rotted-out lifeboats, and inoperable engines and electronic equipment. As work progressed to repair the ship for its new role as a floating classroom, Nevar Makofka, the acting director of the Oceanics Schools, told United Press International: "We're running behind schedule right now because of all of the work involved in getting her ready to sail. The engines were flooded and it's taken weeks of work just to get them operating again."[41]

Originally the Gallaghers had planned to have *Antarna* leave Miami in December 1971 for a week in a Jacksonville, Florida, dry dock for hull and bottom painting, to be followed by a student cruise to South America, Africa, and Europe before returning to the United States in June 1972. Among the students reportedly slated to take that cruise were the children of actresses Mary Tyler Moore and Julie Harris.[42]

Ultimately the Gallaghers spent approximately $630,000 in repairs and supplies for *Antarna* and were finally able to begin using the vessel in the school program.[43] Unfortunately, John Blue of OSC, and not Stephanie Gallagher, had retained the ship's papers, so when *Antarna* left Miami without them, she lacked sufficient legal documentation as to her ownership and thus *Antarna* became tantamount to a pirated vessel.

John Blue pursued the ship to Louisiana where *Antarna* had gone after an aborted attempt to dry-dock in Tampa. The vessel's bottom was cleaned of barnacles and marine growth in a New Orleans shipyard, but shortly after that *Antarna* somehow was able to undock and get underway, with Blue unable to prevent it. Later, while en route to the Galapagos Islands, the ship stopped in Panama to replenish its supplies. Blue, who seemed to dashing around the Gulf of Mexico and Caribbean chasing after OSC's ship, caught up with *Antarna* in Panama in March 1972 and had the vessel seized by the local authorities.[44] That "capture" effectively put the kibosh on any further use of *Antarna* by the Gallaghers and their nautical schoolhouse—although it was only the beginning of the legal wars between OSC and the Oceanics Schools.

But now, even after regaining possession of *Antarna*, the owner took no further action to use it as a cruise ship or for anything else, so once again the former *Sea Cloud* was left to slowly molder in the Caribbean heat and humidity. Sadly, this time it sat neglected for six years while anchored in the backwaters of Colon, just a few miles from the entrance to the Panama Canal.

Back to Its Birthplace

It may appear to be counterintuitive, but it is not healthy for a ship or a boat to sit in a slip, alongside a pier, tethered to a mooring or anchored to the bottom for an extended period, especially in tropical climates. Barnacles attach themselves to the hull, propellers, and shafts, aquatic plant growth forms on the vessel below the waterline, paint fades and peels, rubber gaskets and hoses weaken and fail, leaks begin, wires corrode, brass fittings are oxidized, machinery rusts and seizes up. The heat and humidity of Panama and the many years of disuse were taking a serious toll on *Antarna*.

As the yacht was degenerating in the Caribbean, Hartmut Paschburg was at work in Europe acquiring and rebuilding an old three-masted sailing vessel into a cruise ship. Paschburg was an experienced shipmaster, and after hearing accounts of the old *Sea Cloud*, he began to investigate the possibility of acquiring *Antarna* for a similar rehabilitation project.

After inspecting the yacht in Panama and meeting with OSC's John Blue, Paschburg returned to Germany to recommend to his investors, including Dr. Cornelius Liedtke, that they buy *Antarna*, despite its serious material

Antarna, seen here in sad shape on January 8, 1975, while at anchor in Cristobal, Panama. (Neil Harvey)

defects.[45] They agreed and after some months offered OSC an amount that was reluctantly accepted. In the summer of 1978 *Antarna* was sold to the German businessmen for $800,000 and renamed—guess what?—*Sea Cloud*.[46] The proceeds of that sale were passed by OSC directly to Clifford Barbour in repayment of "a portion of the loans to the corporation" by Barbour and thereby transferred to Barbour's personal bank account.[47]

Once Paschburg was in possession of the yacht, his next challenge was to bring it approximately 5,700 miles across the Atlantic to Hamburg, Germany, for a major overhaul and restoration—and he had to do it before winter storms churned up the North Atlantic. To help him in that mission Captain Paschburg recruited a team of thirty-eight men and two women, supplemented by twelve locally hired Panamanian laborers, who went to work on the ship in late July 1978. They did so in oppressive weather conditions in Colon—average high temperatures of 87 degrees and humidity levels of 90 percent.

Facing Paschburg's team were a number of defects and problems. *Sea Cloud* had no running water, electricity, or refrigeration; its cabling was corroded; various mechanical cooling systems, pipes, and electrical switchboards were missing or displaced; the deck's mahogany was bleached; and the Enterprise diesels needed major servicing. Consequently, Paschburg's crew worked twelve hours a day (with time out for a noon siesta), slept out on deck at night, used the harbor as the head, showered from water in an oil drum, stowed their fresh provisions under melting blocks of ice, and used petroleum lamps for illumination below deck.[48]

Despite all these problems and handicaps, Paschburg managed to ready *Sea Cloud* for the voyage to Europe in just three months, and the ship departed Colon in mid-October 1978. This would be no pleasure cruise for Captain Paschburg, the thirty-one crew members, and nine passengers on board. They had to deal with faltering engines, at one point cannibalizing parts of two of the diesels to keep the other two engines running. Then the generator died, and with no electricity to power the refrigerator, they lost their initial supply of fresh foodstuffs. Next they were denied entry into Santo Domingo (*Angelita*'s homeport), where they had hoped to obtain new provisions. After that, the remaining engines failed while en route to Puerto Rico but were restored to operation almost a day later. During four days in San Juan the crew was able to repair the generator and replenish *Sea Cloud*'s food supply. It got underway again on October 19.

But although the barque had returned to sea, its problems had also returned. The generator failed for the third time, the winds that had helped propel it slowed to a bare breeze, fresh food was ruined and had to be tossed overboard, the diesels performed only marginally and sporadically, steering was problematic, navigation was by stars (no GPS back then), and the gas lamps were again employed during electrical outages.[49]

Another problem awaited Paschburg after *Sea Cloud* arrived in the Azores, an autonomous region of Portugal consisting of nine islands approximately 2,770 miles from Puerto Rico and 850 miles west of mainland Portugal. Stephanie Gallagher, who had spent more than $600,000 on the *Antarna* venture and had come away after that considerable investment with no ship, filed suit against Operation Sea Cruise, Inc., in the district court of Ponta Delgada, Azores, for breach of contract. That court issued a judgment against OSC for $929,815.55 plus interest and then filed a rogatory letter (a formal request from a court to a foreign court for some type of judicial assistance) to the circuit court for Knox County, Tennessee, for seizure of OSC properties—i.e., the ex-*Antarna*—and those of any persons liable for OSC obligations.[50]

When *Sea Cloud* arrived in the Azores in late October and anchored outside the harbor of Horta, Paschburg learned of the local district court's ruling and was threatened with arrest by Portuguese officials. He, of course, was not personally involved in the litigation between the Oceanics Schools and OSC, but he had smartly elected not to enter the harbor where his vessel might be seized by the authorities.[51] Instead Paschburg set sail for Germany the next day and arrived with no further incident in Hamburg on November 15, 1978.

In February of the following year, *Sea Cloud* began an eight-month major overhaul, rebuilding, and refurbishment by Howaldtswerke-Deutsche Werft AG in Kiel, Germany. That work, fittingly, was performed in the very shipyard in which the yacht had been built almost a half century earlier. *Sea Cloud* was back in its birthplace undergoing a rebirth.[52]

The yard constructed twenty-five new passenger cabins on the main deck to add to the fifteen original staterooms. Each new cabin was equipped with two beds, a private bath, and air conditioning.[53] In addition, the vessel's auxiliary diesels and pressure pump systems were replaced. New sprinkler systems and smoke alarms were placed in each cabin, and the engine room was fitted with the Halon gas fire extinguishing system. (Halon is a liquefied, compressed gas that stops the spread of fire by chemically disrupting combustion.) At the same time, *Sea Cloud*'s teak deck was partially replaced.[54] The cost of all this work amounted to approximately $6.5 million.[55]

In 1979 Sea Cloud Cruises GmbH was formed, and *Sea Cloud* left the Kiel shipyard that September.[56] It set out on its first voyage for Sea Cloud Cruises in October, heading for Oporto, Portugal, but had to abort the remainder of the trip on November 4 because of another legal maneuver engineered by Stephanie Gallagher in a Portuguese court. As a result, *Sea Cloud* ended up stuck in Oporto for three months.

After that forced time-out, *Sea Cloud* got back to work in 1980, providing seven- and fourteen-day voyages out of Port-de-France, Martinique, for eighty passengers on each cruise. For visits to St. Lucia, the Grenadines, Grenada, and Trinidad, the passengers paid from $1,260 to $2,520 each for the seven-day itinerary and from $2,520 to $5,040 for the two-week cruise.[57]

Sea Cloud crossed the Atlantic in 1981 with crew of fifty-five from seventeen countries. The barque was then taking one-week cruises in the Mediterranean Sea in the summer and in the Caribbean Sea in the winter.[58] The following year *Sea Cloud* cruised through the Lesser Antilles, sailed from Nice around the western Mediterranean, visited the Adriatic and Tyrrhenian, and then operated around the Greek Islands. Trips lasted from eleven to thirteen days, with one week on board, and passengers spent anywhere from $3,300 to $5,700 a person, including air fare from New York.

Between November 1981 until May 1982 *Sea Cloud* sailed minus its distinctive figurehead because the carved eagle that had been installed on *Antarna* by OSC had been lost in a storm. But under Sea Cloud Cruises, a new golden eagle was carved in Naples, Italy, and fitted on the barque in the fall of 1982 at a cost of more than $100,000.

In 1983 *Sea Cloud*'s former skipper, Carlton Skinner, came aboard—but this time not as the captain but as a passenger-cum-educator. He was one of three guest lecturers sponsored by the Smithsonian National Associate Program who were enlisted to discuss marine biology, oceanography, and the vessel's wartime service during a cross-Atlantic cruise from the Canary Islands off northwestern Africa to Martinique in the Caribbean.[59]

Skinner paid still another return visit to his old command in May 1987. *Sea Cloud* had been on a voyage to the South Pacific at that time, visiting Easter Island, Tahiti, Fiji (twice), the Solomons, Papua New Guinea, Palau, Bali, and Cairns. When it pulled into Suva, Fuji, on May 30, Skinner attended a reception held on the ship and said to the guests in a tone of sweet nostalgia: "I welcome you to the legendary *Sea Cloud*, the most fascinating ship sailing in the world today. . . . Stephen Crane, the American writer, has said that the heart of a ship's master is rooted in her timbers and that is true."[60]

In 1994 ownership of *Sea Cloud* changed yet again when Hermann Ebel and a small group of investors acquired the barque.[61] With that transaction, *Sea Cloud* had been owned by six different people and entities in the half century following World War II. It had been known variously by five names during that time. Since 1945 it had functioned as a conventional motor yacht, a sailing vessel, a presidential yacht, a playboy's houseboat, a floating schoolhouse, and a high-end cruise ship. There were days in the postwar period when it was a pawn in a long-running international legal skirmish between one of its owners and an unhappy charterer. In the second-half of the twentieth century it had exhibited the two extremes of majestic beauty and splendid luxury on one hand and disuse and abuse, rot and decay, on the other. Indeed, there were times—especially in the 1970s—when *Sea Cloud* could very well have ended up as an unpowered barge or harbor breakwater or even scrapped or sunk. Fortunately, none of those outcomes ever happened because it was saved in 1978 by Hartmut Paschburg and his German investors. In sum, the years 1944 to 1994 were for *Sea Cloud* momentous, uncommon, colorful, and challenging—certainly in vivid contrast to its earlier service under Marjorie Post's watchful eye and caring command.

At this point, with *Sea Cloud* approaching the advent of the new millennium, we'll pause in our chronicle of the yacht's history and resume it in chapter 9 with an account of its activities in the twenty-first century. But before doing so, we need to step back in time to 1944 to follow the postwar government service and business career of Carlton Skinner, who played such an important part in *Sea Cloud*'s life. In several ways, for him and his country, the best was yet to come.

8 Governor Skinner

From Dress Blues to Mufti

With Japan's surrender on August 15, 1945, the global war that had begun in 1939 finally came to an end. Two months later, on October 3, Carlton Skinner, then age thirty-two, was released from active duty as a Coast Guard lieutenant commander and became a civilian again after three years in uniform. When he last wore civvies, Skinner had been serving as the acting director of the promotion and information division in the US Maritime Commission, the agency he had joined in 1939. And it was to the commission that he returned in 1945 to head up its sales and charter organization.

During World War II the Maritime Commission had acquired—through new construction and purchases of existing hulls—several hundred passenger ships, tankers, and cargo vessels for the nation's use in the war against the Axis. But now with the war over, most of these ships were no longer needed and the government set about to dispose of the surplus vessels through various means, including returning them to their prior owners, selling or leasing them to commercial and private operators, storing them in the various anchorages of the "mothball" National Defense Reserve Fleet, or transferring them to other nations. Skinner and his team would have been heavily involved in arranging the sale and chartering of many of the unneeded ships. He served in that post for just a short time, only until April 1946, when he moved over to the US Department of the Interior.

Interior Insider

Established in 1849, the cabinet-level Department of the Interior manages the nation's natural and cultural resources and administers various federal programs related to Native Americans, Alaskan Natives, and Native Hawaiians, as well as the territorial and insular areas of the United States.

In February 1946 President Harry Truman nominated the thirty-nine-year-old Julius A. Krug to succeed the long-serving Harold L. Ickes as secretary of the interior. A native of Wisconsin, Krug had worked at the Tennessee Valley Authority and War Production Board before becoming the thirty-third interior secretary on March 18. Just a few weeks after being sworn in, Krug announced on April 28 the appointment of Carlton Skinner as his director of information.[1] With that appointment, Skinner resumed his career in government public relations, a role he had performed in the late 1930s with the Department of Labor and the Maritime Commission and with the Coast Guard in 1943.

The arrival of Krug and Skinner in their new positions coincided with a strike by 400,000 coal miners that had begun on April 1. The United Mine Workers (UMW), led by John L. Lewis, had walked out in an effort to obtain improved wages, health benefits, and safety regulations. With the stoppage of coal production threatening the nation's economy, Truman assigned Krug —whose department then administered US mines—to lead negotiations between Lewis and the mine owners. Those negotiations resulted in a contract signed on May 29 by Lewis and Krug at the White House, with Truman looking on. In announcing the agreement to the waiting press corps, Krug said: "I am sure Mr. Lewis will agree that the contract is fair to the operators and the men alike. It's too bad we didn't have it two months ago."[2] Skinner then dutifully provided the terms of the contract to the White House reporters. (A second walkout by the miners on November 21 and Lewis's rejection of an injunction to resume work led to a finding by a US judge that Lewis was in contempt of court, and a fine of $3.5 million was imposed on the UMW. Lewis ended that strike on December 7, 1946.)

During his time at the Interior Department, Skinner continued to pursue his interest in art with regular visits in the evening to the Phillips Memorial Gallery, located in the Dupont Circle neighborhood of Washington. The Phillips collection contains the works of many celebrated artists, including Renoir, El Greco, van Gogh, Matisse, Monet, Picasso, Homer, and Whistler.

Skinner's after-work and weekend visits to the gallery as an adult replicated in some way the many hours he had spent as a child looking at paintings in Boston's Museum of Fine Arts.

Carlton Skinner's involvement in Democratic politics later in his life might have had its beginnings in 1946 when he accompanied his boss to a Democratic fund raiser in California. It seems that Secretary Krug, the after-dinner speaker, did not do well at that event. He talked much too long (during which someone in the audience yelled out in exasperation: "Where's the last page of the speech?"). John P. McEnery, the vice chairman of the California Democratic State Central Committee, later recalled that he tried to tell Krug that he was taking too much time, but "he kept grinding away on something that nobody was interested in, telling about the wonderful things Interior was doing."[3] But while Krug had bombed with the local Democrats, Skinner on the other hand had made a favorable impression, at least on the state party's vice chairman. Twenty-four years after the event, McEnery remembered that "[Skinner] was very close to Secretary Krug. He was in Washington with him—a very outstanding man, too, great ability."[4]

Of course, serving as Krug's special assistant and Interior Department spokesman was giving Skinner exposure to many men of influence in Washington and national politics. For example, as we saw in chapter 7, in May 1948 Skinner had the opportunity to socialize with Secretary of the Navy John L. Sullivan over two days at a dinner and ceremony on board Skinner's former command, USS *Sea Cloud*, in Annapolis. As Skinner recalled his experience with Sullivan: "I later knew him in my business life. He was a senior partner in a law firm I retained, and we had a number of reminiscences about it [the Annapolis event]. He remembered the occasion very well and was very happy with it."[5]

The young bureaucrat even got to spend some time with the president of the United States. Two cases in point: Skinner lunched with Harry Truman and Krug at the Interior Department on February 2, 1947, and in February 1948 cruised with the president, Krug, and others for two days on the presidential yacht USS *Williamsburg* (AGC-369) from San Juan, Puerto Rico, to St. Croix, Virgin Islands.[6] These incidental contacts with Truman may have factored in a decision the president made in August 1949 that significantly changed Skinner's life. (In his later years, Skinner came to regard Truman as a father figure.)

On July 26, 1948, Truman established the President's Committee on Equality of Treatment and Opportunity in the Armed Services. The committee was to recommend revisions to military regulations to implement the government's policy of equality for all armed forces personnel regardless of "race, color, religion or national origin." Chaired by Charles Fahy, former solicitor general of the United States, the committee had six other members: Alphonsus J. Donahue, Lester Granger, Charles Luckman, Dwight Palmer, John H. Sengstacke, and William E. Stevenson. The Fahy committee held hearings and meetings throughout 1949 before issuing its final report to Truman on May 22, 1950.

Among the people who testified before the committee was the director of information of the Department of the Interior. Skinner appeared "as a civilian drawing on his background on naval experience" at an April 25, 1949, hearing held at the Pentagon. He told the committee in a formal opening statement that his "contribution to your work will be valuable to the extent that my experience can be used in helping to attain the goal of equality of treatment and opportunity."[7]

In reviewing that experience with the committee, Skinner recounted the Oliver Henry incident on the cutter *Northland*, his letter to the Coast Guard commandant, and the subsequent *Sea Cloud* experiment of 1944. Then he offered some conclusions and recommendations: First, African American sailors and officers "should be used interchangeably with white [personnel] in all general duty positions; no position in the naval force should be barred to a Negro." Second, there should be no segregation of any kind on ships or in any working, messing, berthing, or training facility ashore. Third, black and white sailors should have equal opportunity for all advanced training and be admitted to service schools on the basis of ability and aptitude, with no racially based quotas for training. And, fourth, "a quota system should be established requiring every ship or unit to have a certain percentage of Negroes, but not more than another percentage."[8]

Skinner acknowledged that this last point "will be a slightly controversial recommendation." Certainly, by today's standards it was. Nevertheless, he went on to explain his reasoning. He believed, he said, there should be no quotas on advancement in rank or service school attendance. In addition, he opposed the creation or maintenance of any all-black units and provided a number of solid reasons for that view. Similarly, he thought all-white units would be "segregation in reverse." Based on his experience, he suggested that "five to 25 percent" of a ship's crew be comprised of African-Americans, as a ratio in that range would best facilitate acceptance by the white majority, provide adequate opportunities for training and advancement, and lead to the total integration of the sea services. He stated: "If every naval unit were required to have 25 percent Negroes, coupled with a system of complete freedom for advancement, of complete freedom to go into different special assignments, of complete availability of service schools, I think that problem would handle itself."[9]

Since he was still a lieutenant commander in the Coast Guard Reserve, Skinner had provided an information copy of his April 25 statement to Coast Guard headquarters. In July 1949 he received notification that Adm. Joseph F. Farley, the Coast Guard's commandant, concurred with his recommendations: "Your straightforward account of Coast Guard experience with this controversial subject reflects highly on your own and this service's treatment of personnel without regard to race, creed, color or national origin. Your action and testimony in this instance is most commendable."[10]

One month after receiving the commandant's endorsement, Carlton Skinner got an even bigger and much more significant accolade. Harry Truman selected him to be the governor of Guam.

The George Washington of Guam

Located in the western Pacific Ocean, Guam is the largest and southernmost of the Mariana Islands as well as the largest island in Micronesia. It is approximately 4,000 miles west of Hawaii, 2,700 miles north of Australia, and 1,500 miles east of the Philippines. Twenty-five miles long and five to ten miles wide, the island has an area of 210 square miles. In 1950 some 59,000 people lived on Guam, including: 25,000 Guamanians, 30,000 US military personnel and their dependents, and several thousand Filipino contract laborers and US workers, businessmen, and their dependents. Today the population is approximately 167,000.

Following the Spanish-American War, Guam was ceded by Spain to the United States under the terms of the Treaty of Paris on December 10, 1898. During World War II Japan captured Guam in December 1941 and occupied the island for thirty months until it was recovered by US forces in Operation Forager in July 1944.

Over the years Guam had been governed by a series of forty-eight Spanish army officers dating from the 1600s to 1898, twenty-eight different US Navy officers from 1899 to 1942, five Japanese army and naval officers in 1942–44, a US Marine Corps general in 1944 and 1945, and a US Navy admiral from 1945 to 1949.[11] Those three centuries of military rule ended in 1949 in the person of Carlton Skinner.

At the conclusion of World War II Harry Truman had asked his secretaries of state, war, navy, and interior to recommend how the United States should govern Guam and the other Pacific Islands then under US administration. In 1946 Truman appointed a Civil Rights Commission to propose actions by the government to eliminate discrimination and foster civil rights among its citizens and nationals. Skinner then advised Secretary Krug that the Interior Department "had some very special civil rights problems," including those of American Indians, and that "there was no adequate governmental procedure for taking care of the civil rights of . . . the Pacific territories of Guam, American Samoa and the Trust Territory of the Pacific Islands," which were all under military rule.[12]

In 1947 the Civil Rights Commission recommended US citizenship and "organic acts" for the inhabitants of Guam and American Samoa. (An organic act is a law passed by Congress to establish local government in a territory that is governed by the United States.) The people of those two islands, said the commission, "are in the anomalous position of being neither citizens nor aliens, but nationals of the United States."[13] Although owing allegiance to the United States, Guam's inhabitants had none of the rights of citizenship (unlike, say, the people of Hawaii, Alaska, Puerto Rico, and the Virgin Islands, who were deemed US citizens either by birth or naturalization), and Guam did not have an organic act creating a local government that would guarantee civil liberties.

In June 1947 Secretary Krug and the three other cabinet members recommended separate congressional legislation to provide civil government and citizenship for the people of Guam. That August, Krug led an inspection team—which included Carlton Skinner and H. Rex Lee, the assistant director of the Division of Territories—on a visit to the Pacific islands. They traveled to Hawaii (which, like Alaska, was then a territory and not yet a state), met there with R. Adm. Charles A. Pownall, the naval governor of Guam, and then went on to American Samoa and later to Guam. On Guam, Skinner and Lee met with civilians who urged the formation of a civil government. From Guam the team flew to Tokyo and met with Gen. Douglas MacArthur, who was serving as the US proconsul of Japan. As Skinner later noted, MacArthur "enthusiastically endorsed civil government for the U.S. Pacific territories, saying it would be helpful to him in demonstrating to the

Japanese people that the United States did not seek to perpetuate military rule over civilians and that the U.S. occupation of Japan would end when a civil government with a democratic constitution could be established and maintained."[14]

When Krug and his team returned to the United States, they recommended that a civilian be appointed governor of Guam on July 1, 1949, "with the Navy Department heading the Naval Government of Guam for one year as a transitional and preparatory period, with responsibility transferring to the Interior Department on July 1, 1950. This civilian governor was to be proposed by the Secretary of the Interior to the Secretary of the Navy, who would then nominate him to the President."[15]

Accordingly, in late August 1949, Krug designated his special assistant, protégé, and information director—Carlton Skinner, then thirty-six years old —as the first civilian governor of Guam and sent his name to the Navy Department, which was still administering the island.[16] Skinner was to succeed Rear Admiral Pownall, who was to retire on or about September 1. President Truman then formally named Skinner as governor on September 3.[17] Skinner told an interviewer in 1970 that his appointment required two political endorsements. He received one from, not too surprisingly, former ambassador Joseph Davies, owner of *Sea Cloud*, and the other from Max O'Rell Truitt, grandson of Vice President Alben W. Barkley and a member of the US Maritime Commission (where Skinner had served three years earlier).[18]

On September 7 Truman issued an executive order formally transferring administrative responsibility for Guam from the secretary of the navy to the secretary of the interior, to be effective on July 1, 1950.[19] Nine days later the president sent a letter to the newly appointed governor in which he wrote, in part:

> I am happy, through you, to greet the people of Guam on this historic occasion when you become the first civilian Governor of our island possession. This is another step in our program for extending a full measure of civil rights to all its people. I hope it will be followed soon by the passage of organic legislation to carry out our fifty-year-old obligation to define the civil rights and political status of the inhabitants. Guam is an important part of our United States. Its prosperity and its security will remain our concern.[20]

Skinner arrived on Guam on September 26 and was greeted by hundreds of Guamanians, US military and naval personnel, civilian workers, and a chorus of young girls who sang two songs of welcome at the airport.[21] At the same time, Krug back in Washington expressed his support of the orderly transfer of Guam from naval to civilian administration and sent a congratulatory radiogram to Skinner.[22]

At 4:00 p.m. on Tuesday, September 27, 1949, Carlton Skinner delivered his inaugural address in the Plaza d'Espana in Agana, Guam. He pledged to work "unceasingly for the passage of organic legislation for this island and for all other measures which will bring about increased self-government." Skinner said that self-government should not only be applied to islandwide matters but extend down to the community and village levels. He advocated for the establishment of a sound economy and indicated that rehabilitation, reconstruction, and new construction following the Pacific war would be essential to creating a new and better postwar Guamanian economy. The governor's policies, he told his audience, would be predicated on what was best for the entire island population. He concluded his remarks by evoking American democracy, calling it a "flowering of the spirit—a spirit that is free in the knowledge of free men that they control their own destinies—free from fear, free from want, free to speak and free to worship" (i.e., Roosevelt's "Four Freedoms" from his 1941 state of the union address). "It is my humble pledge to do everything in my power to gain and maintain those freedoms for the people of Guam."[23] As we shall see, over the next four years, Carlton Skinner did his best to make good on that pledge.

But first he had to deal with a mighty wind. On November 17, 1949, Guam was struck by Typhoon Allyn, which lashed the island with gusts of 125 miles an hour. Large Quonset huts—corrugated metal wartime structures housing many of Guam's private homes, government buildings, schools, and warehouses—broke apart, and several boats were damaged. Roads and bridges were washed out, and power lines were knocked down. In all, Allyn cost an estimated $1.6 million in damages to civilian property, not including losses to the island's crops. Fortunately, no lives were lost and there were only a few injuries.[24] Skinner flew to Washington on November 24 to request federal assistance for Guam but was refused by the Office of Emergency Management.[25] According to Skinner's account of the storm and its aftermath, that agency did not help the island, "contending that it had no authority. Guam, it said, was 'legally attached to but not part of the United States.' The irresponsibility of such a reply was beyond belief, even if technically correct."[26] For Skinner, this experience "had a salutary effect in making the new Guam government realize that it must be self-reliant. It had to stop its former instinctive dependence on the occasional benevolence of the U.S. Government . . . And accept that with its more mature political status would come the obligation to make its own decisions and provide for itself. From this stemmed a whole new series of actions and programs, large and small."[27]

The governor most likely had an additional objective for his November trip to Washington: to meet with Oscar L. Chapman. After Julius Krug had resigned as interior secretary over political differences with Truman, the president selected Chapman—who had served under Harold Ickes for thirteen years as assistant secretary and as acting secretary for a few months in 1946—to succeed Krug on December 1, 1949. An Associated Press report at the time suggested that while Skinner was in the nation's capital, he was "expected to take time to find out how he stands" with Chapman.[28] Apparently, he was in good standing with his new boss, as both he and Chapman went on to serve in their respective jobs until the end of the Truman administration in 1953.

The first and top priority for Oscar Chapman and Carlton Skinner was to draft and get enacted an organic act for Guam. Interior's draft provided for three branches of government for the island. The executive branch would be led by the governor, with a government secretary as deputy. Both posts would be appointed by the president, and the governor would be confirmed by vote of the US Senate. The legislative branch would be given exclusive territorial authority to adopt laws affecting Guam, while the judicial branch would have authority under both US laws and local laws established on Guam.

The proposed organic act was introduced in Congress and referred to the respective Committees on Public Lands of the House and Senate. Hearings on Guam were held by a subcommittee of the House Public Lands Committee in November 1949, and hearings in Washington were convened by the Senate Interior and Insular Affairs Committee in April 1950. Skinner testified before the Senate committee on April 15 and obviously urged passage of the legislation.[29]

In early June 1950 Secretary of Defense Louis Johnson made an inspection visit to Guam—the navy at that point still holding authority over Guam—and followed his visit with an attempt to persuade the White House to retain the military's control over the island. The Korean War had broken out on June 25, and Johnson believed that the Navy Department should continue to govern Guam because it was the nation's most important naval and air base in the western Pacific. Chapman countered that argument and reminded Truman of MacArthur's advice to Krug in 1947.

Meanwhile, there were some clever political maneuvers—too intricate to enumerate here—in the House and Senate to get around Johnson's position. In the end, the Senate, which had been considering Senate Bill 1862, accepted the House version of the organic act (House Resolution 7273).[30] Once signed into law by Truman, the Organic Act of Guam transferred the administration of Guam from the Navy Department to the Interior Department at the end of July 1950.

The enacted legislation accomplished the following:

- Defined Guam as an unincorporated territory of the United States, ended military rule, and assigned the island's relations with the federal government to be conducted by the civilian department directed by the president.
- Extended US citizenship to all persons born or residing in Guam after April 11, 1899.
- Established a comprehensive Bill of Rights, including prohibitions of any discrimination and hazardous child labor, and required a strict separation of church and state and compulsory education for children ages six to sixteen.
- Left the right to a trial by jury to be determined by the Guamanian legislature.
- Assigned legislative powers to a single house not to exceed twenty-one members and listed a number of rules for member selection, sessions, and voting.
- Defined the role of governor, including authorization to coordinate all activities of a civil nature by the US agencies in Guam.
- Created a district court under the jurisdiction of a US district court in the continental United States.
- Transferred title to all property owned by the United States and used by the naval government "in the administration of civil affairs" to Guam's government.
- Required the governor of Guam to establish public health services and to provide for a public educational system.

- Directed that taxes collected in Guam were to be conveyed to Guam's treasury and expended for Guam's benefit.

There have been some criticisms of the Organic Act of Guam with respect to the formulation and implementation of the legislation. For one thing, the milestone law did not originate with, nor was it drafted by, the people of Guam but instead was created in the halls of Congress in Washington, DC. For another, the final legislation was not voted on by the Guamanian people themselves.[31] Notwithstanding these criticisms, the enactment in 1950 of the Organic Act of Guam was a transformational event in Guam's history as it paved the way for significant changes in the island's governance, economy, and society.

Three months after the Organic Act came into effect, Guam held its first-ever election under civil rule. In that voting, the island's Popular Party shut out both the Democratic and Republican Parties and won eighteen of the twenty-one seats in the unicameral legislature.[32]

Once Guam had acquired self-governing authority and had a legislative body, the Skinner administration developed and submitted to the legislature a series of laws covering such activities as voting, civil service, public utilities, construction and zoning, the courts, civil defense, shipping, medical care, and education. In addition, the governor arranged for the construction of a new Guam Memorial Hospital and proposed the creation of the Territorial College of Guam—the first tertiary-level educational facility in the Pacific Islands. The college opened in 1952 and is now the University of Guam with more than 3,700 students. It offers twenty-five undergraduate and fifteen graduate programs and has graduated more than 18,200 students.[33]

In a program to foster and promote local private enterprise, Skinner privatized the former navy-run Bank of Guam (there are now more than fifteen banks on Guam) and sold the island's navy-owned newspaper, *Guam Daily News*, to Joseph Flores, a Guamanian (the paper is now known as the *Pacific Daily News* and is part of the USA Today network).[34]

On January 13, 1951, Skinner established a "free port" on Guam whereby customs duties were canceled on products coming to the island from foreign ports. This step in effect facilitated the importation of food and construction materials from sources other than the United States and thereby ended the mainland's monopoly as Guam's only supplier.

Six months later, on July 5, Skinner spoke to the World Trade Club of San Francisco and told his audience about the benefits US companies could

Governor Skinner poses at his desk in Agana in 1950. (Solange P. Skinner)

gain from locating their businesses on the island. Referring to Guam as "the Hong Kong of the future"—obviously a bit of a stretch—Skinner listed a number of potential advantages to Guam-based US businesses, including duty-free entry into the United States of products manufactured in Guam (provided half the value of the manufactured goods were added in Guam), the availability of an US banking system, and the island's proximity to major markets in the Far East.[35]

Carlton Skinner's term as governor was not without some rough spots and controversies. For instance, in June 1951, some critics of his administration alleged that he had exercised improper influence over the Guam legislature by providing federal employment to many of its members. Skinner called the allegations unfounded, saying that "there is not one legislator now in government work who was not in such employment when I took office."[36] In another case, two former Guam employees charged the governor in 1952 with maladministration. He responded by telling the US House Interior Affairs Committee that "there is no fraud, graft, corruption or mismanagement in the government of Guam" and provided a detailed rebuttal of the charges made by the discharged civil servants (one had been laid off after his job had been eliminated, and the other had been fired for insubordination).[37] In a third instance, the Sailors' Union of the Pacific—a labor union of unlicensed sailors who work in the deck, engine, and steward departments of US-flag vessels—went on strike on the West Coast in the summer of 1952, thereby restricting the importation of refrigerated food to Guam. Skinner reacted by arranging for the navy to use military transports to carry vital shipments of foodstuffs to the island for the duration of the strike and by screening all orders for food shipments to ensure that they were in fact essential.[38]

Skinner's four-year term as governor was due to expire on September 9, 1954, but political developments in the United States during the summer and fall of 1952 would ultimately end his term nineteen months early. President Truman had decided not to run for reelection that year and backed Illinois governor and fellow Democrat Adlai Stevenson to be his successor. But on November 4, 1952, Dwight D. Eisenhower defeated Stevenson in a landslide election, turning the White House over to the Republicans for the first time since 1932.

Skinner waited five weeks to announce on December 18 that "conforming to established American political custom," he would resign his post on January 20, 1953, "to allow the newly elected national administration to appoint its own choice."[39] According to Skinner's 1970 interview, he and Secretary Chapman briefed Eisenhower on their areas of responsibility during the transition. On February 12, 1953, the Eisenhower White House accepted Skinner's resignation and new Secretary of the Interior Douglas McKay said that Randall S. Herman, who had been serving as government secretary of Guam, would become acting governor.[40] Eisenhower followed up by appointing Ford Quint Elvidge, a sixty-one-year-old Seattle attorney, as the second civilian governor of Guam. Elvidge assumed that office on April 23, 1953.

On January 12, 1953, Carlton Skinner delivered his farewell address to the Guam legislature. He, of course, reviewed some of the achievements he and the people of Guam had made during his term. He warned the legislators against possible future attempts to undermine governmental institutions, and he offered formal and detailed proposals for future government actions in 1953. It was almost as if Skinner were giving a traditional state of the union address rather than a valedictory speech.[41]

Forty-six years later Skinner summed up his tenure as governor by saying that, in a little less than four years, he "had been able, with the support of the President of the United States and the people of the United States, acting through their Congress and the people of Guam, to bring civilian government and representative democracy to the people of Guam for the first time in 300 years. It was an act of principle."[42]

Truman wrote to Skinner on January 16, 1953, to thank him for his service and for "the good job you have done in establishing civilian government" on Guam. "Under your leadership," Truman said, "the people of Guam have made tremendous strides. . . . The achievements of the Government of Guam since 1950 are, I believe, ample testimony to the value of civil government under organic law."[43] Recognizing the governor's significant contributions, Oscar Chapman bestowed on Skinner his department's highest honor, its Distinguished Service Award.

But perhaps the most meaningful tribute Skinner received for his service came in 1961. Speaking at the dedication of the Skinner Plaza in Agana (later known as Hagatna), Guam, Manuel Lujan, then vice speaker of the Guam legislature, called Skinner "the most revered governor this territory has ever had. . . . Had he not been the man he was and still is, our experiment in civil government might have failed completely. . . . He is not only the faithful friend of the territory, he is the friend and comrade of all of us."[44] Skinner was then presented with a small walking stick, "hand crafted," Skinner later wrote, "by an anonymous Guam silversmith, capped with the Guam seal in silver and with a silver band at the top carrying the inscription . . .*Gov. Carlton Skinner, George Washington of Guam*."[45]

The silver band with Guam's accolade equating Skinner to America's first president. (Solange P. Skinner)

And Now for Something Different

After leaving Guam in March 1953, the unemployed Carlton Skinner had to decide what he would do next. Presumably, he could return to his first profession as a journalist. That certainly would be one option. Another would be to follow in his father's footsteps and take up a career in academia. We could easily see him teaching political science and government at, say, UCLA or Stanford. A third option would be to enter politics. Skinner, a Democrat, said in his 1970 interview for the John F. Kennedy Presidential Library and Museum that when he got back to California after leaving Guam he had been encouraged to run for Congress (perhaps by John P. McEnery, the former vice chairman of the California Democratic State Central Committee). Skinner had attended the 1952 Democratic National Convention at the invitation of Oscar Chapman and in his capacity as the governor of a US territory, and presumably had retained some ties to the Democratic establishment after working in the Roosevelt and Truman administrations. But Skinner told his Kennedy Library interviewer, James A. Oesterle, that he voted against running for office because he lacked sufficient funds to mount a campaign. Resuming his service in the federal government was still another option that Skinner considered, but this too was ruled out: "I concluded that it would be very difficult, if not impossible, to work effectively again within the civil service in Washington. So I came to San Francisco and began to hunt for employment. It was not easy because the openings for unemployed governors are not very frequent."[46]

By deciding to focus his vocational efforts instead on the private sector, Skinner for the first time in his life became a player in the corporate world of business and industry, a realm in which he would excel over the next thirty years.

His business career began in 1953 when he was hired by American President Lines (APL) in San Francisco. Formerly known as the Dollar Steamship Company, APL had been acquired by the US government in 1938 and had operated numerous cargo and passenger ships during World War II. At war's end the company's assets were valued at $40 million. In 1952, the year before Skinner joined the business, US oilman Ralph K. Davies and a group of investors purchased APL from the government for $18 million. After that APL added several new vessels to its fleet, with eleven ships built between 1952 and 1954.

APL was a logical fit for Skinner. After all, he had a degree in finance, had served in the Maritime Commission and was therefore very knowledgeable about the US merchant marine, and was familiar with business in the Pacific region, a prime operating area for APL. In his first year with the company Skinner worked in the freight traffic department, but in 1954 he became executive assistant to APL's president, a role he performed until 1958.

In mid-August 1956 Skinner attended his second Democratic National Convention, held in the International Amphitheater in Chicago—this time as an official member of the California delegation. However, he participated as an alternate delegate and as such did not cast a vote for the party's presidential nominee, Adlai Stevenson. That may have been just as well, as Stevenson again lost to Eisenhower in another landslide election on November 6.

Two years after the convention, Skinner weighed anchor at APL and traveled 3,000 miles east to New York City to become the financial vice president, treasurer, and a director of the Fairbanks Whitney Corporation. That organization had been formed in 1958 in a merger of the Fairbanks-Morse Company—a manufacturer of industrial equipment such as locomotives and diesel engines—and the Penn-Texas Corporation. In August 1958 Skinner was named a director, vice president, and treasurer of Penn-Texas.[47] Four years after that, Skinner became the chairman of Pratt & Whitney Company, Inc., a subsidiary of Fairbanks Whitney, while continuing in his post as the latter's CFO.[48] Pratt & Whitney at that time was a manufacturer of machine tools and factory automation equipment.[49]

In July 1960 Skinner went to his third and the party's thirty-third Democratic National Convention, which was held at the Los Angeles Memorial Sports Arena and Coliseum. Based largely on his friendship with Senator Clair Engle of California and Don L. Bradley, the manager of the California Democratic State Central Committee, Skinner attended as a guest of the state's delegation.

On July 14 Skinner had an unexpected and very brief brush with presidential politics. He had gone to the 7300 wing of the Biltmore Hotel in Los Angeles—Senator Lyndon B. Johnson's convention headquarters—to deliver a campaign contribution to the majority leader. Just by chance as he was leaving LBJ's suite, he was passed by Robert F. Kennedy, who was then entering to see Johnson. Bobby had been engaged in the backstage discussions and maneuvers by the Kennedy team throughout that day over the selection of John F. Kennedy's vice presidential running mate. According to noted

Johnson biographer Robert A. Caro, Bobby had made more than one trip (the exact number is fuzzy) rushing up and down the hotel's two floors separating the Kennedy and Johnson suites while serving as an intermediary between his brother and the various men involved in that selection.[50] The final nod, as history shows, went to Johnson rather than to either Senator Henry M. Jackson of Washington or Senator Stuart Symington of Missouri.

Whether it was the climate or the people or the pace of the town, we don't know. What we do know is that in 1963 Skinner had concluded that he "didn't enjoy the New York life" and decided to leave the city and his job to return to San Francisco. He already owned a house there, purchased when he was serving as Guam's governor.[51]

Once back in the Bay Area, the former governor formed his own management consulting firm—Skinner & Company—and located his offices at 110 Sutter Street (and later at 660 Market Street) in San Francisco. He described his firm as a "very unusual business," as it engaged, while under retainer, in various corporate dogfights to defend or elect or defeat a corporation's board of directors. According to Skinner, there were only four other firms like his in the United States, and those four were in New York City. He was alone west of the Hudson River. He told his interviewer in 1970: "It's been described sometimes as very much like selling bridges. You don't sell very many of them but when you do, it's a good sale."[52]

Mister Commissioner

The South Pacific Commission (SPC) was established in Sydney, Australia, in 1947 by six nations that were then administering territories in the Pacific Ocean: Australia, France, New Zealand, the Netherlands, the United Kingdom, and the United States. The commission had been formed to "restore stability to a region that had experienced the turbulence of the Second World War, to assist in administering their dependent territories and to benefit the people of the Pacific."[53] That region covered 20 percent of the Earth's surface.

In 1949 the SPC's headquarters was moved from Sydney to Noumea, New Caledonia (a collection of islands administered by France), and the first formal South Pacific Conference convened there in the following year. In 1951 the area served by the SPC was enlarged to include Guam and the Trust Territory of the Pacific Islands in Micronesia. (Randall S. Herman, Guam's gov-

Carlton Skinner at his desk at Skinner & Company. Numerous mementos of his years on Guam and in the Pacific region decorate the office. (Solange P. Skinner)

ernment secretary and later acting governor, represented the island at the 1952 SPC meeting.)

The South Pacific Commission consisted of six voting commissioners, one from each nation, who were termed "senior commissioners," and all SPC decisions were based on the votes of those six members. Each participating nation also had a second commissioner and, in the case of the United States, a third commissioner.

In the early 1960s the SPC had two entities—the South Pacific Conference, with representatives from each of the territories who met every three years to confer on common problems and make recommendations to the commission; and the Research Council, made up of technical and scientific experts who considered and proposed projects for consideration by the commission. A secretary-general appointed by the SPC served for a five-year term and oversaw the principal staff officers, who in turn managed a staff of fifty-nine people. The United States provided about $88,000 or 15 percent of the SPC's annual expenditures of about $700,000 (in 1963 dollars).

On August 11, 1961, President John F. Kennedy appointed Carlton Skinner as an SPC commissioner. Kennedy had met Skinner at a dinner in April 1960, and the two men had discussed Guam and various issues involving the Pacific Ocean area.[54]

The SPC post was not a full-time position, and it paid only $25 a day plus expenses on days when Skinner was actually working as a commissioner.[55] In his SPC role, therefore, Skinner was able, and more or less financially required, to keep his day job as a corporate executive. As a commissioner Skinner would have attended biannual meetings of the governing body of the SPC, along with annual meetings of a committee made up of representatives of governments and administrations that convened in the years when the governing body conferences were not held. Hence, there was at least a little bit of traveling halfway around the world required for the US commissioner.

In August 1962 the first South Pacific Conference held on US soil took place in Pago Pago on American Samoa. Attending that meeting, in addition to Skinner, were Secretary of the Interior Stewart Udall, Governor H. Rex Lee of Samoa, and seventy representatives of more than 3 million Pacific islanders.[56] Among other topics, the delegates discussed the changing role of women in the South Pacific territories, and they set an agenda for the 1965 meeting to include the care and rehabilitation of handicapped inhabitants, the problems of juvenile delinquency, and the establishment of new industries.[57] (Samoa became an independent state in 1962, and three years later became the first Pacific Island nation to become a full-fledged member of the SPC. Also in 1962 the Netherlands withdrew from the SPC when it relinquished its control of Irian Jaya.)

Central to Skinner's geopolitical thinking during his service on the SPC was the global competition between the Soviet Union and communism on the one hand and the United States and the Western democracies on the other. Skinner believed that the economic development and enhancement of the Pacific Island community was of strategic importance in the long-running Cold War contest. He pointed out that whereas communism had made inroads in Europe, Africa, mainland Asia, and South America, "there is not in the Pacific Island area . . . a Communist government . . . political party . . . newspaper or even an active Communist trade union."[58] Skinner said the absence of communist influence on the islands was because the Western nations had "constantly encouraged self-government."[59]

Moreover, the US commissioner drew an important distinction between self-government and full independence. He believed that despite the move toward decolonization in the postwar period, certain of the island territories were better served by remaining a self-governing part of the "metropolitan" nation, as, for example, Guam was—and is today: a US territory. While some former colonies and territories possessed economies that could make them self-sustaining and viable as independent nations, others did not, and those islands should stay aligned with the "mother country." Today this stance probably appears paternalistic and somewhat anachronistic, but in the international context of the early 1960s one could argue that it was prudent and pragmatic.

Two years after becoming a commissioner, Skinner wrote an article for the prestigious international relations journal *Foreign Affairs*, published by the Council on Foreign Relations. Entitled "Self-Government in the South Pacific," the 1963 piece provided an overview and account of the colonial history of the region served by the SPC, described the various functions of the SPC and its personnel, and discussed the strategic situation in Oceania vis-à-vis the communist countries.

In the article Skinner restated one of the guiding principles behind his actions on the Coast Guard cutter *Northland* and USS *Sea Cloud* and as governor of Guam. "If we believe both in the equality of man and in the dignity of man," he wrote, "it follows that a man must be allowed and encouraged to develop to the limit of his own capacity."[60] That is why he supported Oliver Henry's case to become a motor machinist's mate; encouraged Steward's Mate Jacob Lawrence's talents as an artist; fought for his African American crewmen's rights to train, perform, and live in full equality with their white counterparts; and arranged for native Guamanians to fully develop and expand their own government and businesses.

With respect to the Cold War as it pertained to the South Pacific, Skinner argued:

> If we of the Western nations see to it that there are means and opportunities for personal advancement, we will build in the enormous Pacific Ocean area a stable political economy and society which will strengthen us both internally and externally. We will have demonstrated to the people of the non-aligned nations (as well as the unhappy peoples of the Eastern alliance) that they can fulfill their legitimate aspirations for freedom, self-government and a better life for their children without flirting with Communism or venturing on the tightrope of independence unsupported by economic, educational or national defense viability.[61]

In 1964 Skinner received his third presidential appointment when Lyndon Johnson named him the senior US commissioner on the South Pacific Commission. He served in that role through the remainder of Johnson's term and the first two years of Richard Nixon's first administration. During his service he met a few times with Dean Rusk, who was secretary of state under Presidents Kennedy and Johnson. Skinner was greatly impressed by Rusk, recalling in 1970 that the secretary "had a very clear understanding of the problem in the Pacific, a very broad vision, and certainly I came away with an enormous respect for Dean Rusk as a government servant and a political leader."[62] Rusk resigned his position in January 1969, and Skinner left the SPC in the following year.

Other Hats

Carlton Skinner wore many hats during the first five decades of his life, including journalist, student, civil servant, Coast Guard officer, corporate executive, ship captain, father, governor, consultant, writer, and entrepreneur. He would go on to add still more hats and titles in his later years.

In 1966 Continental Airlines approached Skinner for advice and assistance in establishing airline service in the Trust Territory of the Pacific Islands. On behalf of Continental and in response to a 1967 request for proposals,

In one of his last meetings as senior US commissioner, Skinner speaks at a 1969 conference in Noumea, New Caledonia. (Solange P. Skinner)

Skinner pitched the establishment of six hotels in Micronesia. That proposal was approved. In 1968 Air Micronesia was formed as a joint venture of Continental, the United Micronesia and Development Corporation (UMDA), and Aloha Airlines. Skinner subsequently became a director of UMDA and represented the 30 percent stake that Continental took in UMDA.[63] (He later became chairman of Air Micronesia, although he told a reporter in 1984 that he was "not actively involved in running the airline."[64])

Skinner also was a consultant to and later a director of Micronesian Inter-Ocean Line Incorporated (MILI), a shipping company owned jointly by Marine Chartering, a US shipping business, and various Micronesian interests. MILI provided ocean shipping services from Japan and the United States to Micronesia.[65]

Additionally, he worked with various governments in the region. As he told a Kennedy Library interviewer in 1970: "I am consulted from time to time by some of the leaders of territories or independent countries in the Pacific, among them are Nauru, Western Samoa and Fiji. . . . I have been asked to assist in one way or another based on my long experience in the Pacific."[66]

One of those countries, Nauru, is an island in the central Pacific that, following a postwar United Nations trusteeship, gained its independence in 1968. As the new Republic of Nauru, the eight-square-mile nation handled its foreign relations with a string of consuls. In Nauru's case, it maintained consuls and representatives in Australia, Japan, Taiwan, the United Kingdom, Hawaii, New Zealand, Guam, and Saipan, and one official of note in San Francisco. His name? Who else? Carlton Skinner—appointed as Nauru's honorary consul general on December 6, 1971.[67] As he explained in a very detailed article he wrote about the island in 1976, Nauru's minimal foreign service handled "diplomatic and foreign commercial problems, as directed from Nauru by the president and his staff."[68] Working out of his 110 Sutter Street offices in San Francisco, Skinner served as Nauru's consul in the United States until 1981.

Even at a time when he was running his own consulting company in San Francisco, serving on the South Pacific Commission, and working with various businesses and governments in Oceania, Carlton Skinner was able to significantly enhance his personal curriculum vitae by marrying Solange Petit. When he met Solange in 1967, she was a Sorbonne-trained anthropologist and psychologist—with doctorates in both disciplines—and the director of the French Ethnological Mission in Fiji. Funded by France's Ministry of Foreign Affairs, the mission trained Fijians to create an archive of materials on indigenous culture and traditions and to publish monographs documenting that information. Carlton and Solange were joined in matrimony in San Francisco on April 6, 1970.

Between Skinner's longtime interests and experiences in the South Pacific and his bride's academic and professional accomplishments, it is easy to see how a union between the two was a natural combination. Nevertheless, in an interview for this work, Solange Skinner made it clear that for many years she had no interest in marrying anyone and that she "did not want to become [merely] Madame Skinner."[69] Instead she wanted the freedom to continue to pursue her own professional life fully while sharing with her partner the rewards of both their separate and mutual experiences. The two of them obviously achieved a successful merger because they remained happily together for all of the final thirty-four years of Carlton Skinner's life. It could be said that theirs was an arrangement that not only worked but may have been preordained.

In the mid-1970s Skinner's personal life also included another lady: his sailboat *Yark*.[70] Wearing his captain's hat as a member of the St. Francis Yacht

Club, Skinner sailed and raced *Yark* in the beautiful waters of San Francisco Bay, enjoying again the same pleasures and excitement of working with the wind and seas that he had known as a seventeen-year-old with his first boat in 1930 and later as *Sea Cloud*'s skipper during the war. Robert C. Keefe, staff commodore and historian of the yacht club—whose place of business was in the same building as Skinner & Company—fondly remembers that he and Skinner avidly discussed their weekend sailing experiences on Monday mornings as they rode the same elevator together to their respective quarters.[71]

Carlton Skinner undertook still another role in the early 1980s—that of guest lecturer. And to his enormous pleasure, the stage on which he performed was his beloved *Sea Cloud*. In 1983 under the aegis of Travel Dynamics of New York, the barque carried thirty-one passengers, a professional crew of forty, and twenty young people serving as apprentice seamen and stewards on a southwesterly 2,800-mile crossing of the Atlantic from the Canary Islands to Martinique in the Caribbean. According to one of the passengers, Paul Donovan Kigar, *Sea Cloud* also had three men on board who, as part of the Smithsonian National Associate Program, spoke to the passengers about various nautical topics. One speaker discussed marine biology

Skinner at the helm of *Yark* in San Francisco Bay off the shores of Marin County in the mid-1970s. (Solange P. Skinner)

and oceanography, the second, a retired navy captain, covered old ships and marine preservation, and the third lecturer, Skinner, "who captained the vessel during her World War II service, told us about her wartime duty."[72]

Fortunately, naval historians and aficionados still have available for their research the recorded text of one of Skinner's 1983 *Sea Cloud* lectures, which includes a wide-ranging narrative of the vessel's history from its construction into the postwar years, humorous and colorful anecdotes about life on board the ship, background on the pioneering racial integration "experiment" on *Sea Cloud*, and Skinner's relationship with Marjorie Post and Joseph Davies.[73] In Kigar's account of the cruise, Skinner was somewhat emotional at the end of his brief tenure as a guest lecturer. Upon arrival in Martinique, a "moist-eyed Commander Skinner said a second farewell to his ship, as a tribute to him her commission pennant was again hauled down, and the bosun piped 'over the side.'"[74] But that was not to be the last time Skinner spoke about *Sea Cloud* while on board.

On May 30, 1987, the sailing yacht *Sea Cloud* stood into the Suva harbor on the island nation of Fiji and tied up at King's Wharf. It had been cruising in the western Pacific, with stops at such ports of call as Easter Island, Tahiti, Tonga, and Bali. Upon its arrival, Carlton Skinner and his wife Solange presented the ship with a tabua—the polished tooth of a sperm whale that is an esteemed gift in Fijian culture—to honor *Sea Cloud*'s visit to Fiji.

The former commanding officer and SPC senior commissioner then donned his figurative lecturer's cap during an evening reception on board and delivered a warm, poetic, and admiring history of the vessel and its attributes. Among other comments Skinner offered these:

> While you are aboard today study the exquisite cabinet work in the deck houses, not in straight lines but gentle curves required to parallel faithfully the camber and sheer of the vessel. After nearly sixty years afloat, the metal of the hull is thicker and stronger than that of ships built in 1987. Her hull form is so beautifully shaped that she rides easily in any weather. I know because for two years I kept her on patrols in the stormy North Atlantic, where she rode gracefully over the mountainous seas.[75]

In a bit of gentle lobbying, Skinner told the guests (and indirectly the ship's owners) that the South Pacific is "the true and proper home for the *Sea Cloud*" and "Suva is the true and proper home port for such a magnificent product of the shipbuilder's art, the spiritual home from which it can derive inspiration and sustenance. It would be fitting if some day her crew were

Fijians." Suffice to say, *Sea Cloud*'s German owners have not yet followed up on Skinner's suggestion.

He concluded his remarks that evening with something of a valedictory, positioning the barque's visit in the context of the prior forty years of his life:

> As most of you know, my own career after the war was in the Pacific as Governor of Guam and as U.S. Senior Commissioner on the South Pacific Commission. Then I was fortunate enough to be accepted as a partner by a distinguished anthropologist, who specialized in Pacific island cultures. So, all three of these emotional attachments happily converged in one place and at one time in the arrival of the *Sea Cloud* in Fiji today.[76]

Over the years Carlton Skinner would from time to time sit at a typewriter and turn out articles, papers, and books of professional quality. His skill as a writer shouldn't be surprising since as a younger man he had been both a journalist and public relations practitioner. For example, an article he authored on Arctic navigation was published in *Yachting* magazine in 1943; his monograph on Nauru, originally published in *Oceanistes* in 1976, was reprinted a year later by the University of California, Santa Cruz; and a memoir about his World War II experiences was recently included in a 2013 anthology.

One of the most important works Skinner authored was his book *After Three Centuries: Representative Democracy and Civilian Government for Guam*, published in 1997 by San Francisco's Macduff Press. In 177 pages Skinner provided a comprehensive account and a verbal documentary on the history of Guam and the mid-twentieth-century transformation of the island's civic, economic, and social life. Referring to himself in the third person in the book, he catalogued all the actions he took as governor to help Guam become a more self-governing and self-sustaining territory of the United States, comparable in some respects to Hawaii and Alaska before they achieved statehood. You get the feeling reading the book that Skinner was writing not only for the benefit of future historians and students of government and public affairs, but also to create a durable written record of his own achievements. In some respects that puts him in the same company as Lyndon Johnson, Henry Kissinger, Jimmy Carter, Bill Clinton, George W. Bush, and other prominent figures who published their memoirs following their governmental service.

Ebb Tide and Sunset

In his later years Carlton Skinner frequently traveled to Guam with his wife, Solange. She remembers that when her husband gave a speech on the island in 2000, marking the fiftieth anniversary of the Organic Act, "He said all he did back then was because he wanted to liberate all the energy there. It was what he wanted to do for everyone—give them the freedom to liberate all their energy."[77]

That same year, Carlton and Solange Skinner left their San Francisco home to relocate to Marblehead, Massachusetts. Perhaps not so coincidentally, they settled at Grover Landing, a condominium development located on the site of the former Rickmere Hotel where Skinner and his mother had often stayed when he was a boy.[78] Appropriately, since the retired *Sea Cloud* captain still had saltwater in his veins, Grover Landing was adjacent to the shores of Marblehead Harbor and the waters of the Atlantic Ocean. The couple also spent considerable time in Paris in the summer months.

During the ensuing years in the Bay State, Carlton Skinner's advancing age and failing health began to take their toll. Eventually, no longer able to nimbly tack into the wind on land or sea, the former governor fell victim to heart disease, and on June 22, 2004, he died in Boston at the age of ninety-one. In the final seconds of his life, Skinner asked his doctor for the "golden number" Those were his last words. After speaking them, he closed his eyes and cast off from this earth forever.

We, of course, will never know the meaning of this enigmatic deathbed request. One possible interpretation is that it referred to a mathematical ratio said to have been used by the ancient Greeks in the building of the Parthenon. Artists throughout history, including Botticelli and da Vinci, have employed the so-called golden rectangle, or variations of it, as the basis for their paintings. So perhaps in his last moments Skinner was thinking of the works of art he had admired and loved as a child and as a man.

A second theory is that the "golden number" referred to a given year's position in the nineteen-year lunar Metonic cycle that was the basis for the ancient Greek calendar and was used to fix the date of Easter for that year. If that were the case, perhaps Skinner had resurrected a memory of being at sea in cold Arctic waters using a sextant for celestial navigation, and maybe at the end of his life he was trying to fix his own place in a heavenly constellation.

Whatever was behind Skinner's final "Rosebud" words, it originated in the recesses of his complicated mind. He was, after all, an intellectual, and his mind, to paraphrase Walt Whitman, was large; it contained multitudes. Regardless of what he was thinking in that most ultimate moment, as Solange put it in 2015, Carlton Skinner "died like a prince."[79]

In Memoriam

After Carlton Skinner's death, Solange said in an interview for this volume that her husband had had "three loves in his life: *Sea Cloud*, Guam and me—in that order." On the other hand, as she saw it, Skinner had some hates: all forms of oppression, and he "worked his whole life trying to rid the world of it." She believes that Skinner's actions on *Sea Cloud* and Guam convincingly make that case. In summing up her husband's life, Dr. Skinner recalled something the prime minister of Fiji once said to France's Minister of Foreign Affairs: "Governor Skinner was a man of conviction, not ambition."[80]

On learning of his predecessor's passing, Felix P. Camacho, Guam's governor in 2004, told Solange that "Governor Skinner will forever be remembered by our people. He brought great beginnings to Guam and has left his mark with the establishment of our Organic Act. He provided a solid foundation for future generations by establishing the University of Guam, allowing Guam's children access to higher education. For these blessings, we want to express our honor and appreciation to his legacy."[81]

Governor Camacho and first lady Joann Camacho sponsored a memorial service for Guam's first civilian governor on September 19, 2005. Attended by Solange Skinner along with government, community, and business leaders, and the public, the service fittingly was held on Skinner's Plaza in Guam's capital, Hatgatna.

Manuel Lujan, the vice speaker of the Guam legislature, recalled that Skinner's record was "unparalleled in the history of territorial governments. He presided over a complete and basic change in our whole way of life, economically, socially and politically."[82]

Joe Murphy, a retired journalist on Guam, provided probably the best summary appraisal of his friend: "Anybody who knew Skinner quickly realized that he was a man of great integrity. He fought injustice wherever he found it, wanting everyday people to have their chance. He also had a great sense of humor, foresight and sensitivity. He made a huge mark on Guam."[83]

More than that, Carlton Skinner made a lasting mark on the US Navy and Coast Guard and on the country he and they defended. In his lifetime of service to the United States in various federal agencies and executive departments, as a Coast Guard officer, as the governor of a US territory, and as a US diplomat in the South Pacific, Skinner represented the better angels of our nature and personified the best of human qualities and values to be found in this nation. Drawing on his keen intelligence, extraordinary decency, and pragmatic idealism in the pursuit of justice and equality, Skinner made a lasting difference in the lives of so many men and women at home, at sea, and in distant lands. It can be fairly said that his was a life well lived and his legacy will be the generations of people who benefited from it.

On July 8, 2019, Adm. Karl Schultz, commandant of the Coast Guard, announced to his personnel around the world that a new cutter support facility on Guam would be named the Commander Carlton Skinner Building. Calling Skinner a "Coast Guard hero," Admiral Schultz said that *Sea Cloud*'s captain had "championed desegregation efforts by successfully sailing with the first fully integrated crew in the history of the Coast Guard and Navy."[84] Two weeks later, on July 22, the commandant and Guam's governor and lieutenant governor participated in a groundbreaking ceremony at Naval Base Guam for the new building honoring Skinner's legacy.

Taking part in the July 2019 groundbreaking ceremony for the Skinner Building are (left to right) Adm. Karl Schultz, Coast Guard commandant; Capt. Christopher Chase, USCG, commander of Sector Guam; the Honorable Lou Leon Guerrero, governor of Guam; and the Honorable Josh Tenorio, Guam's lieutenant governor. (US Coast Guard)

9 *Sea Cloud* in the New Millennium

Peering at the four tall masts, wind-filled sails, and gleaming 360-foot white hull on the distant horizon, mariners on the bridge of the 1,200-foot diesel-powered container ship could have thought they were seeing an apparition, a nautical ghost from the nineteenth century. Sure, there were still sailing vessels of various sizes and types afloat on the high seas these days, even a few windjammers like this one; but still, this magnificent beauty out there far off their port bow had to be an absolute rarity. No one aboard had ever seen anything quite like it. As the lookouts on the container ship got closer and were able to check out the tall ship with their binoculars, they noticed that it had a gorgeous golden eagle figurehead under the bowsprit and just aft of that was the name on its bow: *Sea Cloud*. Amazing! Here they were in the second decade of the twenty-first century, hauling thousands of containers in the Mediterranean Sea, and they were about to pass abeam of a fully manned four-masted square-rigger that had been built in the early twentieth century. And this was no apparition or ghost; instead what they were seeing was today's splendidly preserved and fully operational incarnation of *Hussar* of 1931 and "Marjorie's Baby" of 1947—still sailing after all these years.

Unchanged . . . But Better

"Some things never change, you're still the same," sang rocker Bob Seger in a hit single from the *Stranger in Town* album. Those lyrics, written and recorded in 1978, could be applied to the *Sea Cloud* of today—only now with the addendum "but better." Let's take a brief verbal walking tour of the barque to see why that is so.[1]

Sea Cloud underway with the wind filling all of its sails. (Sea Cloud Cruises GmbH)

A closeup view of the figurehead, decorative scrolling, and ship's name on *Sea Cloud*'s bow. (Sea Cloud Cruises GmbH)

The modern *Sea Cloud* now has thirty-two outside cabins, including ten original staterooms equipped with either a bathtub or a shower, and twenty-two rooms providing a shower. All of the cabins have individually adjustable air conditioning and safes for securing the guests' valuables. Two of the cabins are designated by the operators as Category A or "luxury."

Luxury Owner's Cabin 1, located amidships on the starboard side of the main deck, is a 410-square-foot suite that was originally decorated and first occupied by Marjorie Post Hutton. It offers an ample seating area, a large Louis XIV–style double bed, a decorative marble fireplace, a desk, nightstands, a walk-in closet, and a 97-square-foot bathroom with a marble sink and golden swan fixtures. Luxury Owner's Cabin 2, located amidships on the port side of the main deck, was originally occupied by Edward Hutton. The handsome wood-paneled 366-square-foot stateroom also has a decorative marble fireplace, a walk-in closet, an antique secretary, and two antique nightstands.

Six of *Sea Cloud*'s original cabins are designated as Category B or de luxe. Cabin 3 is decorated in colonial style, and many famous guests of Marjorie Post stayed in this room. Cabin 4 is on the port side of the main deck and contains several pieces collected by Marjorie Post. Aft of Cabin 3 on the starboard side is the 215-square-foot Cabin 5. Cabin 6, aft of Cabin 4 on the port side of the main deck, is a 194-square-foot stateroom outfitted similarly to Cabin 5 except that its 43-square-foot bath has a shower rather than a tub.

Cabin 1 looks more like a suite in a five-star hotel than a stateroom on a sailing ship, which is exactly what Marjorie Post would have wanted. (Sea Cloud Cruises GmbH)

Right, above. Edward Hutton's former quarters are now enjoyed by passengers traveling on board *Sea Cloud*. (Sea Cloud Cruises GmbH)

Right, below. Cabin 3, a cozy, tastefully furnished stateroom. Its two portholes help to remind passengers that they are on a ship and not guests at a well-appointed country estate ashore. (Sea Cloud Cruises GmbH)

A partial view of the bathroom in Cabin 5. (Sea Cloud Cruises GmbH)

Located on the starboard side of the main deck, Cabin 7 is the room in which Dina Merrill, the daughter of Edward Hutton and Marjorie Post, spent much of her childhood (see chapter 1). In 2006, when *Sea Cloud* marked its seventy-fifth year, Merrill, then age eighty-three, returned to the ship to join in the birthday celebration in Hamburg, Germany.[2] Doubtless she paid a nostalgic visit to Cabin 7. Aft of Cabin 6 on the port side is Cabin 8. Situated as it is on the main deck, Cabin 8's passengers can access the promenade deck by an interior staircase leading to the restaurant/lounge.

Sea Cloud has two Category C de luxe outside cabins that were previously single staterooms for crew members and converted to original guest cabins in 2002. Cabin 9 is on the starboard side of the main deck, back near the fantail. It is 215 square feet in size and has its own staircase to the promenade deck. Cabin 10 is on the port side across from, and is equipped similarly to, Cabin 9, except that the room's 39-square-foot bathroom has a shower rather than a tub.

In addition to the original cabins described above, *Sea Cloud* has two Category 1 double-bed cabins, six Category 2 twin-bed cabins, eight Category 3 twin-bed cabins, two Category 4 twin-bed cabins, and four Category 5 upper- and lower-bed cabins.

Cabins 28 and 29, designated Category 4, are located back aft near the fantail. They are 113 square feet in size, with two single beds, and are similar to Cabins 18–25. Cabins 14–17, designated Category 5, were formerly occupied by *Sea Cloud*'s officers. Located far forward on the promenade deck, they provide 102 square feet of space, an upper and lower single berth, a small sofa, a desk, and a closet. Sea Cloud Cruises says that—although the cabins have individually adjusted air conditioning and a porthole—the room's occupants can sleep in fresh air "with the door open." We can safely assume that the thickly perfumed aroma that once permeated these rooms back when Carlton Skinner commanded the ship has long since departed.

Guests in Cabin 25 are able to easily view the open ocean and shoreside scenery through two large windows. (Sea Cloud Cruises GmbH)

In the ship's lounge, located on the promenade deck, passengers can enjoy a collection of books, board games, and a writing desk equipped with a laptop. In the adjoining oak-paneled restaurant—originally a salon when Marjorie owned the yacht—guests dine on fine cuisine as did their predecessors in the 1930s and 1940s. Under fair skies the passengers sit out on the lido deck at lunchtime for buffet snacks or under the stars for drinks in the evening, occasionally entertained by a pianist providing background music. In addition, passengers relax in deck chairs and mahogany benches located on the weather decks while reading or simply monitoring the sails' response to varying wind conditions. As *Sea Cloud* sails from port to port, guests are able to watch its seamen performing some of the same tasks practiced by sailors for centuries or visit the ship's bridge to speak with officers handling the barque.

Final adjustments are being made to the place settings in *Sea Cloud*'s restaurant. (Sea Cloud Cruises GmbH)

The canvas-topped lido deck awaits its first guests. (Sea Cloud Cruises GmbH)

A happy passenger takes the helm during a visit to *Sea Cloud*'s bridge. (Sea Cloud Cruises GmbH)

Today's *Sea Cloud* has many of the same specifications and characteristics as it did in its early years—number of sails, length, draft beam, and the like (see appendix B for specification details)—but in several other ways it has changed, and for the better, thanks to a major renovation in 2011.

Although *Sea Cloud* is very much a vessel of the early twentieth century, it nevertheless has to meet and maintain the maritime standards of the early twenty-first century. Accordingly, in November 2010, the barque entered the Motorenwerke Bremerhaven (MWB) AG shipyard in Bremerhaven, Germany, for extensive work to bring it into compliance with the October 2010 international Safety of Life at Sea (SOLAS) regulations.

Over the ensuing five months MWB performed the following tasks:

- The yacht's original wooden panels were removed, coated, and underfilled with fire protection insulation. Wooden staircases were replaced with metal staircases. The substructure of the deck in the original cabins was replaced with fire protection material. Additional local fire alarms and sprinklers were installed, extending the coverage provided by the unique fire detection and alarm system that had been installed in *Sea Cloud* by the Friedrich Krupp Germaniawerft shipyard in Kiel eighty years earlier. Two separate insulated zones in the ship were created by fitting a fireproof bulkhead amidships.

- The core of the crew deck was totally dismantled and rebuilt to SOLAS standards. Escape routes and storeroom layouts were redesigned. The electrical system in the crew's area was replaced, and a new air conditioning system for *Sea Cloud*'s personnel was installed.

- By means of ultrasound imaging the vessel's material thickness was measured. According to the operators at the time, "The plate thicknesses still comply with the new building regulations in force, indicating the high building standard and soundness of the ship."[3]

- Two new, high-performance auxiliary diesel engines were installed. Used for generating power, the new diesels have lower fuel consumption and emission ratings than their predecessors. *Sea Cloud*'s SKL main engines were completely overhauled, and the exhaust pipes were reinsulated. The ship's bridge was enlarged, and its radar system and navigation equipment were replaced

- *Sea Cloud*'s top hamper was substantially refurbished. The jib boom, foremast, main mast, parts of the mizzenmast, and central portions of several steel yards on masts were replaced, and the rigging that controls the sails received a general overhaul. Meanwhile below, the vessel's teak deck, teak benches, and handrails were sanded down and resealed.

- Of course, as all of this work had the safety and comfort of the passengers in mind, the yacht's passenger cabins were also redone by the yard. Specifically, Cabins 30–37 on the lido deck and Cabins 14–17 on the promenade deck received new heads. Those cabins, along with Cabins 9 and 10 on the main deck, were furnished with new carpets, upholstery, and other materials, and all of the antiques in the original staterooms were restored.

As a Sea Cloud Cruises press release explained, "The aim of the complete renovation was to retain the original character of the four-masted bark despite the extensive work."[4] After the job was completed in April 2011, the

The bridge of today's *Sea Cloud* features a mixture of original and modern equipment. In the foreground is the engine order telegraph, first installed by the Krupp shipyard in 1931. (Sea Cloud Cruises GmbH)

barque's operators could legitimately claim that they had met that goal and that *Sea Cloud* was now, in the words of the press release, "resplendent in all her new glory."

Captain and Crew

The physical properties, layout, characteristics, and specifications of a ship do not, by themselves, fully portray or indicate its qualities. A vessel's basic statistics do not count for much unless that vessel has competent officers and a skilled crew to maintain and operate it. Put another way, a ship is only as good as its captain and personnel. Thus it is fortunate that *Sea Cloud* has been commanded over the years by world-class mariners and cared for by dedicated professionals.

Vladimir Pushkarev has served as one of *Sea Cloud*'s masters since 2009. (Sergey Komakin is the other captain; the two men have alternated every three months between duty on board the barque and time ashore.)

Born in landlocked Belarus in 1967, Pushkarev was nevertheless drawn to the sea as a young man. Perhaps he had been influenced by his uncle, a Soviet naval officer, during summer visits to see him in Kaliningrad on the Baltic coast. But rather than follow his uncle into the Russian navy, Pushkarev attended the civilian Kaliningrad Maritime Academy, graduating at age twenty-five in 1992. He spent the next seven years sailing on the Russian square-rigger *Kruzenshtern*, literally learning the ropes as both a deck officer and a ship handler.[5] On January 30, 1999, Pushkarev reported aboard *Sea Cloud* as the barque's third officer. Over the next ten years, he honed his skills and broadened his knowledge under the guidance of such masters as Capt. Richard T. Shannon and Capt. Richard Choinsky, finally moving up to become a captain himself in April 2009.

Pushkarev obviously loves his job and his ship. "*Sea Cloud*," he said in 2016, "has a timeless elegance of windjammers and majestic pride. If even she has given 84 years of faithful service, she is [a] real working square-rigger. I am proud to be a captain of the ship [of] such captivating beauty."[6]

Captains Pushkarev and Komakin command an international crew of approximately sixty men and women, largely from eastern and central Europe and Asia. Included among them are engineers, riggers, seamen and deckhands, oilers, chefs and cooks, stewards, a sailmaker, and a carpenter (see appendix C for a complete list of the various billets on board *Sea Cloud*). This complement is almost equal in number to the maximum of sixty-four pas-

Vladimir Pushkarev exudes pride as he stands alongside his ship. (Sea Cloud Cruises GmbH)

Members of *Sea Cloud*'s crew lash down the jib sails on the bowsprit. (Sea Cloud Cruises GmbH)

sengers who cruise on the barque at any one time, an impressive ratio of approximately 1 to 1 that enables the staff to provide maximum service and support to guests.

Bicontinental Voyager

In recent years *Sea Cloud* has transported a total of approximately 10,000 passengers on cruises to some of the most beautiful and exotic locales in the world.[7] For example, the barque spent much of 2011 in the Mediterranean and Adriatic Seas. In May 2011 it visited Hamburg for the first time in thirty-three years to participate in the Hamburg Port Anniversary celebration, considered by some to be the greatest harbor festival in the world. Later that month it went to Bremerhaven and then on to southern England. In November 2011 *Sea Cloud* cruised from Larnaca in Cyprus to Piraeus in Greece. It departed European waters in December to cross the Atlantic, transiting from Lisbon to Antigua, and spent the winter months in the Lesser Antilles. (*Sea Cloud* had been scheduled to winter in Egypt and the Red Sea that year, but the political situation in Egypt forced a change to that plan.[8])

In 2012 the yacht passed the summer months in the Adriatic and the Aegean before proceeding to the western Mediterranean and on to the Canary Islands in the Atlantic. This schedule allowed passengers to visit Sicily —including an excursion to Mount Etna—in August and to play golf at three courses in Spain in October and November.

On August 5, 2013, Sea Cloud Cruises offered its passengers the opportunity to tie the matrimonial knot in style aboard their windjammers, including a special wedding ceremony performed by the ship's captain followed by an on-board honeymoon. To date, at least thirty-six couples have taken their vows on *Sea Cloud*.[9] (There is no record that Carlton Skinner ever performed even one wedding on the ship during his captaincy in 1944.) *Sea Cloud* and its windjammer "sibling" *Sea Cloud II* cruised together for two days in November from Gran Canaria to La Gomera in Spain's Canaries.[10] Both vessels then sailed westward, with *Sea Cloud* heading for Barbados in the eastern Caribbean.

In 2014 the operators sent their vessel on a new sailing route to the Sporades, an archipelago along the eastern coast of Greece, where "fine sandy beaches and whitewashed chapels radiate under a deep blue sky illustrates a Greece that one only knows from picture books."[11] In July *Sea Cloud* sailed from Kusadasi, Turkey, to Istanbul. That voyage included an exclusive classical concert for guests at the Library of Celsus in Ephesus, Turkey. Four months later the barque once again headed west, sailing from Las Palmas in the Canaries to Barbados.

Also in 2014 Daniel Schafer was named managing director of Sea Cloud Cruises GmbH, joining Hermann Ebell, chairman of the board, and Klaus Gerken, on the management board.[12]

Right after New Year's in 2015 *Sea Cloud* shifted to the Atlantic side of Central America to visit Mexico and Belize. Later in January it took passengers on a round-trip voyage out of Havana, Cuba, and then on a cruise from Havana to Santo Domingo in the Dominican Republic, its homeport while operating as Rafael Trujillo's presidential yacht, *Angelita*. Following a round trip out of Barbados in March and April, the barque departed the Americas and headed to the Mediterranean. Once back in Europe, *Sea Cloud* provided travelers with a visit to the French Riviera, with stops in Nice, Hyeres, Sanary-sur-Mer, and St. Tropez. In August it sailed on a short round trip from Venice to Rab and Rovinj in Croatia, with a run up to Trieste, Italy. Following the practice of prior years, the barque headed west across the Atlantic late in the year to spend the winter of 2015–16 in the warm waters of the Caribbean.

In January 2016 *Sea Cloud* made a ten-day round-trip voyage out of Barbados; in February it sailed to Aruba, Curacao, and Bonaire (the so-called ABC islands); in March the yacht cruised to Costa Rica, Nicaragua, Honduras, Belize, Mexico, Cuba, and the Dominican Republic. In April *Sea Cloud* celebrated its eighty-fifth birthday along the southern coast of Spain, featuring a five-day cruise in company with *Sea Cloud II*. That voyage began in Lisbon, Portugal, with subsequent stops in Cadiz and Malaga and ended in Barcelona. During the trip Patricia Witzigmann performed in the same role played by Carlton Skinner in 1983 by lecturing about the ship's history to embarked passengers. Three months later *Sea Cloud* departed Istanbul for a week-long voyage to Athens. The two Sea Cloud Cruises windjammers got together again for six days in October, beginning with a voyage from their homeport of Valletta, Malta.

The pace and area of *Sea Cloud*'s operations have continued in recent years. For example, in 2017 the ship visited Cuba, the British Virgin Islands, Lesser Antilles, Venice, Sicily, Athens, Corsica, Malta, Central America, Panama, and Curacao. In 2018 *Sea Cloud* transported passengers to various ports in the Caribbean and Mediterranean, including Costa Rica, Barbados, Antigua, Lisbon, Nice, Casablanca, Barcelona, and Monte Carlo. In 2019 the yacht's itinerary took it to St. Barths to watch the Bucket Regatta yacht races, Cape Verde (for the first time), and Palma de Mallorca. It would cruise together with *Sea Cloud II* in November on an eight-day voyage from Casablanca to Las Palmas.

On January 17, 2020, Sea Cloud Cruises announced that under the command of Capt. Sergey Komakin, *Sea Cloud* had recently crossed the Atlantic from Cape Verde to the Caribbean powered by just the wind. After the crew set thirty sails encompassing 32,000 square feet of canvas and shut down the engines, the windjammer was propelled solely by northeast trade winds at speeds of 15–20 knots for seventeen days, a Sea Cloud Cruises record.[13]

▪ ▪ ▪ ▪

Since 1931 *Sea Cloud* has been the largest privately owned motor-sailing yacht in the world, an ersatz US consulate in the Soviet Union, a naval warship during World War II, a historic test bed for the racial integration of the US Navy and Coast Guard, the presidential yacht of the Dominican Republic, a floating high school and college, an unwanted quasi-derelict, and, more recently, a majestic four-masted sailing yacht and luxury cruise ship. It has been kept alive, rejuvenated, and upgraded by resourceful and caring owners. As a result, thousands of men and women in this century are able to have the same wonderful experiences that Marjorie Merriweather Post enjoyed on board *Sea Cloud* in the last century. All you need today is a few thousand dollars and a valid passport. Welcome aboard.

epilogue

On July 26, 1948—three years after the Japanese surrender ceremony on board USS *Missouri* (BB-63) formally ended World War II and four years after Carlton Skinner had successfully demonstrated full racial integration on a US naval ship—President Harry Truman signed Executive Order 9981. It created the President's Committee on Equality of Treatment and Opportunity in the Armed Forces (see chapter 8) and ordered "equality of treatment and opportunity for all persons in the armed forces without regard to race, color, religion or national origin."[1] Needless to say, the full implementation of Truman's directive was neither immediate nor smooth. Far from it. Indeed, in some respects, it took decades to totally fulfill the intent and requirements of Executive Order 9981.[2]

For example, as late as December 1970—more than two decades after Truman's directive—Adm. Elmo R. Zumwalt Jr., the navy's chief of naval operations, told all of his officers and men in a message that he had been struck by "the depth of feeling of our black personnel that there is significant discrimination in the Navy . . . We do have problems and it is my intention and that of Secretary [of the Navy John] Chafee to take prompt steps toward their solution."[3] In that message Zumwalt outlined a number of specific actions that naval commanders and organizations should take to address racial discrimination. "It is evident," he said, "that we need to maximize our efforts to improve the lot of our minority Navymen. . . . We are counting on your support to help seek out and eliminate those demeaning areas of discrimination that plague our minority shipmates. Ours must be a Navy family that recognizes no artificial barriers of race, color or religion. There is no black Navy, no white Navy—just one Navy—the United States Navy."[4]

Over time, as racial barriers were broken and removed individually and collectively, the naval establishment reached the goal that Skinner had essentially met back in 1944. A few selected examples help to mark some of the milestones along that long journey toward equality:

- In 1949 Wesley A. Brown became the first black graduate of the US Naval Academy, joining the navy's Civil Engineer Corps and eventually retiring at the rank of lieutenant commander. He died on May 22, 2012, after a distinguished career both in the navy and in the civilian workforce.

- Alex P. Haley, who had served as ship's cook on the Coast Guard cutter *Mendota* (WPG-69), transferred to the journalist rate in 1949 and then became the Coast Guard's first chief journalist in 1950. Haley served as the assistant to the service's public relations officer at Coast Guard headquarters until 1959, when he retired. He later became well known as the author of *Roots*, a bestseller and winner of a special Pulitzer Prize in 1977.

- Edna Young was the first black woman to enlist in the regular navy and later the first black woman to achieve the rank of chief petty officer. She had joined the navy after the passage of the Women's Armed Services Integration Act on July 7, 1948.

- Carl Brashear became the navy's first African American master diver in 1949. The 2000 film *Man of Honor* portrayed his struggle to overcome racism in the navy.

- In January 1961 Samuel Gravely Jr. became the first black officer to command a navy ship, the destroyer USS *Theodore F. Chandler* (DD-717). He later rose to the rank of vice admiral and led the navy's Third Fleet.

- In December 1996 J. Paul Reason was the first black naval officer to wear the four stars of a full admiral. He took command of the Atlantic Fleet and its nearly 200 warships, 1,400 aircraft, and 122,000 service men and women based at eighteen major shore facilities.

- On March 12, 1999, Michelle Howard became the first African American woman to command a navy vessel, the dock landing ship USS *Rushmore* (LSD-47).

Today black men and women make up 19 percent of the navy's active duty personnel, and they serve in all roles, ships, and stations, thanks in part to the achievements, humanity, patriotism, common sense, and uncommon intelligence of Lt. Cmdr. Carlton Skinner, USCGR.

In addition to the notable men and women cited above, all of the principal figures in this book have also experienced significant changes and developments in their lives before and after the events reported in these pages. Here are just a few:

Carlton Skinner's executive officer on USS *Sea Cloud*, Wallace B. Bishop, was a noted cartoonist even before he joined the Coast Guard in World War II. After his naval service, Bishop continued to draw his cartoon *Muggs and Skeeter* until his retirement in 1974. He died in St. Petersburg, Florida, on January 15, 1982, following a long illness.[5]

Oscar L. Chapman succeeded Julius Krug as secretary of the interior in 1949 and headed that department for the remainder of the Truman administration. After leaving government he practiced law in the firm of Chapman, Duff, and Paul in Washington, DC. Chapman died in Washington on February 8, 1978, at the age of eighty-one and was buried, like his Interior Department predecessor, in Arlington National Cemetery.

President Franklin Roosevelt's friend, Joseph E. Davies, who had served as FDR's ambassador to the Soviet Union in 1936–38, married Marjorie Merriweather Post in 1935, and often sailed on *Sea Cloud* until 1950. The couple was divorced five years later, and Davies, who did not remarry, died in Washington, DC, on May 9, 1958 at the age of eighty-one.

Eugene S. Duffield, an assistant to Secretary of the Navy James Forrestal—and whom Skinner briefed about the *Sea Cloud* experiment—went on to become an officer and director of the McGraw-Hill Publishing Company, assistant publisher of the *Cincinnati Enquirer*, and vice president of Federated Department Stores. He died in September 1974 at the age of sixty-six.[6]

James V. Forrestal succeeded Frank Knox as secretary of the navy in May 1944 and was named by President Truman as the nation's first secretary of defense three years later. He resigned his cabinet post on March 28, 1949, and died in an apparent suicide at Bethesda Naval Hospital in Maryland on May 22 of that year. The navy's first supercarrier (CVA-59), commissioned in 1955, was named for him posthumously.

The accomplishments of Robert Earl ("Rocky") Hammond did not end with his retirement from the Coast Guard in 1963. He went to work as a control operations manager and marketing manager at Pepsi-Cola and was very active in various veterans' organizations. Hammond died on September 28, 2013, in Jersey City, New Jersey.[7]

Following his 1935 divorce from Marjorie Merriweather Post, Edward F. Hutton married again the following year. He resigned as chairman of General Foods in February 1937, served on the boards of major corporations, and died on July 11, 1962, in Westbury, New York, at the age of eighty-six. He was described in a *New York Times* obituary as a man who could "look back on a long life of dedication to the American principle of enterprise."[8]

Following his wartime active duty in the Coast Guard, Joseph Charles Jenkins served as a captain in a segregated engineering unit of the Michigan National Guard until 1947. He resigned his commission as a lieutenant (junior grade) in the Coast Guard Reserve on June 27, 1947, and died in 1959.[9]

William Franklin "Frank" Knox, like Carlton Skinner, began his career in journalism. In 1936 he ran unsuccessfully as a Republican for vice president of the United States. President Roosevelt appointed him secretary of the navy in July 1940. Knox died while still serving as SecNav on April 28, 1944, and was buried in Arlington National Cemetery.

Skinner's patron, Interior Secretary Julius A. Krug, resigned his cabinet portfolio in December 1949 and became a Washington-based utilities consultant. In addition, he served as the chairman of the board of textile manufacturer Brookside Mills and co-founded the Volunteer Asphalt Company, both in Knoxville, Tennessee. He died in that city on March 26, 1970, at the age of sixty-two and was interred at Arlington.

After the war Jacob Lawrence continued to paint. He joined the faculty of the University of Washington (where Skinner's father, Macy, had been a professor), was commissioned to paint murals for the Munich Olympic Games in 1972 and the United States Bicentennial in 1976. He also created artwork for *Time* magazine, including a 1970 cover portrait of Jesse Jackson. He died in Seattle on June 9, 2000. In the autumn of 2016 several of his paintings in "The Migration Series" were displayed in Washington, DC, at the Phillips Collection, where Skinner had often visited as a young man.

From the summer of 1942 to the spring of 1943, Carlton Skinner served as executive officer under Lt. Cmdr. Francis C. Pollard on board the cutter *Northland* on the Greenland Patrol. During his Coast Guard service Pollard earned the Legion of Merit with Combat "V," the Navy-Marine Corps Medal, the Order of the British Empire, and the Order of the Fatherland First Degree from the Soviet Union. He died in December 2011.[10]

Three years after selling *Sea Cloud* in 1955, Marjorie Merriweather Post married her fourth husband, Herbert A. May, a Pittsburgh businessman. They were divorced in 1964. In her later years Marjorie continued to entertain guests at her Hillwood estate in Washington, DC—sometimes with lavish dinner parties seating fifty people—and was regarded by some as the top hostess in the nation's capital. She also engaged in philanthropy and funded a growing art collection. The Post heiress died at Hillwood on September 12, 1973, at the age of eighty-six.[11]

Ellis Reed-Hill, Skinner's boss at Coast Guard headquarters in 1943, served as chief of the public information division from August 1940 to August 1946 and retired as a rear admiral in 1950. He died in February 1975 in Charleston, South Carolina, at the age of eighty-five.

After his service in the Coast Guard, Harvey Clarence Russell joined the Pepsi-Cola Company in 1950 as a field representative, responsible for coordinating franchise bottler activity around the United States. He advanced through various executive positions in the company, including vice president of corporate planning and vice president of community affairs. Russell retired from PepsiCo in 1983 and died in 1998 at the age of seventy-nine.[12]

Sea Cloud damage control officer Lt. (j.g.) Clarence Lorenzo Samuels retired from the Coast Guard in 1947 in the Philippines. Years later he moved to Sonoma, California, where he died on April 4, 1983.

Carlton Skinner's second wife and widow, Solange Petit Skinner, is today an anthropologist and psychologist living in Boston, Massachusetts. She has published eleven books—most recently *Birds of the Wind, People of the Wind: Frigatebirds and Polynesians* in 2012—and numerous articles on Oceania culture.[13]

R. Adm. Edward H. "Iceberg" Smith, under whose operational command Skinner served on the cutter *Northland* and USS *Sea Cloud*, was highly regarded as an expert on the Arctic and oceanography. After the war he became commander of the Third Coast Guard District, based in New York City, and subsequently worked on the staff of the Applied Physics Laboratory of Johns Hopkins University and as a project leader for the Defense Department's Weapons System Evaluation Group. He retired on June 30, 1950. The next month he was named director of the Woods Hole Oceanographic Institution and remained in that post until 1956. Smith died on his birthday, October 29, 1961, in Quisset, Massachusetts. He was seventy-two.

When James Forrestal became defense secretary in 1947, he was succeeded as secretary of the navy by John L. Sullivan. Sullivan had been a lawyer in the 1920s and 1930s and joined the government in 1939 as assistant secretary of the treasury. He served as SecNav for only two years, resigning that post over Secretary of Defense Louis A. Johnson's 1949 decision to cancel the construction of what was to have been the navy's first supercarrier, *United States* (CVA-58). Sullivan then resumed his career as an attorney, and at one point Carlton Skinner retained the services of Sullivan's law firm. Sullivan was active in Democratic politics, served on various corporate boards, and died in Exeter, New Hampshire, on August 8, 1982, when he was eighty-three years old.

After his father's death in 1961, Ramfis Trujillo fled the Dominican Republic—initially on board *Angelita* with his father's body—to begin a life in exile. He ultimately ended up in Spain in 1962. On December 16, 1969, Trujillo was driving his Ferrari 330GT when he crashed into another vehicle, killing its driver and badly injuring himself. He died eleven days later from pneumonia and was buried near Madrid.

Carl Christian von Paulsen commanded the cutter *Northland* in 1941 and early 1942 and was Carlton Skinner's first captain during his service on the ship. Before that, von Paulsen, who had begun his career in 1913, established himself as one of the most accomplished aviators in the Coast Guard. Following his command of *Northland*, he served on the attack transport USS *Samuel Chase* (APA-26) and commanded the troop transport USS *General George M. Randall* (AP-115). Von Paulsen retired in June 1945 after thirty-five years in the Coast Guard but went on to assist the National Park Service in mapping the Florida Everglades. He died on March 10, 1979, in Miami at the age of seventy-eight.[14]

Russell R. Waesche, who as Coast Guard commandant enabled Skinner's experiment on *Sea Cloud*, was commissioned in 1906 and became commandant in June 1936. Having held that post through 1945, Admiral Waesche was the longest-serving head of the Coast Guard. He retired on January 1, 1946, and died on October 17 that same year.

Appendix A | Chronology

1875
September 7. Edward Francis Hutton is born in New York City.

1876
November 29. Joseph Edward Davies is born in Watertown, Wisconsin.

1887
March 15. Marjorie Merriweather Post is born in Springfield, Illinois.

1913
April 8. Carlton Skinner is born in Palo Alto, California.

1920
Edward Hutton marries Marjorie Post.

1926
Preliminary work begins on Hutton's *Hussar* V.
Skinner begins his high school studies at Tilton School in Tilton, New Hampshire.

1930
Skinner graduates from Tilton and begins his college education at Wesleyan University in Middletown, Connecticut.

1931
April. *Hussar* is launched in Kiel, Germany.
November 30. Marjorie Post Hutton boards *Hussar* for the first time (in Bermuda).

Skinner continues his college studies at the University of California, Los Angeles.

1932

January. *Hussar* begins an 11,680-mile voyage in the Caribbean, Atlantic, and Pacific.
February 11. *Hussar* crosses the Equator.

1933

July. King Gustav V of Sweden cruises on board *Hussar*.
King Haakon VII and Queen Maud of Norway visit the ship in Oslo.

1934

February. *Hussar* arrives in Miami following yard work in Germany.
March. The yacht sails to Tahiti and Hawaii and also visits San Pedro, California, and Juneau, Alaska.
Carlton Skinner graduates from the UCLA with an A.B. degree. He goes to work as a reporter for the United Press in Washington, DC.

1935

September 7. Edward Hutton and Marjorie Post Hutton are divorced.
September 8. Hutton passes title to *Hussar* to his ex-wife. The yacht is renamed *Sea Cloud*.
December 15. Marjorie Post marries Joseph Davies.

1936

Skinner begins his second employment as a reporter for the *Wall Street Journal* in Washington, DC.
January 16. Joseph and Marjorie Davies begin a honeymoon cruise on *Sea Cloud* to the Dominican Republic.
May. *Sea Cloud* makes a second trip to that nation.
November 7. Marjorie Post Davies formally registers *Sea Cloud*.
November 16. Joseph Davies is appointed US ambassador to the Soviet Union.

1937

July 6. *Sea Cloud* arrives in Leningrad, Russia, and serves as an adjunct to the ambassador's residence in Moscow.
July. *Sea Cloud* sails to Sweden.

1938

Skinner joins the federal government as assistant director of information in the US Department of Labor's Wage and Hour Division.

March. *Sea Cloud*'s hull is repainted from black to white.
March 14. Joseph Davies is appointed US ambassador to both Belgium and Luxembourg.
October. Marjorie Post Davies returns to the United States to reside in Washington, DC.

1939
Skinner joins the US Maritime Commission as assistant director of information.
September 1. World War II begins.
November 30. Davies leaves Brussels to take up his new State Department post in Washington.

1940
Skinner becomes acting director of the Maritime Commission's Division of Promotion and Information.

1941
Spring. Davies explores the possibility of selling *Sea Cloud*. He subsequently offers the yacht for government service.
June 17. Carlton Skinner is commissioned as a lieutenant (junior grade) in the US Coast Guard Reserve.
July 7. Skinner reports aboard the Coast Guard cutter *Northland* (WPG-49) and serves initially as a watch officer.
September. Skinner, another officer, and twelve *Northland* crewmen capture four Germans at their clandestine radio station in Greenland. The station is destroyed.
December 4. The Navy's Auxiliary Vessels Board determines that *Sea Cloud* can be acquired for use as either a weather ship or training vessel for the Coast Guard or as a patrol boat for the navy.
December 7. The Japanese attack Pearl Harbor. The United States goes to war against Japan, Germany, and Italy.
December 15. The navy bareboat-charters *Sea Cloud* for conversion into a Coast Guard weather ship.

1942
January. Skinner becomes *Northland*'s navigator.
January 11. *Sea Cloud* enters the Coast Guard's Curtis Bay shipyard to begin its conversion.
April 4. *Sea Cloud* is commissioned as a Coast Guard vessel and designated as WPG-284.
June. Skinner becomes *Northland*'s executive officer.
June 15. Skinner is promoted to lieutenant.

June 16. *Sea Cloud* rescues eight survivors of the sunken schooner *Maria da Gloria*.
June 18. *Northland* attacks a German submarine off the southwestern coast of Greenland.
November. *Northland* rescues two survivors from a downed B-17 bomber in Greenland.

1943

January 15. Skinner is detached from *Northland* to become the commanding officer of an LST crew in training.
March 20. Skinner becomes executive officer of the cutter *Gresham*. He serves in that billet until April 8.
April 9. *Sea Cloud* is transferred to the navy, commissioned as a naval vessel, and designated as IX-99.
Spring. Skinner is assigned as executive officer of the Coast Guard's Public Relations Office in Washington, DC.
May 1. Skinner marries Ensign Jeanne Rowe.
July 23. Skinner proposes the creation of an experimental racially integrated ship to the Coast Guard commandant.
November 18. Skinner reports on board *Sea Cloud* in Boston as executive officer.
December 22. Skinner is promoted to lieutenant commander.

1944

January 26. Skinner becomes commanding officer of *Sea Cloud*.
February 5–26. *Sea Cloud* performs its first weather patrol with Skinner as captain.
April 5. *Sea Cloud* attacks the German submarine U-856.
May 20. *Sea Cloud* arrives in Argentia, Newfoundland, its new homeport.
August 2. *Sea Cloud* is ordered to proceed to Boston "for disposition."
September. *Sea Cloud* enters the Bethlehem Atlantic Works shipyard for decommissioning and reconversion projects.
November 4. The navy's Board of Inspection and Survey officially completes its inspection of *Sea Cloud*, finding that the ship is "considered in a seaworthy condition for return to the owner."
November 4. USS *Sea Cloud* is decommissioned and returned to Joseph Davies.
December. Skinner briefs an assistant to the secretary of the navy on the racial integration experiment on *Sea Cloud*.

1945

January–February. Skinner attends a navy command training course in Miami.
March 8. Skinner assumes command of USS *Hoquiam* (PF-5) in Alaska.

May 20. The navy secretary advises the president that African Americans will be assigned to general service on large auxiliary ships.
June. *Hoquiam* is designated for transfer to the Soviet Union.
August 14. World War II ends with Japan's surrender.
August 16. *Hoquiam* is transferred to the Soviet navy, and Skinner is relieved as its commanding officer.
October 3. Skinner is released from active duty by the Coast Guard. He returns to the US Maritime Commission as head of its sales and charter organization.

1946
April 28. Skinner is named director of information of the US Department of the Interior.
July 4. *Sea Cloud* makes its first postwar "pleasure" cruise.
Sea Cloud enters Bethlehem Shipbuilding Sparrows Point shipyard in Baltimore for reconditioning, refitting, and upgrades.

1947
April 7. *Sea Cloud* departs the Baltimore shipyard en route to Florida.
Spring. *Sea Cloud* undertakes a two-week shakedown cruise to the Bahamas.

1948
March. Rafael Trujillo visits *Sea Cloud* and presents Marjorie Post Davies with the Juan Pablo Duarte Order of Merit.
March–April. The Duke and Duchess of Windsor cruise on board *Sea Cloud*.
May 22. The secretary of the navy awards Joseph Davies the Naval Reserve Yacht Owners Distinguishing Pennant in a ceremony on board *Sea Cloud* in Annapolis, Maryland. Skinner attends the ceremony.

1949
February. *Sea Cloud* is fitted with new sails.
April 25. Skinner testifies before the President's Committee on Equality of Treatment and Opportunity in the Armed Forces.
September 3. President Truman names Skinner as the first civilian governor of Guam. He arrives on the island on September 26 and is inaugurated the next day.

1950
August–November. Marjorie Post Davies takes her last cruise on *Sea Cloud*.

1951
January–May. *Sea Cloud* is deactivated and decommissioned in Jacksonville, Florida.

March. Marjorie Post Davies visits *Sea Cloud* to direct the disposition of her personal property. (She comes aboard only once more, in 1953.)
Sea Cloud is offered for sale.

1953

January 20. Skinner resigns as Guam's governor.
March. Skinner leaves Guam and returns to the United States. He is initially employed by American President Lines.

1955

March. Marjorie Post Davies and Joseph Davies are divorced.
August 15. *Sea Cloud* is sold to George W. Gibbs. Gibbs, in turn, sells the yacht to Rafael Trujillo. He renames it *Angelita*.

1958

Skinner becomes vice president of finance for Fairbanks Whitney Corporation in New York City.
February. Trujillo's son, Ramfis, entertains Zsa Zsa Gabor on board *Angelita* in New Orleans.
June 21. Ramfis Trujillo hosts Gabor and Kim Novak on board *Angelita* in Los Angeles.
July. *Angelita* visits San Diego and Acapulco with Trujillo on board.
August. *Angelita* returns to the Dominican Republic.
August. Skinner is named as a director, vice president, and treasurer of Penn-Texas Corporation.

1959

March–July. Four new Enterprise diesel engines are installed in *Angelita*.

1961

May 30. Rafael Trujillo is assassinated.
August 11. Skinner is appointed by President Kennedy as a US commissioner in the South Pacific Commission. He later serves as chairman of the commission in 1964 and 1969.
November 18. *Angelita*, with Ramfis Trujillo and the body of his father on board, departs the Dominican Republic en route to France. The Dominican government orders the yacht to return.
November 29. *Angelita* returns to the Dominican Republic without Ramfis, who has flown to France from Martinique. The next day Trujillo's body is flown to Paris.

1962

Skinner becomes chairman of Pratt & Whitney Company, Inc.
Spring. *Angelita*, now renamed *Patria*, is offered for sale by the Dominican government.

1963

Skinner leaves Fairbanks Whitney and establishes his own business—Skinner and Company—in San Francisco.

1964

October 1. President Johnson appoints Skinner as the senior US commissioner in the South Pacific Commission.

1965

Clifford E. Barbour Jr. forms Operation Sea Cruise, Inc., in Panama for the purpose of acquiring *Patria*.

1966

Skinner provides advice and counsel to Continental Airlines in establishing airline service in Micronesia.

1967

Barbour purchases *Patria* and renames the yacht *Antarna*. It is sent to Naples, Italy, for repairs and reconditioning.
February. Jeanne Rowe Skinner sues Carlton Skinner for divorce.

1968

Antarna returns to the United States and makes one voyage as a luxury cruise ship for Operation Sea Cruises. The vessel is subsequently impounded in Miami by the US Customs Service for nonpayment of import duties.

1970

April 6. Skinner marries Solange Petit, a French anthropologist.
Stephanie and Charles Gallagher form the Oceanic Schools to offer students academic and nautical education on board large sailing vessels.
Skinner leaves the South Pacific Commission.

1971

Gallagher charters *Antarna* as a floating schoolhouse.
December 6. Skinner is appointed honorary consul general of the Republic of Nauru. He serves in that capacity until 1981.

1972

March. Following several incidents and disputes between Operation Sea Cruise and the Gallaghers, *Antarna* is seized in Panama by its owner. The yacht then sits unused and deteriorating in Colon for the next six years.

1978

Hartmut Paschburg and a group of German investors purchase *Antarna* from Barbour. The barque is given its former name, *Sea Cloud*.
July–October. Paschburg and a small team prepare *Sea Cloud* for a transatlantic voyage to Germany for restoration work. It departs Panama in mid-October.
November 15. *Sea Cloud* arrives in Hamburg, Germany.

1979

Sea Cloud Cruises GmbH is formed.
February–September. *Sea Cloud* undergoes a major overhaul and refurbishment in the same shipyard in Kiel, Germany, where it had been built in 1930–1931.
October. *Sea Cloud* makes its first voyage for Sea Cloud Cruises.

1980

Sea Cloud provides one- and two-week cruises in the Caribbean.

1981

Operating under charter to Travel Dynamics, *Sea Cloud* cruises in the Mediterranean during the summer and in the Caribbean in the winter.

1983

Skinner serves as a guest lecturer on *Sea Cloud* during a cruise from the Canary Islands to Martinique.

1987

May 30. Skinner boards *Sea Cloud* in Fiji during a South Pacific cruise.

1994

Hermann Ebel and investors acquire ownership of *Sea Cloud*. The ship is operated by Sea Cloud Cruises GmbH.

1997

Macduff Press publishes Skinner's *After Three Centuries*, an account of the formation of civilian government and his governorship in Guam.

2000

Skinner delivers a speech on Guam marking the fiftieth anniversary of the Organic Act.

Skinner leaves San Francisco and moves to Marblehead, Massachusetts.

2004

June 22. Carlton Skinner dies in Boston at the age of ninety-one.

2005

September 19. Guam memorializes Skinner in a ceremony held in its capital.

2006

Dina Merrill, Marjorie Post's daughter, visits *Sea Cloud* in Hamburg, Germany, to help celebrate the ship's seventy-fifth anniversary.

2010

November. *Sea Cloud* begins a five-month major renovation in a Bremerhaven shipyard to bring it into compliance with SOLAS regulations.

2011

May. *Sea Cloud* participates in the Hamburg Port Anniversary celebration.

2013

August. Sea Cloud Cruises offers wedding ceremonies for *Sea Cloud* passengers.

November. *Sea Cloud* and *Sea Cloud* II cruise together in Spain's Canary Islands.

2016

April. *Sea Cloud* marks its eighty-fifth birthday and cruises with *Sea Cloud* II along the southern coast of Spain.

2019

July 22. The commandant of the Coast Guard and governor of Guam break ground for the Commander Carlton Skinner Building, a new cutter support facility on Guam.

Appendix B | Specifications

***Sea Cloud / Angelita / Patria* Specifications**

Call sign[a]	WCEQ[b] HIJA[c]
Length (overall)	359.25 feet
Length (hull)	315.28 feet
Beam	49.01 feet
Freeboard	27.98 feet
Draft	16.83 feet
Displacement	3,075 tons
Gross registered tonnage	2,492
Main mast height above deck	177.82 feet
Length of standing and running rigging	82,020 feet (approximately)
Rigging weight	110 tons (approximately)
Sail area (30 sails)	32,291 square feet (approximately)
Engines	4 Enterprise eight-cylinder diesels, each with 1,500 hp[d]

Speed (under engine power)	12 knots (approximately)
Crew	60–90[e]

[a] A unique designation for a radio transmitter station assigned by a national licensing authority.
[b] Registered for *Sea Cloud* by Marjorie Post Davies in 1939.
[c] Assigned to *Angelita* during Trujillo ownership.
[d] Installed in 1959 as replacements for *Sea Cloud*'s original four six-cylinder Krupp diesels, each with 800 hp.
[e] Number varied with owners. In 1950 the crew rostered about 75 personnel under Marjorie Post; in the late 1950s it consisted of as many as 90 people, including 17 musicians, under Rafael Trujillo.

USS *Sea Cloud* (WPG-284) (IX-99) Specifications

Length	316 feet
Beam	49 feet, 2 inches
Draft	19 feet
Displacement	3,077 tons
Propulsion	Diesel-electric; twin screws
Speed	14 knots
Cruising radius	20,000 miles at 12 knots
Fuel capacity	590 tons of diesel oil
Complement	21 officers 1 warrant officer 13 CPOs 160 enlisted
Weapons	2 3-inch/50 guns 8 20 mm guns 4 K-guns 1 Mk10 hedgehog projector 2 depth charge racks 44 depth charges
Radars	1 ET 80198-2-22MC 1 ET 8010C 375–500 KC 1 ET 8012B 2100–3000 KC

Other electronics	Sound equipment Echo ranging equipment (active sonar) Range recorder (measures distance to the target on sonar) Sub-Sig fathometer

SY *Sea Cloud* Specifications

Ship identification number[a]	IMO 8843466
MMSI number[b]	256084000
Call sign[c]	9HOM2
Flag	Malta
Length (overall)	360 feet
Beam	50 feet
Draft	17 feet
Height of main mast above deck	178 feet
Total sail area	32,000 square feet
Number of sails	30
Main engine	2 SKL diesel engines
Engine output	3,000 hp
Maximum speed	10 knots (approximately)
Range	10,000 nautical miles at 8 knots
Gross register tonnage	2,532
Voltage	220 volts/50 hertz
Satellite	Very small aperture terminal (VSAT)
Passengers	64 (maximum)

Crew	60 (approximately)
Cabins	32 outside cabins (including 10 original)
Passenger furnishings	Bathrobes, hair dryer, telephone, air conditioning, private safe
Public areas	Lido deck with bar Restaurant (69 seats) with open seating and one-sitting dining Lounge with library and desk area with laptop Hospital

[a] The International Maritime Organization (IMO) ship identification number scheme was introduced in 1987 to assign a permanent number to each ship for identification purposes.
[b] Maritime Mobile Service Identity (MMSI) is a nine-digit number used by maritime digital selective calling (DSC), automatic identification systems (AIS), and certain other equipment to uniquely identify a ship or a coast radio station.
[c] A unique designation for a radio transmitter station assigned by a national licensing authority.

USS *Hoquiam* (PF-5) Specifications

Length	303 feet, 11 inches
Beam	37 feet, 6 inches
Draft	13 feet, 8 inches
Displacement	2,415 tons (full load)
Propulsion	2 three-drum expansion boilers 2 5,500 ihp J. Hendy Iron Works vertical triple-expansion engines 2 shafts and screws
Range	9,500 nm at 12 knots
Maximum speed	20 knots
Complement	190
Armament	3 3-inch/50 dual-purpose guns 2 twin 40 mm guns 9 20 mm guns 2 depth charge racks 8 depth charge projectors 1 hedgehog projector

Appendix C | Personnel

USCGC *Sea Cloud* (WPG-284) Officers and Crew, 1942

The officers and enlisted men in the original ship's company (plank owners) as listed in the ship's log in April 1942.

Lieutenant Commander G. N. Bernier
Lieutenant R. G. Jenkins
Lieutenant (junior grade) Frank Bronski
Lieutenant (junior grade) Clyde D. Goodwin
Ensign W. S. Nevins
Ensign Alexander N. Standish
Machinist Marcus B. Dalton

Chief Boatswain's Mate Ralph H. Joline
Chief Quartermaster Harold R. Rodgers
Chief Machinist's Mate Roger W. Brown
Chief Machinist's Mate Frank D. Holbrook
Chief Machinist's Mate Vino Mixon
Chief Radioman David Levin
Chief Yeoman Wayne C. Wallace
Chief Commissary Steward John T. Suski
Boatswain's Mate 1st Class William A. Partridge
Gunner's Mate 1st Class Frank M. Smith Jr.
Machinist's Mate 1st Class Johnie McPherson
Machinist's Mate 1st Class Harry E. Nielson
Machinist's Mate 1st Class Ronald C. Oldenburg
Machinist's Mate 1st Class Warren H. Jett
Electrician's Mate 1st Class Hubert G. Meadors
Radioman 1st Class William H. Yates
Pharmacist's Mate 1st Class Douglas H. Shiflet

Boatswain's Mate 2nd Class Frank M. Batha
Boatswain's Mate 2nd Class Walter S. Gillen
Boatswain's Mate 2nd Class Ernest C. Powell Jr.
Boatswain's Mate 2nd Class Carl M. Smith
Gunner's Mate 2nd Class John A. Pasillis
Gunner's Mate 2nd Class Clayton R. Wiley
Quartermaster 2nd Class Lowell D. Mead
Quartermaster 2nd Class Edward J. Zaletel
Machinist's Mate 2nd Class Tom Hilton
Machinist's Mate 2nd Class Raymond E. Miller
Machinist's Mate 2nd Class Donald L. Xander
Electrician's Mate 2nd Class Thomas E. Hutchins Jr.
Electrician's Mate 2nd Class Melvin C. Latham
Radioman 2nd Class John L. Bonomo
Radioman 2nd Class Woodrow H. Mason
Radioman 2nd Class Robert Shute
Radioman 2nd Class John C. Soltesz
Yeoman 2nd Class Max D. Barbour
Coxswain Floyd E. Halstead
Quartermaster 3rd Class Marshall F. Brown
Gunner's Mate 3rd Class Robert A. McKenzie
Radioman 3rd Class Floyd J. Daeley
Radioman 3rd Class Charles C. Jones
Yeoman 3rd Class Clyde R. Johnson
Ship's Cook 3rd Class Louis W. Blitch
Ship's Cook 3rd Class Vladimir G. Cucura
Ship's Cook 3rd Class John B. McCarthy
Ship's Cook 3rd Class Earl W. Skoglund
Seaman 1st Class Kenneth S. Duvall
Seaman 1st Class Richard M. Epstein
Seaman 1st Class Elwood H. Cabara
Seaman 1st Class Ilko Grech
Seaman 1st Class Charles D. Hamilton
Seaman 1st Class Ralph P. Hudlow
Seaman 1st Class Roy F. Johnson
Seaman 1st Class Joseph P. Lutman
Seaman 1st Class Charles M. McCollum Jr.
Seaman 1st Class Howard E. Moore
Seaman 1st Class Thaddeus Nowakowski
Seaman 1st Class Charles J. Palmisano
Seaman 1st Class Raymond I. Sawyer
Seaman 1st Class Edward C. Scheffler

Seaman 1st Class James W. Smith
Seaman 1st Class Rollin H. Wilson
Fireman 1st Class Clifton M. Daniels Jr.
Fireman 1st Class Quentin Roark
Seaman 2nd Class Cecil E. Barrington
Seaman 2nd Class Donald R. Beaton
Seaman 2nd Class Dennis D. Boyles
Seaman 2nd Class Edward A. Carroll
Seaman 2nd Class Edward S. Chestnut
Seaman 2nd Class Christian N. Christensen
Seaman 2nd Class Robert H. Cowley
Seaman 2nd Class Reuben H. Crowley
Seaman 2nd Class John H. Dunn
Seaman 2nd Class Howard J. Dwyer
Seaman 2nd Class William Greenawalt
Seaman 2nd Class Ernest J. Haberer
Seaman 2nd Class John J. Hlastawa
Seaman 2nd Class Delbert S. Jackson
Seaman 2nd Class Howard J. Jenkins
Raymond D. Krohn [no rating listed; presumably Seaman 2nd Class]
Seaman 2nd Class Albert Le Grow
Seaman 2nd Class William W. Leininger
Seaman 2nd Class Richard Lycan
Seaman 2nd Class Frederick R. Means
Seaman 2nd Class Joseph W. Morin
Seaman 2nd Class Richard J. Northridge
Seaman 2nd Class Edward M. Polhemus
Seaman 2nd Class Stewart J. Pomeroy
Seaman 2nd Class Willis W. Rhoades
Seaman 2nd Class Eugene B. Roskey
Seaman 2nd Class Salvatore A. Tartaglia
Seaman 2nd Class George W. Vance
Fireman 2nd Class Richard H. Sumner
Apprentice Seaman Raymond F. Bernstein
Apprentice Seaman Lawrence F. Carlson
Appentice Seaman Joseph M. Hines
Apprentice Seaman John J. Kennedy Jr.
Appentice Seaman Stanley Koshmosky
Apprentice Seaman Harold Lawner
Apprentice Seaman Stephen Lazarek
Apprentice Seaman Ralph L. Mohr
Apprentice Seaman George Peros

Apprentice Seaman Henry M. Roko
Apprentice Seaman George B. Tekulsky
Fireman 3rd Class Ed K. Bo
Fireman 3rd Class Percy J. Cooper
Fireman 3rd Class Guy L. Jensen
Fireman 3rd Class William A. Marks
Fireman 3rd Class Thomas M. McBride
Fireman 3rd Class Wilfred J. Miller
Fireman 3rd Class James C. Roland*
Fireman 3rd Class Lester H. Roland*
Fireman 3rd Class Irwin C. Rostrup
Fireman 3rd Class John P. Tobin
Officer's Steward 2nd Class Charles Carter
Officer's Steward 2nd Class Paul E. Reyes
Mess Attendant 1st Class Allen J. Hebert
Mess Attendant 1st Class Milton Lewis
Mess Attendant 1st Class Willie Simms
Mess Attendant 2nd Class John T. Gray
Mess Attendant 3rd Class Andrew A. Boiseau
Mess Attendant 3rd Class James Vincent
Fireman 1st Class Kenneth J. Snyder

*As their serial numbers are sequential, these men are presumed to be brothers.

USS *Sea Cloud* (IX-99) Officers and Crew, 1944

The officers who served in 1944 include:

Lieutenant Commander Carlton Skinner (commanding officer)
Lieutenant Commander Wallace B. Bishop (executive officer)
Lieutenant Chester Caton
Lieutenant Robert M. Wadewitz (navigator)
Lieutenant Clarence C. Samuels
Lieutenant (junior grade) Joseph C. Jenkins
Ensign Michael L. Karmazin
Ensign Harvey C. Russell
Electrician Charles E. Cunniff

The enlisted men who served in the ship's final months of naval service include:

Chief Pharmacist's Mate Clarence C. Chrittenden Jr.
Chief Storekeeper Andrew J. Donaldson
Chief Machinist's Mate Daniel R. Engelgau
Chief Yeoman Leo E. Forrest

Chief Motor Machinist's Mate Erling H. Hantho
Chief Electrician's Mate Thomas B. Hutchins Jr.
Chief Electrician's Mate Roy R. Johnson
Chief Motor Machinist's Mate Stanley Kosmoski
Chief Commissary Steward Eugene Lassister
Chief Motor Machinist's Mate Ronald C. Oldenburg
Chief Radioman Harvey A. Schaller
Chief Radio Technician Fredrick Scheffler
Motor Machinist's Mate 1st Class Walter B. Ballance
Steward's Mate 1st Class R. E. Bird
Boatswain's Mate 1st Class Tommy C. Burnett
Carpenter's Mate 1st Class Norman Christy
Ship's Cook 1st Class Bernard J. Dudley
Storekeeper 1st Class George E. Greeley
Specialist 1st Class Francis L. Griffin
Boatswain's Mate 1st Class Marion Hudkins Jr.
Steward's Mate 1st Class Richard U. Mitchell
Quartermaster 1st Class William G. Morley
Radarman 1st Class Joe W. Naud
Boatswain's Mate 1st Class Paul L. Perkins
Motor Machinist's Mate 1st Class Joseph V. Rider Jr.
Yeoman 1st Class Carlton B. Still
Quartermaster 1st Class Paul P. Storer
Steward's Mate 1st Class Grover Taylor
Radionman 2nd Class Walter Alkavich
Motor Machinist's Mate 2nd Class Salvatore Alonge
Motor Machinist's Mate 2nd Class Clarence I. Arno
Yeoman 2nd Class John R. Barrows
Quartermaster 2nd Class James Boyd Jr.
Gunner's Mate 2nd Class Ward E. Broady
Motor Machinist's Mate 2nd Class Harold L. Case
Motor Machinist's Mate 2nd Class Ralph I. Cogan
Soundman 2nd Class Arthur S. Duxbury
Motor Machinist's Mate 2nd Class Irving Goldstein
Soundman 2nd Class Solomon Greenman
Radioman 2nd Class Norman W. Grigsby
Electrician's Mate 2nd Class John R. Kimball
Sonarman 2nd Class Gerald Marc-Aurele
Ship's Cook 2nd Class James McCarthy
Radarman 2nd Class Warner C. Palmer
Storekeeper 2nd Class Ivan A. Riddick
Boatswain's Mate 2nd Class Robert Smith

Photographer's Mate 2nd Class Jewel P. Word
Signalman 3rd Class Henry L. Bagby
Carpenter's Mate 3rd Class Henry E. Banks
Motor Machinist's Mate 3rd Class Otto A. H. Barber
Coxswain Floyd W. Beane
Motor Machinist's Mate 3rd Class Benjamin H. Bechtold
Hospital Apprentice 3rd Class Albert Berrian
Motor Machinist's Mate 3rd Class Harold Cuffee
Coxswain Vincent Edwards
Motor Machinist's Mate 3rd Class Ralph A. Farina
Carpenter's Mate 3rd Class Fredrick W. Fauntleroy
Motor Machinist's Mate 3rd Class Harold L. Fischer
Motor Machinist's Mate 3rd Class Mirko E. Gillia
Radioman 3rd Class Robert M. Graves
Coxswain Robert E. Hammond
Signalman 3rd Class John E. Hall
Coxswain Luther C. Hicks
Sonarman 3rd Class Lewis W. Holloway Jr.
Sonarman 3rd Class Welsford J. Hovey
Sonarman 3rd Class George E. Jackson
Specialist 3rd Class Jacob A. Lawrence
Gunner's Mate 3rd Class Edward L. Lewis
Machinist's Mate 3rd Class Robert F. Nelson
Radarman 3rd Class Joseph I. Noel
Radioman 3rd Class Charles D. Patterson
Motor Machinist's Mate 3rd Class Earnest Roberts
Gunner's Mate 3rd Class Roy L. Rucker
Motor Machinist's Mate 3rd Class Demetreos L. Stamowlaros
Radarman 3rd Class Charles B. Stenhouse
Coxswain James W. Teate
Electrician's Mate 3rd Class William E. Travers
Yeoman 3rd Class William Vancamp
Gunner's Mate 3rd Class Ernest Walker
Quartermaster 3rd Class Charles A. Ward Jr.
Ship's Cook 3rd Class James E. Weekly
Seaman 1st Class Morris N. Anderson
Seaman 1st Class Albert Ballard Jr.
Seaman 1st Class William D. Braxton
Seaman 1st Class James H. Brown
Seaman 1st Class Allan B. Cohen
Fireman 1st Class Samuel Daniels
Seaman 1st Class Arthur L. English

Seaman 1st Class Leon Gadson
Seaman 1st Class John I. Gray
Seaman 1st Class Melrick Griffith
Seaman 1st Class Edgar A. Johnson
Seaman 1st Class Irving J. Jones
Seaman 1st Class William L. Kennedy
Seaman 1st Class Edward A. Keyes
Seaman 1st Class Paul L. Lancaster
Seaman 1st Class Raymond Lively
Seaman 1st Class James J. Marguis
Seaman 1st Class William E. Martin
Seaman 1st Class John L. McFerrin
Fireman 1st Class Glenn L. Nuck
Seaman 1st Class Ismael N. Ortiz
Seaman 1st Class Lawrence W. Pankey
Seaman 1st Class Charner Patterson
Seaman 1st Class Clyde Rayford Jr.
Fireman 1st Class Henry Rhodes
Seaman 1st Class Leonard E. Roundtree
Seaman 1st Class Arthur Saunders
Seaman 1st Class John W. Sieminski
Seaman 1st Class Ernest Spiller
Fireman 1st Class Edward I. Thoman
Fireman 1st Class Mark White Jr.
Steward 1st Class Robert Woldon
Seaman Sercond Class Marcus Alexis
Seaman 2nd Class Davis O. Banks
Seaman 2nd Class Elworth Blumenberg
Seaman 2nd Class John W. Bowman
Seaman 2nd Class Fitz G. Boyce
Seaman 2nd Class Robert L. Bozeman Jr.
Seaman 2nd Class Lemos S. Brannon
Seaman 2nd Class Cloris Brown
Seaman 2nd Class Costello Bullock
Seaman 2nd Class George W. Burrell
Seaman 2nd Class Calvin C. Burton
Seaman 2nd Class Harold Carr
Seaman 2nd Class Leon G. Carter
Seaman 2nd Class Iva Coakley
Seaman 2nd Class Armsted Collins Jr.
Seaman 2nd Class Thomas I. Coombs Jr.
Seaman 2nd Class John H. Davis Jr.

Seaman 2nd Class Clifford N. Decreney
Seaman 2nd Class Harris Garmon Jr.
Fireman 2nd Class Norman F. Greer
Fireman 2nd Class Theron L. C. Hale
Seaman 2nd Class Alfred B. Handy
Seaman 2nd Class Julius S. Harris
Seaman 2nd Class Charles W. Hayes
Seaman 2nd Class Rudolph D. Hurt
Seaman 2nd Class Willard Johnson
Seaman 2nd Class Frank M. Martin
Seaman 2nd Class Phillip H. McKennon
Fireman 2nd Class James E. Mitchell
Seaman 2nd Class Auzheal L. Merrell
Seaman 2nd Class George W. Morris
Seaman 2nd Class Hampton B. Ridley
Seaman 2nd Class Robert Sands
Seaman 2nd Class Irwin L. Scott
Seaman 2nd Class Everett Thompson
Seaman 2nd Class Honh N. Thornton
Seaman 2nd Class Lewis Tucker
Seaman 2nd Class Jesse West

SY *Sea Cloud* Personnel, 2016

The following is a listing of the various billets or positions filled by the ship's officers and crew:

Captain (one on board and one ashore on a rotating basis)
Chief Officer
2nd Officer
3rd Officer
Chief Engineer
2nd Engineer
3rd Engineer
Electrician
Boatswain
Sailmaker
Carpenter
Rigger (three assigned)
Able Seaman
Ordinary Seamen (three assigned)
Deckhand (seven assigned)

Engine Fitter
Oiler (three assigned)
Hotel Manager
Purser
Chief Steward
Service Steward (three assigned)
Housekeeper
Cabin Steward (three assigned)
Barkeeper
Bar Steward
Chef de Cuisine
Sous Chef
3rd Cook
4th Cook
Baker/Patissier (two assigned)
Head Laundryman
Laundryman (two assigned)
Service Assistant (four assigned)
Cruise Director
Musician
Assistant Cook
Deck Fitter
Electrotechnical Officer

Glossary of Naval Terms and Abbreviations

Abaft: Behind, toward the stern.

AG: Miscellaneous auxiliary vessel.

AGC: Amphibious force flagship.

AK: Cargo ship.

AKA: Amphibious cargo ship.

AOG: Aviation gasoline tanker.

AP: Transport ship.

availability: A period of repair, maintenance, upkeep, or overhaul, usually either in a shipyard or alongside a tender.

bareboat charter: An arrangement for the hiring or leasing of a ship or boat that does not include the provision of a crew or supplies by the vessel's owner.

bark, barque: A ship of three or more masts with square sails on the forward masts and fore-and-aft sails on the aftermost mast.

beam: The maximum width of a ship or boat.

bhp: Brake horsepower (for diesel engines).

binnacle: A stand holding a compass and other navigational devices.

BMCM: Master chief boatswain's mate.

boatswain's mate: A petty officer who trains and supervises members of a ship's deck force (seamen) in the performance of duties involving marlinspike, activities on deck, boat seamanship, painting, and upkeep of the vessel's external structure, rigging, deck equipment, and boats.

bow: The front of a ship or boat.

bowsprit: A large spar running out forward from the stem (the bow) of a sailing ship.

brow: A gangway connecting a ship to a pier.

bulkhead: A vertical structure or wall separating compartments on a ship.

call sign: In radio transmission a designation used to identify the transmitter.

captain: A commissioned officer in the US Navy and Coast Guard one rank higher than commander; equivalent to an army colonel. Also, a ship's commanding officer regardless of rank.

CFO: Chief financial officer.

CGC: Coast Guard cutter

Charley Noble: Galley smokestack.

chief petty officer: A senior enlisted man or woman in the US Navy and Coast Guard.

Class A School: A program that provides education and training in specialized job fields and occupations.

CO: Commanding officer.

commander: A commissioned officer in the US Navy and Coast Guard one rank higher than a lieutenant commander; equivalent to an army lieutenant colonel.

commodore: A commissioned officer in the US Navy and Coast Guard one rank higher than captain and one rank below rear admiral. Also, the officer commanding a group of vessels such as a squadron or flotilla.

companionway: A stairway or ladder within a boat or ship.

complement: The officers and crew of a naval vessel.

conn: The person, or act of, controlling the movement of a ship while underway.

CVE: Escort aircraft carrier.

DD: destroyer.

DE: Destroyer escort.

displacement: The weight of water that a ship displaces when it is floating; thus a measurement of the ship's weight (including its contents).

draft: The vertical distance between a vessel's waterline and its hull, indicating the minimum depth of water in which that vessel can operate.

dynamo: A device that converts energy produced by movement into electrical energy.

ensign: The lowest rank for a commissioned officer in the US Navy and Coast Guard; equivalent to an army 2nd lieutenant.

fantail: The rounded area on the main deck at the stern of a vessel.

fathometer: A device using sound waves to measure the depth of the water under a ship's keel.

figurehead: A carving, typically a bust or a full-length figure (in *Sea Cloud*'s case, a golden eagle) set at the prow of a sailing ship.

fleet admiral: A commissioned officer in the navy, one rank higher than a full admiral.

foremast: The mast nearest the bow.

40 mm gun: A naval gun used as an antiaircraft weapon capable of firing projectiles 40 mm (1.57 inches) in diameter hundreds of times a minute.

freeboard: The height of a vessel's side between the waterline and the main deck.

general quarters: The situation in which a ship's crew is sent to their battle stations preparatory to engaging in combat.

general service: Typical ordinary and regular duties performed by naval personnel aboard ship.

gross register tonnage: A ship's total internal volume in "register tons," each of which is equal to 100 cubic feet. Gross register tonnage uses the total permanently enclosed capacity of the vessel as its basis for volume. This is not a measure of the vessel's displacement.

head: Bathroom.

hedgehog: A naval weapon for firing up to twenty-four mortar projectiles ahead of ship to attack a submerged submarine.

hp: Horsepower.

ihp: Indicated horsepower, the theoretical power of a reciprocating engine if it is completely frictionless in converting the expanding gas energy in the cylinders.

IX: Unclassified miscellaneous vessel.

J2F-5: An amphibious single-engine propeller-driven biplane known as the Duck. It was powered by a 1,050 hp R-1820-54 engine. The 144 J2F-5s built by Grumman were used primarily for rescues at sea and various utility operations.

jib boom: A spar run out as an extension of the bowsprit.

Jim Crow: Laws and regulations for enabling segregation in the South; first enacted during the post–Civil War period (Reconstruction) and remaining in effect until the mid-1960s.

K-gun: A depth-charge projector used for firing depth charges from either side of a ship's main deck.

keel: The structural center member of a ship at the bottom of a hull.

knot: A measurement of speed equal to about 1.151 miles per hour.

lash down: To secure with ropes.

launch: The process for putting a boat or ship into the water.

lido deck: An open deck, usually containing a pool. (There is no pool on *Sea Cloud*.)

lieutenant: A commissioned officer in the US Navy and Coast Guard one rank higher than lieutenant (junior grade); equivalent to an army captain.

lieutenant commander: A commissioned officer in the US Navy and Coast Guard one rank higher than a lieutenant; equivalent to an army major.

lieutenant (junior grade), lieutenant (j.g.): A commissioned officer in the US Navy and Coast Guard one rank higher than ensign; equivalent to an army 1st lieutenant.

LST: Tank landing ship.

master: The captain of a civilian or merchant marine vessel.

mizzenmast: The third mast from forward in a vessel with three or more masts.

MY: Motor yacht.

NCO: A noncommissioned officer; in the US Navy and Coast Guard of World War II; in ascending order, petty officers 3rd class, 2nd class, and 1st class and chief petty officers.

nm: Nautical mile (about 6,076.1 feet or 1.1508 statute miles).

PC: Patrol craft.

petty officer: In the US Navy and Coast Guard a noncommissioned officer in a specialized rating or occupation (e.g., signalman 2nd class).

PF: Patrol frigate.

pilot: A person qualified to guide and direct the movement of a ship in and out of port or harbor.

plank owners: The officers and enlisted personnel of a vessel at the time it is placed in commission.

port: The left side of a ship or boat.

PR: Public relations.

promenade deck: An upper deck used by passengers to stroll outdoors.

prow: The part of a ship's bow above the waterline.

PY: Patrol yacht.

Q-ship: A merchant ship with concealed weaponry used to lure submerged submarines to the surface so they could be sunk by the Q-ship's guns.

radiosonde: A battery-powered telemetry package carried aloft by balloons to record meteorological data.

rating: The specific occupation or specialty of an enlisted man or woman in the US Navy and Coast Guard.

rear admiral: A commissioned officer in the US Navy or Coast Guard, equivalent to a major general in the army.

schooner: A sailing vessel with two or more masts with sails rigged fore-and-aft and the foremast smaller than the main mast.

sealer: A ship engaged in hunting seals.

SecNav: Secretary of the navy.

shipway: The structure supporting a ship during its construction.

sick bay: A compartment on a ship for the treatment of ill or injured personnel.

slop chute: A chute near the stern for dumping garbage.

spar: A stout rounded wood or metal pole used to support rigging.

SPARS: US Coast Guard Women's Reserve.

square-rigger: A vessel carrying its sails perpendicular to the keel and its masts.

starboard: The right side of a ship or boat.

stem: The most forward part of a vessel's bow and an extension of the keel itself.

step (noun): A block that receives the heel of a mast set into it on a boat or ship.

step (verb): To set the mast into its step.

stern: The back of a ship or boat.

SY: Sailing yacht.

TAD: Temporary additional duty.

TBF: Grumman Avenger torpedo bomber.

3-inch/50: A gun with a barrel 50 calibers (150 inches) long that fires projectiles 3 inches (76 mm) in diameter.

top hamper: The sails, rigging, and other gear on the upper part of a ship.

transom: The flat surface forming the stern of a ship or boat.

20 mm gun: A gun with an interior barrel diameter of 0.787 inch (20.0 mm) capable of firing projectiles or bullets 75 mm to 127 mm (3 to 5 inches) long against large targets, such as aircraft, vessels, vehicles, or buildings.

USCGR: United States Coast Guard Reserve.

vice admiral: A commissioned officer in the US Navy or Coast Guard one rank higher than a rear admiral; equivalent to a lieutenant general in the army.

WAG: Miscellaneous auxiliary vessel.

WAGL: Auxiliary vessel lighthouse tender.

WAVES: Women's Auxiliary Volunteer Emergency Service.

windjammer: A cargo-hauling large sailing ship with an iron hull; built in the 1800s and early twentieth century.

WPB: Patrol boat.

WHEC: Coast Guard high-endurance cutter.

WPG: Patrol gunboat.

WYTL: Small harbor tug.

XO: Executive officer, the second in command of a naval ship.

yard: A horizontal spar on which sails are set.

yeoman: A ship's clerk or secretary.

Notes

Chapter 1

General information in this chapter was obtained from the following sources:

- Grobecker and Neumann, *Sea Cloud*.
- Sea Cloud Cruises, "A Windjammer Writes History."
- Wright, *Heiress*.

1. "Germania-Werft Actien-Gesellschaft."
2. "Friedrich Krupp Germaniawerft"; "Shipyards: Germaniawerft, Kiel."
3. Comment attributed to banker J. P. Morgan.
4. Wright, *Heiress*, 106.
5. Ibid., 2.
6. Ibid., vi.
7. MacKay, *Great Yachts*, 123.
8. "History of Gibbs & Cox."
9. Maassen, *Floating Luxury*, 13.
10. Grobecker and Neumann, *Sea Cloud*, 35.
11. Ibid., 34.
12. Ibid., 35.
13. Ibid., 16.
14. Wright, *Heiress*, xii.
15. Ibid., 106.
16. Ibid., 118.
17. Ibid., xiv.
18. Grobecker and Neumann, *Sea Cloud*, 68.
19. Williams, *World War II U. S. Navy Vessels*, 179.
20. "Marjorie P. Hutton Receives a Divorce."
21. "Mrs. Post Hutton Wed to J. E. Davies."
22. Grobecker and Neumann, *Sea Cloud*, 77.

23. Wright, *Heiress*, 173.
24. Williams, *World War II U. S. Navy Vessels*, 68.
25. Grobecker and Neumann, *Sea Cloud*, 80.
26. "Davies Will Inspect South Russian Areas."

Chapter 2

General information in this chapter was obtained from the following sources:

- "Northland, 1927."
- Skinner, interview by Oesterle.
- Skinner, "U.S.S. Sea Cloud, IX-99."
- Solange P. Skinner, interview by Hurley.
- Willoughby, *U.S. Coast Guard.*

1. University of Washington, *The 1922 Tyree.*
2. Harvard College, Class of 1894, *Fiftieth Anniversary Report* (Norwood, MA: Plimpton Press, 1944), quoted in Lythgoe, "Macy Millmore SKINNER."
3. Howes, "BEACH, Marian Weymouth."
4. "Mrs. Marion Beach, 84, Dies."
5. "Private Services Were Held for Dr. Selby M. Skinner, 96, of Kirtland."
6. "Mrs. Max Mandellaub."
7. Decatur, "Marblehead Man Not Afraid to Make Waves at Sea."
8. Tilton School, "Our Mission and Vision."
9. Tilton School, "Affording Tilton."
10. Wesleyan University, "Wesleyan University: A Brief History."
11. UCLA, "Mission & Values."
12. Delta Upsilon, "The Cornerstone."
13. Manchester, *The Glory and the Dream*, 33.
14. US Department of Labor, "A Brief History."
15. Maritime Administration (MARAD), "A Short History of the Maritime Administration."
16. Skinner, "U.S.S. Sea Cloud, IX-99," 2.
17. Skinner, "Greenland, North Atlantic and North Pacific."
18. Morison, *History of United States Naval Operations*, 60.
19. Ibid., 61.
20. Polmar, "If It Flies Like a Duck . . . "
21. Skinner, "Arctic Navigation," 28.
22. Ibid.
23. Ibid.
24. Skinner, letter to Bunch, March 31, 1999.
25. Skinner, "Greenland, North Atlantic and North Pacific." 59
26. Willoughby, *U. S. Coast Guard*, 101; "U-Boat Fates."

27. Skinner, 1943 notebook.

28. Skinner, letter to Bunch, March 31, 1999.

29. Kaplan, "Half a Century of Coast Guard Wings."

Chapter 3

General information in this chapter was obtained from the following sources:

- MacGregor, *Integration of the Armed Forces*.
- Miller, *Kelly Miller's History*.
- US Coast Guard Historian's Office, "African Americans in the United States Coast Guard."
- US Navy, Bureau of Naval Personnel, *The Negro in the Navy*.

1. Department of the Navy, Bureau of Naval Personnel, "Guide to Command of Negro Naval Personnel."

2. Miller, *Kelly Miller's History*, 203.

3. US Coast Guard Historian's Office, "African Americans in the United States Coast Guard," 2.

4. The 420-foot icebreaker USCGC *Healey* (WAGB-20) was commissioned in 1999 with a complement of eighty-five officers and men. It is still in service and operates in Arctic waters.

5. Sayers, *Uncommon Warriors*, 122.

6. Miller, *Kelly Miller's History*, 204–5.

7. Data on the racial composition of the nineteenth-century navy are difficult to locate. See, for example, MacGregor, *Integration of the Armed Forces*, 4n3.

8. The term "general service" encompasses all of the usual and typical occupations, ratings, and specialties of US Navy and Coast Guard personnel, as opposed to the few "service" occupations, such as mess attendant and steward, to which blacks had been restricted for many years.

9. MacGregor, *Integration of the Armed Forces*, 5.

10. Miller, *Kelly Miller's History*, 214.

11. MacGregor, *Integration of the Armed Forces*, 5.

12. Ibid, 58.

13. Ibid, 112.

14. Thiesen, "Change Hastened by Conflict," 27.

15. US Navy, Bureau of Naval Personnel, "The Negro in the Navy," 5.

16. MacGregor, *Integration of the Armed Forces*, 59.

17. White, *A Man Called White*, 191.

18. Department of the Navy, "Navy to Accept Negroes for General Service."

19. Department of the Navy, Bureau of Naval Personnel, "Guide to Command of Negro Naval Personnel."

20. Ibid.

21. MacGregor, *Integration of the Armed Forces*, 69.

22. Thiesen, "Change Hastened by Conflict," 27.

23. MacGregor, *Integration of the Armed Forces*, 117.

24. Issued by President Abraham Lincoln on January 14, 1863, the proclamation granted that "all persons held as slaves" within the Confederacy shall be "forever free" and that the military and naval authorities of the United States "will recognize and maintain the freedom of any such persons, and will do no act or acts to repress such persons . . . in any efforts they may make for their actual freedom." "Emancipation Proclamation, U.S. Navy General Order No. 4 of 14 January 1863," https://www.history.navy.mil/research/library/online-reading-room/title-list-alphabetically/e/emancipation-proclamation-navy-general-order-no-4-1863.html (accessed May 25, 2020).

25. Ship data were sourced from Naval History and Heritage Command, "U.S. Ship Force Levels, 1886–Present."

Chapter 4

General information in this chapter was obtained from the following sources:

- Dinsmore, "Ocean Weather Ships 1940–1980."
- Grobecker and Neumann, *Sea Cloud*.
- Naval History and Heritage Command, "DANFS: Sea Cloud."
- Roberts, "Class: USS Sea Cloud (IX-99)."
- Sea Cloud Cruises, "A Windjammer Writes History."
- Skinner, "U.S.S. Sea Cloud, IX-99."
- "USS Sea Cloud, 1942."

1. Lupiano and Sayers, *It Was a Very Good Year*, 325–27; Manchester, *The Glory and the Dream*, 239.

2. Grobecker and Neumann, *Sea Cloud*, 92.

3. Morison, *History of United States Naval Operations*, 266.

4. Ibid., 268.

5. Ibid., 275.

6. Secretary of the Navy, to All Bureaus and Offices of the Navy Department, January 23, 1941, reproduced in Roberts, "Appendix 2: The Auxiliary Vessels Board, 1941–1948."

7. "Class: USS Sea Cloud (IX-99)."

8. On April 21, 1942, the navy informed Davies that it no longer would be required to reconvert those vessels that had been leased for $1.00 per annum when they were eventually returned to their owners and, further, that the navy's liability would be limited to the $1.00 fee in case of the vessel's loss. Davies disputed this amendment to the original charter agreement, and on December

5, 1942, the navy's vice chief of naval operations ordered *Sea Cloud* to be requisitioned outright via a purchase by the US War Shipping Administration. "Class: USS Sea Cloud (IX-99)"; memorandum from Lt. Cmdr. John W. Chapman, USNR, (Op-23-J-JWC/pw), procurement officer, to the WSA, March 9, 1943, collection of the US Coast Guard Historian's Office, Washington, DC.

9. "A Vessel Built in Germany Is Chartered to U.S. Navy."

10. The US Maritime Service was established in 1938 under provisions of the Merchant Marine Act of 1936 to train officers and men for an adequate merchant marine.

11. "23 Yachts Given to 3 U.S. Services."

12. V. Adm. Lloyd T. Chalker, Coast Guard memorandum (OP-209, 601, 701) to Commander of Coast Guard base in Charleston, SC, January 2, 1942, collection of the US Coast Guard Historian's Office, Washington, DC.

13. Skinner, "USS Sea Cloud, IX-99."

14. Ibid. The meteorological data would be collected by a radiosonde—a battery-powered telemetry instrument package carried by the balloon into the atmosphere. It would measure such conditions as altitude, barometric pressure, temperature, relative humidity, wind speed and direction, and the balloon's position and then transmit those data back down to the ship.

15. Tidwell, "The Best Democracy I've Known," 34.

16. A memorandum from the Coast Guard assistant commandant to the chief of naval operations placed the cost of operating and maintaining *Sea Cloud* from January 6, 1942, to October 1, 1943, as follows: $396,519 for maintenance, repair, and alteration; and $27,554 for operational expenses exclusive of personnel pay. R. Adm. Merlin O'Neill to Adm. Chester W. Nimitz, June 19, 1947, collection of the US Coast Guard Historian's Office, Washington, DC.

17. *Bibb* was commissioned on March 10, 1937; after a long and distinguished history of service it was decommissioned on September 30, 1985, and sunk as an artificial reef off the Florida Keys on November 28, 1987. *Duane* was commissioned on August 1, 1936, and like *Bibb* served long and well; it was decommissioned on August 1, 1985, and, like *Bibb*, was sunk as an artificial reef off Florida the day before *Bibb* was scuttled. *Alexander Hamilton* was commissioned in March 1937, but its service was cut short on January 30, 1942, when it was sunk off Iceland following a torpedoing by the German submarine U-132. *Spencer* was commissioned on March 1, 1937, decommissioned on December 15, 1980, and sold to North American Smelting Company of Wilmington, Delaware, on October 8, 1981, for scrapping.

18. Sayers, *Uncommon Warriors*, 21–28.

19. *Evergreen* was commissioned on April 30, 1943, decommissioned on June 13, 1990, then transferred to the navy and expended as a target on November 25, 1992. *Sorrel* was commissioned April 15, 1943, decommissioned June 20, 1996,

and subsequently sold to a private purchaser. *Conifer* was commissioned on July 1, 1943, decommissioned on June 23, 2000, and later used as a training hulk at Seattle.

20. *Nourmahal*, like *Sea Cloud*, had been built by the Krupp shipyard in Kiel, Germany. It was completed and delivered to its owner, William Vincent Astor, in 1928. The yacht was taken into the Coast Guard on August 21, 1940, and converted into a weather station vessel in September–December 1941. It was ultimately transferred to the Maritime Administration on July 18, 1948, and sold by MARAD on September 11, 1964, to Hughes Brothers, Inc., for scrapping.

21. Willoughby, *U S. Coast Guard*, 120.

22. *Monomoy* was built as a cargo ship in 1918, acquired by the navy on September 15, 1941, commissioned in that service, and designated as AG-40 on December 24, 1941. It damaged a German U-boat in July 1942, was transferred to the Coast Guard on October 22, 1943, and redesignated as WAG 275; it was decommissioned on October 12, 1945, and reportedly sold by the Maritime Commission to Patapsco Scrap Company on March 21, 1951. *Manasquan* was built in 1918 as the steamship *Lake Catherine*, carried cargo and coal in Europe that year, served in the merchant marine following World War I, was acquired by the navy on October 14, 1941, and was designated AG-36 the next day. It was lent to the Coast Guard and commissioned on April 2, 1942, as WAG-273, formally transferred to USCG on October 22, 1943, assigned as a training ship at the Coast Guard Academy from August 1944 to February 1945, decommissioned on February 22, 1945, and sold on March 11, 1946. *Manhassett* was built as the cargo ship *Wilton* in 1923, acquired by the navy on January 2, 1942, designated as a miscellaneous auxiliary (AG-47) on May 30, 1942, loaned to the Coast Guard, and commissioned as WAG-276 on August 8, 1942. It attacked German submarines in 1943, was formally transferred to USCG on October 22, 1943, decommissioned on October 15, 1945, and sold on October 16, 1946.

23. Coast Guard message (201525) to *Sea Cloud*, July 20, 1942, collection of the US Coast Guard Historian's Office, Washington, DC.

24. IX was the navy designation for unclassified miscellaneous vessels. Today that designation indicates "non-commissioned vessels designed to provide support to combat ships and other naval operations but not involved with combatant forces, Navy warfighting or support missions, and are not part of the battleforce inventory." Sayers, *Uncommon Warriors*, xv.

Chapter 5

General information in this chapter was obtained from the following sources:

- "Gresham, 1897."
- Skinner, "Greenland, North Atlantic and North Pacific."
- Skinner, interview by Oesterle.

- Skinner, lecture delivered on board *Sea Cloud*.
- Skinner, testimony before the President's Committee on Equality of Treatment and Opportunity.
- Skinner, "U.S.S. Sea Cloud, IX-99."
- US Coast Guard Historian's Office, "African Americans in the U.S. Coast Guard."

1. Fractal Foundation, "What Is Chaos Theory?"
2. Skinner, "U.S.S. Sea Cloud, IX-99."
3. Skinner, interview by Oesterle, 4.
4. Skinner, "U.S.S. Sea Cloud, IX-99."
5. Skinner, interview by Oesterle, 4.
6. Skinner, "U.S.S. Sea Cloud, IX-99"; Morison, *Oxford History of the American People*, 884–85.
7. Given the short duration of his time on board, it is likely that Skinner was sent to the ship on a Temporary Additional Duty (TAD) basis (i.e., an assignment to a location other than a person's permanent duty station). The TAD assignment would allow him to fill in temporarily for an XO who was either away or yet to report aboard.
8. Skinner's characterization was apt because *Gresham* was unable to steam faster than 7 knots, too slow for convoy escort. It was taken out of service and decommissioned on April 7, 1944. The old vessel was then sold, renamed *Tradewinds*, and later acquired by the Jewish Haganah. Renamed *Hatikva*, it carried 1,414 Jewish refugees on a voyage from Italy to Palestine but was intercepted and rammed by a Royal Navy destroyer on May 17, 1947. "Gresham, 1897."
9. "Coast Guard-Manned LSTs."
10. Handwritten notes that Skinner made on February 22 and March 4, 1943, suggest that he was already engaged in planning activities for "Coast Guard Crew #10" (LST 10?) and the organization of an LST. Undated notes also detail some thirty-one specific "desired changes for LST," including raising the Charley Noble, constructing a wind protector for the bow lookout, building a locker in the chart room for navigational gear, acquiring an ice cream machine, and building a slop chute. Skinner, 1943 notebook.
11. Willoughby, *U.S. Coast Guard*, 174.
12. In a search of the Coast Guard ship histories of the various LSTs manned by USCG personnel, the author was unable to find Carlton Skinner's name among the listings of their commanding officers. It is likely, therefore, that although he had undergone training as a prospective LST CO, Skinner's orders were subsequently changed and he was reassigned to other duties before formally assuming command of a commissioned LST. This view is partially confirmed by Skinner himself when he wrote in a memoir ("Greenland, North Atlantic and North Pacific") that after "commanding an LST crew in training and

briefly helping to commission a ship [*Gresham*?]," he was transferred to Coast Guard headquarters. That phrasing implies that he did not officially serve as CO of a commissioned LST, rather that he was in charge of the precommissioning crew but departed to take up his new post in Washington prior to the crew's assignment to a newly built LST.

13. Skinner, "Arctic Navigation."

14. "Ensign Rowe Is Bride of Lieut. Skinner."

15. "Jeanne R. Skinner."

16. Skinner, "U.S.S. Sea Cloud, IX-99,"4

17. Ibid. 5

18. Ibid.

19. Waesche was born in 1886, commissioned in 1906, and became Coast Guard commandant in June 1936. With the longest tenure as commandant, Admiral Waesche served in that post through 1945, retired from the Coast Guard on January 1, 1946, and died on October 17 that year.

20. Reed-Hill was commissioned as an ensign in January 1912, served as chief of the public information division from August 1940 to August 1946, and retired as a rear admiral in 1950.

21. Skinner, "U.S.S. Sea Cloud, IX-99," 5.

22. Skinner subsequently was given a copy of the memo on which had been noted in Waesche's handwriting: "Send Skinner to Sea Cloud." The original memorandum has been lost. However, the US Coast Guard Historian's Office holds Skinner's reconstructed copy of it.

23. Skinner, "U.S.S. Sea Cloud, IX-99," 5.

24. Skinner, lecture delivered on board *Sea Cloud*, 24.

25. The commanding officers of naval ships are referred to as "captain" regardless of their actual rank.

26. Built in 1874 in Boston's Copley Square, the landmark Hotel Brunswick was demolished in 1957 to make room for a new office building.

27. Nicholas Rossi, telephone interview by author, January 12, 2017. Rossi said that he had reported aboard *Sea Cloud* as an apprentice seaman following graduation from boot camp in March 1943. He sailed on the ship for two patrols—calling it "tough duty" because of the foul weather and heavy seas—and was transferred to a navy oiler early in 1944. Rossi later served ashore in Greenland and was discharged from the Coast Guard at the end of the war as a yeoman 2nd class. He died on June 12, 2018, in Florida. See also Tidwell, "The Best Democracy I've Known," 36.

28. Skinner, testimony before the President's Committee on Equality of Treatment and Opportunity, 5. Smith had previously been in command of the Greenland Patrol and carried his flag in the cutter *Northland*, on which Skinner was navigator and later XO.

29. Skinner, "U.S.S. Sea Cloud, IX-99," 5–6.

30. Skinner, interview by Oesterle; Skinner, testimony before the President's Committee on Equality of Treatment and Opportunity, 5.

31. Skinner, "Greenland, North Atlantic and North Pacific," 61.

32. "Jacob A. Lawrence."

33. Miller, "Art of History," 26.

34. Tidwell, "The Best Democracy I've Known," 36.

35. Miller, "Art of History," 26–27.

36. Capt. J. S. Rosenthal, the ship's CO, had specifically requested that Lawrence be assigned to his ship as combat artist. Rosenthal had encouraged the artist at boot camp, reportedly offering Lawrence a place in his quarters in which to paint. See ibid., 26. The troop transport had been acquired by the navy on October 31, 1944, commissioned on November 2, 1944, served with the army during the Korean War, eventually operated as a commercial vessel for several years, and was dismantled in 2005.

37. Skinner, "Lost Wartime Paintings of Jacob Lawrence."

38. Miller, "Art of History," 27; Whitney Museum of American Art, "Jacob Lawrence, 1917–2000."

39. Tidwell, "The Best Democracy I've Known," 36.

40. "BMCM Robert E. Hammond, USCG."

41. Evanson, "Looking Back," 46.

42. Ibid., 47.

43. Commissioned on April 15, 1944, the ship's first commanding officer was Capt. Carl C. von Paulsen, USCG, who coincidentally was Skinner's CO on the cutter *Northland* in 1941–42. Among the troops it carried during its service was Pvt. Elvis Presley in 1958. *General George M. Randall* was decommissioned June 2, 1961, and sold for $687,000 on May 8, 1975, for dismantling.

44. *Hawser* was commissioned on January 17, 1963.

45. "BMCM Robert E. Hammond, USCG."

46. Thiesen, "Pioneers of Ethnic Diversity."

47. Laughlin, "Mapping the Way to Equality."

48. The 200-foot cutter *Earp* was commissioned into the navy as *Eagle 22* on July 17, 1919, but was transferred to the Coast Guard in March 1920. It served in the Coast Guard for just three years and was returned to the navy on May 22, 1923.

49. Thiesen, "The Long Blue Line: Clarence Samuels.""

50. Lightship No. 115 (a.k.a. Frying Pan) was built in 1929, decommissioned on November 4, 1965, and is now privately owned in New York City. Lightship No. 91 was built in 1908, decommissioned on November 30, 1961, and sold on March 11, 1963.

51. Thiesen, "Pioneers of Ethnic Diversity"; US Coast Guard Historian's Office, "African Americans in the U.S. Coast Guard." The 180-foot cutter *Sweetgum* was commissioned on November 20, 1943, and decommissioned on February 15, 2002.

52. The 190-foot *Tulip* was commissioned on July 14, 1908, and decommissioned on December 1, 1945. It was transferred to the Philippines in July 1947.

53. Thiesen, "Pioneers of Ethnic Diversity."

54. Skinner, lecture delivered on board *Sea Cloud*, 1–2.

55. Ibid., 10.

Chapter 6

General information in this chapter was obtained from the following sources:

- MacGregor, *Integration of the Armed Forces*.
- Naval History and Heritage Command, "DANFS: Hoquiam (PF-5)."
- Naval History and Heritage Command, "DANFS: Sea Cloud."
- Priolo, "Hoquiam (PF 5)."
- US Coast Guard Historian's Office, "African Americans in the U.S. Coast Guard."
- US Navy, Bureau of Naval Personnel, *The Negro in the Navy*.
- Skinner, "Greenland, North Atlantic and North Pacific."
- Skinner, interview by Oesterle.
- Skinner, lecture delivered on board *Sea Cloud*.
- Skinner, testimony before the President's Committee on Equality of Treatment and Opportunity.
- Skinner, "U.S.S. Sea Cloud, IX-99."
- "USS Hoquiam, PF-5."
- "USS Sea Cloud, 1942."

1. Skinner, lecture delivered on board *Sea Cloud*, 13.

2. Skinner, "U.S.S. Sea Cloud, IX-99."

3. Ibid., 6.

4. Ibid.

5. Ibid., 8.

6. Skinner, lecture delivered on board *Sea Cloud*, 33.

7. Ibid., 33–34.

8. Ibid., 35.

9. L. T. Chalker, Assistant Commandant of the Coast Guard, message (CG-001 609) to Commanding Officer of *Sea Cloud*, March 23, 1944, collection of the US Coast Guard Historian's Office, Washington, DC.

10. Dinsmore, "Ocean Weather Ships, 1940–1980."

11. USS *Champlin* was commissioned on September 12, 1942, and placed out of commission in reserve on January 31, 1947.

12. USS *Huse* was commissioned on August 30, 1943, and decommissioned in June 1965.

13. Roscoe, *United States Destroyer Operations*, 302.

14. Skinner, lecture delivered on board *Sea Cloud*, 15. The author was unable to find any reference to *Sea Cloud*'s involvement in this action in the US Navy and Coast Guard World War II histories compiled by Morison, Willoughby, and Roscoe; or in the navy's published ship histories of *Champlin*, *Huse*, and *Sea Cloud*; and only indirectly in the Coast Guard's published history of *Sea Cloud*. The latter does not mention the battle and does not identify the German submarine or its American attackers.

15. USS *Zircon* was built in 1929 as the 235-foot private yacht *Nakhoda*. It was acquired by the navy on December 9, 1940, renamed *Zircon*, and classified as a patrol yacht (PY-16). Converted for naval service at the Brooklyn Navy Yard, *Zircon* was commissioned on March 25, 1941. It was decommissioned on May 10, 1946, transferred to the Maritime Commission for disposal on October 17, 1946, and sold by the War Shipping Administration on April 24, 1947.

16. Skinner, lecture delivered on board *Sea Cloud*, 10.

17. Ibid., 11.

18. Although the Coast Guard's published history of *Sea Cloud* shows it leaving Argentia on May 20, that date appears to be a typo because the ship's official handwritten log book entry indicates that it was still in port several days later. See Ship's Log Book, Record Group 24, National Archives and Records Administration, College Park, MD. In fact, Skinner, seven officers, a Public Health Service officer, and one enlisted man were ordered to assist in the annual material inspection of USCGC *Nourmahal* in Argentia on May 23. See letter from Commanding Officer of *Sea Cloud*, May 22, 1944 (File 68), Record Group 24, National Archives and Records Administration, College Park, MD.

19. Skinner, interview by Oesterle, 50–51; Skinner, "Greenland, North Atlantic and North Pacific," 61–62.

20. USS *Croatan* was commissioned on April 28, 1943, as an auxiliary aircraft carrier (ACV-25) but was reclassified as an escort carrier on July 15, 1943. It was used primarily as an aircraft transport ship in the 1950s, removed from service on October 23, 1969, and sold for $85,888.88 on February 5, 1971, for dismantling by the Southern Scrap Material Company.

21. Roscoe, *United States Destroyer Operations*, 311; Morison, *History of United States Naval Operations*, 320–21.

22. USS *Frost* was an *Edsall*-class DE commissioned on August 30, 1943; it earned a Presidential Unit Citation and seven Battle Stars for service in World War II. It was decommissioned and placed in reserve on June 18, 1946, and sold on December 29, 1966, to be scrapped. USS *Inch* also was an *Edsall*-class DE and was commissioned on September 8, 1943. It served in both the Atlantic and Pacific during the war, was decommissioned on May 17, 1946, and sold on February 26, 1974, to the Southern Scrap Material Company for dismantling.

23. CNO letter signed by V. D. Chapline, Op-23G-mrf Serial 0480523 (SC) L9-3/IX99, Box 421, RG19E1266, National Archives and Records Administration, College Park, MD.

24. "Davies Yacht Released," 15.

25. Ibid.

26. Skinner, lecture delivered on board *Sea Cloud*, 36.

27. Confidential CNO message, October 27, 1944 (0329/27), Box 421, RG19E1266, National Archives and Records Administration, College Park, MD.

28. Confidential message from *Sea Cloud* to INSURV, October 29, 1944 (0745/29), Box 421, RG19E1266, National Archives and Records Administration, College Park, MD.

29. Skinner, lecture delivered on board *Sea Cloud*, 37.

30. Ibid., 37–38.

31. Confidential message from INSURV to CNO, November 4, 1944 (0223), Box 421, RG19E1266, National Archives and Records Administration, College Park, MD.

32. Skinner, lecture delivered on board *Sea Cloud*, 55–56. The author cautions that the latter figure may be a typo in the lecture transcript and that if indeed it is a reference to the navy's compensatory payment to Joseph Davies, it should read $175,000.

33. Skinner, lecture delivered on board *Sea Cloud*, 55–56.

34. Ship's Log Book, November 5, 1944, Record Group 24, National Archives and Records Administration, College Park, MD.

35. Skinner, testimony before the President's Committee on Equality of Treatment and Opportunity, 5–6.

36. Skinner, interview by Oesterle, 5.

37. Skinner, "U.S.S. Sea Cloud, IX-99," 9.

38. Canham had been the *Monitor*'s bureau chief in Washington, the newspaper's editor from 1945 to 1964, and then editor in chief for the next ten years. He died in Agana, Guam, in 1982 at the age of seventy-seven.

39. Skinner, "U.S.S. Sea Cloud, IX-99," 10.

40. Born in 1908, Duffield was a graduate of the University of Wisconsin. He had been first a reporter for the *Wall Street Journal* and later chief of its Washington bureau, and then assistant to the secretary of the navy from 1944 to 1946. He later was an officer and director of the McGraw-Hill Publishing Company, assistant publisher of the *Cincinnati Enquirer*, and vice president of Federated Department Stores. He died in 1974 at the age of sixty-six. "Eugene Duffield, Publisher, Editor."

41. Skinner, lecture delivered on board *Sea Cloud*, 43–44.

42. Skinner, testimony before the President's Committee on Equality of Treatment and Opportunity, 6.

43. Skinner, "Greenland, North Atlantic and North Pacific," 62.

44. The Coast Guard manned eighteen of the navy's seventy-five AOGs during World War II.

45. Skinner, lecture by Oesterle, 52–53.

46. Skinner, "Greenland, North Atlantic and North Pacific," 62.

47. USS *Hoquiam* was recommissioned on September 27, 1950, fought in the Korean War, and earned five Battle Stars for that service. It was decommissioned on October 5, 1951, and leased to the South Korean navy as *Nae Tong* (PF-65). *Hoquiam*'s name was struck from the Naval Vessel Register on August 1, 1972, and the ship was sold to South Korea on October 1, 1973. It was broken up for scrap later that year.

48. MacGregor, *Integration of the Armed Forces*, 60.

49. *Yocona* was a *Kankakee*-class stern paddle-wheeler commissioned on October 19, 1919, for use in flood relief and rescue work on the Ohio and Mississippi Rivers. It had a complement of thirty-five men. The cutter was decommissioned on June 15, 1925, and sold on November 2 of that year for $27,555.

50. Thiesen, "Change Hastened by Conflict," 27.

51. USS *Mason* was decommissioned on October 12, 1945, struck from the Naval Vessel Register on November 1 of that year, and sold on March 18, 1947, to be dismantled.

52. MacGregor, *Integration of the Armed Forces*, 77.

53. "Navy Celebrates 2016 African American/Black History Month."

54. MacGregor, *Integration of the Armed Forces*, 77. PC-1264 was decommissioned on February 7, 1946, struck from the Naval Vessel Register on March 28, 1946, transferred to the Maritime Commission for disposal on March 24, 1948, and sold for scrap.

55. Department of the Navy, Bureau of Naval Personnel, "Guide to Command of Negro Naval Personnel,"

56. MacGregor, *Integration of the Armed Forces*, 78.

57. Carlton Skinner, USS *Hoquiam*, memorandum to Commandant of the Coast Guard, Serial 106, June 30, 1945, collection of the US Coast Guard Historian's Office, Washington, DC.

58. Auxiliary ships support the navy's combat ships and provide a variety of services to the fleet. Large auxiliaries include ammunition ships, oilers, refrigerated store ships, destroyer tenders, and submarine tenders.

59. MacGregor, *Integration of the Armed Forces*, 85.

60. White, *A Man Called White*, 273.

61. MacGregor, *Integration of the Armed Forces*, 85.

62. Ibid., 94.

63. Ibid., 121.

64. "Navy Celebrates African-American/Black History Month."

65. MacGregor, *Integration of the Armed Forces*, 88.

66. Akers, "December 26, 1944."

67. MacGregor, *Integration of the Armed Forces*, 122.

68. Ibid., 121.

69. US Navy, Bureau of Naval Personnel, *The Negro in the Navy*, 76.

70. MacGregor, *Integration of the Armed Forces*, 98.

Chapter 7

General information in this chapter was obtained from the following sources:

- Grobecker and Neumann, *Sea Cloud*.
- May v. Commissioner of Internal Revenue.
- Oceanics Schools Inc. v. Clifford E. Barbour Jr.
- Sea Cloud Cruises, "A Windjammer Writes History."
- Wright, *Heiress*.

1. Grobecker and Neumann, *Sea Cloud*, 98–99.

2. The shipyard was founded in 1887 as Maryland Steel, acquired by Bethlehem Shipbuilding Corporation in 1916, and sold in 1997 to Baltimore Marine Industries Inc.

3. "Refitted for Peacetime Luxury Service," 55.

4. Wright, *Heiress*, 175.

5. "Joseph E. Davies Quits Bermuda," 5.

6. Wright, *Heiress*, 176.

7. "Windsors Visit Bahamas," 35.

8. "Trujillo Presents Medal to Mrs. Davies," 7. The Juan Pablo Duarte Order of Merit was established on February 24, 1931, to be conferred by the Dominican head of state to civilians and military personnel for distinguished services. It was renamed the Order of Merit of Duarte, Sánchez and Mella on September 9, 1954.

9. Skinner, lecture delivered on board *Sea Cloud*, 56.

10. John Sullivan was born in 1899 and appointed secretary of the navy by President Harry Truman in 1947, succeeding James V. Forrestal (see epilogue). R. Adm. James L. Holloway was commissioned in 1918, and became the thirty-fifth superintendent of the US Naval Academy in January 1947. He was promoted to full admiral in 1958, retired in 1959, and died in 1984.

11. The Naval Reserve Yacht Owner's Distinguishing Pennant was authorized in January 1947 to recognize yacht owners who made their vessels available to the navy during the conflict. Recipients were permitted to display the pennant aboard any vessel they owned, whether or not it was the yacht they had provided to the navy.

12. Skinner, lecture delivered on board *Sea Cloud*, 57.

13. Grobecker and Neumann, *Sea Cloud*, 99.

14. "North Florida Notes," 62.

15. Data are from May v. Commissioner of Internal Revenue.

16. Wright, *Heiress*, 204–5.

17. Details regarding the deactivation and decommissioning of *Sea Cloud* were sourced from May v. Commissioner of Internal Revenue.

18. Information regarding the selling of *Sea Cloud* was sourced from May v. Commissioner of Internal Revenue.

19. Grobecker and Neumann, *Sea Cloud*, 108; Wright, *Heiress*, 205.

20. George W. Gibbs was an early shipbuilder in Jacksonville who launched his company in 1908. During World War I his shipyard built sixteen submarine chasers for the navy, and by the 1940s the yard occupied much of the city's riverfront. During World War II the Gibbs Corporation shipyard built navy minesweepers, covered lighters, sub chasers, and tugboats, along with barges and other craft for the army. "Lost Jacksonville: Gibbs Corporation Shipyards."

21. "Trujillo Buys Sea Cloud," 49.

22. "Trujillo's Yacht Firmly Anchored," 4.

23. "Trujillo's Yacht Gets a New Name," 7.

24. Grobecker and Neumann, *Sea Cloud*, 113–14.

25. "Few Big Yachts Left," 29.

26. Grobecker and Neumann, *Sea Cloud*, 115.

27. "Yacht Return Is Demanded," 2.

28. Blackman, *Jane's Fighting Ships*, 66–68.

29. *Presidente Trujillo* was built in 1944 as the Canadian River–class frigate *Carlplace* (K664). It was acquired from Canada in 1946, served as the flagship of the Dominican navy, was modernized in the 1960s, and became a museum ship in 1997.

30. Valbuena, "For Sale: Yacht with Memories."

31. Dubois, "For Sale: One Used Yacht."

32. Valbuena, "For Sale: Yacht with Memories."

33. The ARC *Gloria* was commissioned on September 7, 1968, and is used as both a training vessel and official flagship by the Colombian navy.

34. Berrellee, "Dominican Government Inherits White Elephant," 2.

35. Ibid.

36. Oceanics Schools Inc. v. Clifford E. Barbour Jr.

37. Kigar, "Fair Wind to Martinique," 40.

38. Oceanic Schools Inc. v. Clifford E. Barbour Jr.

39. "Sailing Yacht Now a School."

40. Oceanics Schools Inc. v. Clifford E. Barbour Jr.

41. "Sailing Yacht Now a School."

42. "Salt Air to Add Zest to High School Lessons."

43. Oceanics Schools Inc. v. Clifford E. Barbour Jr.

44. Ibid.

45. Carlton Skinner said Liedtke "imaginatively led" the investors during his

remarks on board *Sea Cloud* on May 30, 1987. "Great Lady of the Sea Arrives in Fiji," 7. Liedtke today is an entrepreneur and partner in the B&L Group in Hamburg.

46. Some published sources state that *Antarna* was sold in 1974 to Klaus E. Oldendorff of Reederie Nord and that the vessel was renamed *Sea Cloud of Cayman* and registered in Malta. (Reederie Nord Group had been established in Hamburg in 1964 by Oldendorff to manage ships owned by the Oldendorff family and other private individuals.) On the other hand, in their own history of the vessel, the current owners of *Sea Cloud* note that the Hartmut Paschburg, "who had breathed new life into old sailing ships before," acquired the yacht along with a group of Hamburg-based businessmen and gave it back its old name of *Sea Cloud*. (Sea Cloud Cruises, "The Renaissance of an Extraordinary Yacht.") It may be that Oldendorff was one of the original Hamburg investors in *Sea Cloud*, but in any event, according to both the current owners' history and the 2003 court records in the United States, the sale of *Antarna* took place in 1978 and the vessel was renamed *Sea Cloud*.

47. Oceanics Schools Inc. v. Clifford E. Barbour Jr.

48. Details on the ship's material problems and the working conditions in Panama are from Grobecker and Neumann, *Sea Cloud*, 133.

49. Details on the ship's material problems after leaving Panama are from ibid., 136–40.

50. Oceanics Schools Inc. v. Clifford E. Barbour Jr.

51. The legal disputes between the Oceanics Schools and Operation Sea Cruise corporately and Clifford Barbour individually continued into the 1990s and early 2000s. Because of its complexity and marginal relevance to *Sea Cloud*'s subsequent history, the technical details of that extended litigation are outside the scope of this account.

52. As successor to Krupp's Germania Werft, Howaldtswerke-Deutsche Werft AG had been formed in 1968 when the old Howaldtswerke shipyard in Kiel merged with Hamburg-based Deutsche Werft. In January 2005 HDW became a subsidiary of ThyssenKrupp Marine Systems (TKMS).

53. Donner, "A Four-Masted Barque That Sails the Caribbean."

54. Grobecker and Neumann, *Sea Cloud*, 142, 147.

55. Donner, "A Four-Masted Barque That Sails the Caribbean."

56. Julia Eble, Sea Cloud Cruises GmbH, email to the author, January 25, 2016.

57. Donner, "A Four-Masted Barque That Sails the Caribbean."

58. Robinson, "Transatlantic by Square-Rigger."

59. Kigar, "Fair Wind to Martinique."

60. "Great Lady of the Sea Arrives in Fiji," 7. Additional information about this visit and Skinner's remarks are provided in chapter 8.

61. Elbe, email to author, January 25, 2016.

Chapter 8

General information in this chapter was obtained from the following sources:

- Skinner, *After Three Centuries*.
- Skinner, interview by Oesterle.
- Skinner, lecture delivered on board *Sea Cloud*.
- Skinner, testimony before the President's Committee on Equality of Treatment and Opportunity.

1. "Krug Appoints Carlton Skinner."

2. Stark, "Lewis Signs Soft Coal Terms with U.S.," 2.

3. McEnery, interview by Fuchs.

4. Ibid., 44.

5. Skinner, lecture delivered on board *Sea Cloud*, 57.

6. "Log of President Truman's Trip to Puerto Rico, the Virgin Islands, Guantanamo Bay, Cuba, and Key West, Florida." *Williamsburg* was built in 1930 as the yacht *Aras* and was acquired and renamed by the navy in April 1941. It served as the presidential yacht from 1945 to 1953, was struck from the list of naval vessels in 1962, and was scrapped in Italy in 2016.

7. Skinner, testimony before the President's Committee on Equality of Treatment and Opportunity, 1–2.

8. Ibid., 9–10.

9. Ibid., 15.

10. Letter from Adm. Joseph F. Farley, Commandant of the Coast Guard, to Skinner, July 12, 1949, file PRA 78, collection of the US Coast Guard Historian's Office, Washington, DC.

11. Skinner, *After Three Centuries*, 7.

12. Skinner, interview by Oesterle, 2.

13. Skinner, *After Three Centuries*, 14.

14. Ibid., 15–16.

15. Ibid., 17.

16. "First Civilian Chief of Guam Designated," 15.

17. "Ex-Reporter Appointed Guam Civilian Governor," 14.

18. Skinner, interview by Oesterle, 5.

19. "Guam Transfer Signed," 9.

20. Skinner, *After Three Centuries*, 143–44.

21. "Guam Greets Skinner," 12.

22. Associated Press report, *New York Times*, September 27, 1949, 12.

23. The full text of Governor Skinner's inaugural address is available in Skinner, *After Three Centuries*, 143–49.

24. "Typhoon Hits Guam," 14; "Guam Storm Cost Large," 3.

25. Skinner "hitchhiked" out of Guam in the aircraft of John W. Snyder,

Truman's treasury secretary. Snyder had been inspecting Coast Guard installations in the Pacific (the Coast Guard was part of the Treasury Department at the time) and had arrived on Guam at 4:45 a.m. on November 24. After breakfast with Skinner and an inspection of the Coast Guard's repaired Loran station, which had been damaged by the typhoon, Snyder's party, now including Skinner, left Guam at 10:20 a.m. Snyder, interview by Hess.

26. Skinner, *After Three Centuries*, 22.

27. Ibid.

28. "Guam Governor Due in Capital," 7.

29. See Skinner, *After Three Centuries*, 123–26, for the governor's statement to the committee.

30. Specific details of some of the congressional actions leading up to passage of the Organic Act are in Skinner, *After Three Centuries*, 46–47; "Action on Guam."

31. Goetzfridt, "Governor Carlton Skinner."

32. "Guam's House Elected."

33. University of Guam, *Academic Year 2015–2016 Fact Book*.

34. "Guam Paper for Sale."

35. The full text of the speech is in Skinner, *After Three Centuries*, 155–60.

36. "Guam Charges Denied," 8.

37. "Guam Corruption Denied," 10.

38. "Navy Aids Guam in Strike."

39. "Skinner, Guam's Governor, Quits," 4; Skinner, *After Three Centuries*, 104.

40. "Governor of Guam Quits; Nebraskan May Get Post"; "Guam Head Steps Out Today."

41. The full text of the farewell address is in Skinner, *After Three Centuries*, 161–72.

42. Skinner, *After Three Centuries*, 104.

43. Ibid., 182.

44. Ibid., 177.

45. Ibid., 104.

46. Skinner, interview by Oesterle, 7.

47. "Silberstein Resigns Directorship in the Penn-Texas Corporation."

48. "New Chairman Elected by Pratt & Whitney Co."

49. Today Pratt & Whitney is a Connecticut-based aerospace manufacturer with global service operations and a subsidiary of United Technologies Corporation. The company's aircraft engines power many civilian and military aircraft. Fairbanks Whitney Corporation was reorganized as Colt Industries in 1964, a year after Skinner had left the business.

50. Caro, *Years of Lyndon Johnson*, 121–34.

51. Solange P. Skinner, interview by Hurley.

52. Skinner, interview by Oesterle, 7–8.

53. "History—SPC—Secretariat of the Pacific Community."

54. Skinner, interview by Oesterle, 60.

55. "President Picks New Labor Aide after Signing Bill Creating Post."

56. Lee had previously been the Interior Department's assistant director of the Division of Territories and had accompanied Secretary Krug and Skinner on their August 1947 inspection visit of the Pacific Islands.

57. "New Values Stir the South Pacific."

58. Skinner, interview by Oesterle, 16.

59. Ibid., 19.

60. Skinner, "Self-Government in the South Pacific," 143.

61. Ibid., 144.

62. Skinner, interview by Oesterle, 57.

63. Ibid., 8–10.

64. Cuff, "Business People."

65. Skinner, interview by Oesterle, 10.

66. Ibid.

67. "Nauru Appoints Honorary Consul."

68. Skinner, *Nauru: The Remarkable Community*, 107.

69. Solange P. Skinner, interview by author, December 8, 2015, and interview by Hurley.

70. The name derives from "You Are Right, Kommander."

71. R. C. Keefe, email to author, December 31, 2015.

72. Kigar, "Fair Wind to Martinique," 37.

73. The typescript is in the collection of the US Coast Guard Historian's Office, Washington, DC.

74. Kigar, "Fair Wind to Martinique," 40. "Over the Side" is piped by a boatswain's mate as a distinguished visitor passes between two rows of sideboys, who salute the VIP.

75. "Great Lady of the Sea Arrives in Fiji," 7.

76. Ibid.

77. Goetzfridt, "Governor Carlton Skinner."

78. Solange P. Skinner, letter to author, September 20, 2016.

79. Solange P. Skinner, interview by Hurley.

80. Ibid.

81. Camacho, letter to Solange P. Skinner, September 16, 2004, copy in author's files.

82. "Governor Carlton Skinner: Pacific."

83. Murphy, "Skinner Shaped Guam's Future."

84. US Coast Guard, "Two Buildings Named for Coast Guard Heroes."

Chapter 9

General information in this chapter was obtained from the following source:

- https://www.seacloud.com/

1. A virtual tour of *Sea Cloud* is available online at https://www.seacloud.com/en/yachts/virtual-tours/.
2. Sea Cloud Cruises, press release, May 2, 2011
3. Julia Eble, Sea Cloud Cruises, email to author, January 22, 2016.
4. Sea Cloud Cruises, press release, May 2, 2011.
5. *Kruzenshtern*, like *Sea Cloud*, is a four-masted barque. It was built in Germany in 1926 and named *Padua*. Acquired by the Soviet navy in 1946 as a war reparation, it still serves today as a Russian sail training ship.
6. Vladimir Pushkarev, email to author, January 11, 2016.
7. Eble, email to author, January 7, 2016.
8. Sea Cloud Cruises, press release, March 29, 2011.
9. Elbe, email to author, October 28, 2016.
10. The 347-foot, three-masted *Sea Cloud II* was built specifically for Sea Cloud Cruises. The keel was laid down on June 24, 1998, and it was commissioned on February 6, 2001.
11. Sea Cloud Cruises, press release, July 5, 2013.
12. Schafer had joined the Hansa Treuhand Group—owners of Sea Cloud Cruises—in 2005 as assistant to Hermann Ebel, the chairman of the board. Five years later Schafer became sales director and vice president of sales for Sea Cloud Cruises.
13. Sea Cloud Cruises, press release. January 17, 2020

Epilogue

1. Executive Order 9981.
2. Morris J. McGregor covers in depth the postwar implementation of Truman's order in his *Integration of the Armed Forces*.
3. Zumwalt, "Equal Opportunity."
4. Ibid.
5."Wallace B. Bishop."
6. "Eugene Duffield, Publisher, Editor."
7. "Robert Earl Hammond."
8. "Edward F. Hutton, Financier, 86, Dies."
9. Laughlin, "Mapping the Way to Equality."
10. "Coast Guard Commandant Admiral Bob Papp's Remarks"; "Francis C. Pollard."

11. "Mrs. Marjorie Merriweather Post Is Dead at 86."

12. "PepsiCo Chairman's Award 2017."

13. "Solange Petit Skinner."

14. Thiesen, "The Long Blue Line: Carl Christian von Paulsen"; "Carl Christian von Paulsen."

Bibliography

Books

Blackman, Raymond V. B. *Jane's Fighting Ships, 1964–1965*. Bucks, England: Sampson Low, Marston & Co., 1965.

Caro, Robert A. *The Years of Lyndon Johnson: The Passage of Power*. New York: Vintage Books, 2013.

Davies, Joseph E. *Mission to Moscow*. New York: Simon and Schuster, 1941.

Gallagher, Stephanie. *True North: A Flickering Soul in No Man's Land*. Bloomington, IN: iUniverse, 2009.

Grobecker, Kurt, and Peter Neumann. *Sea Cloud: A Living Legend*. Hamburg, Germany: Edition Die Barque, 1998.

Lupiano, Vincent dePaul, and Ken W. Sayers. *It Was a Very Good Year: A Cultural History of the United States from 1776 to the Present*. Holbrook, MA: Bob Adams, Inc., 1994.

Maassen, Iwein. *Floating Luxury: The Most Luxurious Cruise Ships*. Tielt, Belgium: Lannoo Publishers, 2014.

MacGregor, Morris J., Jr. *Integration of the Armed Forces, 1940–1965*. Washington, DC: Center of Military History, US Army, 1981.

MacKay, Robert B. *Great Yachts of Long Island's North Shore*. Charleston, SC: Acadia Publishing, 2014.

Manchester, William. *The Glory and the Dream: A Narrative History of America—1932–1972*. New York: Bantam Books, 1975.

Miller, Kelly. *Kelly Miller's History of the World War for Human Rights*. Washington, DC: Austin Jenkins Co., 1919. Reprinted in 2014 by Createspace Independent Publishing Platform.

Morison, Samuel Eliot. *History of United States Naval Operations in World War II: The Battle of the Atlantic, 1939–1943*. Edison, NJ: Castle Books, 2001.

———. *The Oxford History of the American People*. New York: Oxford University Press, 1965.

Paine, Lincoln P. *Ships of the World: An Historical Encyclopedia*. Boston: Houghton Mifflin Company, 1997.

Roscoe, Theodore. *United States Destroyer Operations in World War II*. Annapolis, MD: United States Naval Institute, 1953.

Sayers, Ken W. *Uncommon Warriors: 200 Years of the Most Unusual American Naval Vessels*. Annapolis, MD: Naval Institute Press, 2012.

Schauffen, Otmar. *Great Sailing Ships of the World*. New York: Hearst Books, 2005.

Skinner, Carlton. *After Three Centuries: Representative Democracy and Civilian Government for Guam*. San Francisco: Macduff Press, 1997.

———. *Nauru: The Remarkable Community*. Data Paper No. 5. Santa Cruz, CA: Center for South Pacific Studies, University of California, Santa Cruz, 1977.

Smith, Peter C. *Cruise Ships: The Small Scale Fleet: A Visual Showcase*. Barnsley, England: Pen & Sword Maritime, 2014.

University of Guam. *Academic Year 2015–2016 Fact Book*. [Mangilao, Guam]: Office of Academic and Student Affairs, August 2016.

University of Washington. *The 1922 Tyee* (yearbook). Vol. 23. Seattle: Associated Students of the University of Washington, 1922.

US Navy, Bureau of Naval Personnel. *The Negro in the Navy*. United States Naval Administrative History of World War II, no. 84. Washington, DC: US Navy, 1947.

White, Walter Francis. *A Man Called White: The Autobiography of Walter White*. Athens: University of Georgia Press, 1948.

Williams, Greg H. *World War II U. S. Navy Vessels in Private Hands*. Jefferson, NC: McFarland & Company, 2013.

Willoughby, Malcolm F. *The U. S. Coast Guard in World War II*. Annapolis, MD: Naval Institute Press, 1957.

Wright, William. *Heiress: The Rich Life of Marjorie Merriweather Post*. Washington, DC: New Republic Books, 1978.

Wuerch, William, and Dick Anthony Ballendorf. *Historical Dictionary of Guam and Micronesia*. Lanham, MD: Scarecrow Press, 1994.

Articles

"Action on Guam" (editorial). *New York Times*, April 14, 1950, 22.

Akers, Regina. "December 26, 1944: Navy Commissions First Black Female Officers." Navy News Service, February 20, 2010. https://www.navy.mil/submit/display.asp?story_id=51394 (accessed May 25, 2020).

"Beauty Lies in the Eye of the Beholder: Ramfis Trujillo." http://www.glamourgirlsofthesilverscreen.com/show/272/Ramfis+Trujillo/index.html (accessed December 24, 2015).

Berrellee, Robert. "Dominican Government Inherits White Elephant." *Spokesman-Review*, March 27, 1966, 2.

"Biggest Yacht: 'Sea Cloud' Cruises Caribbean." *Life*, January 3, 1949, 42–43.
"BMCM Robert E. Hammond, USCG." https://www.uscg.mil/history/people/HammondRobertBMCM.asp (accessed March 8, 2016).
"Carl Christian von Paulsen." https://www.geni.com/people/Carl-Von-Paulsen/6000000023574640462 (accessed November 16, 2016).
"Carlton Skinner." http://www.marquiswhoswho.com (accessed December 14, 2015).
"Carlton Skinner, ex-Guam Leader, Dead at 91." http://the.honoluluadvertiser.com/article/2004/Aug/31/In/In54a.html (accessed December 3, 2015).
"Ceremony to Honor Former Gov. Skinner." *Pacific Daily News*, September 19, 2005.
"Civilian Rule of Guam Is Put Off for 30 Days." *New York Times*, June 30, 1950, 8.
"Coast Guard Commandant Admiral Bob Papp's Remarks at the Coast Guard Auxiliary National Conference." San Antonio, Texas, August 25, 2012. https://www.uscg.mil/seniorleadership/SPEECHES/2012-08-25%20NACON%20Remarks.pdf (accessed November 21, 2016).
"Coast Guard-Manned LSTs." https://www.uscg.mil/history/cutters/USN/LST/USCG_LST-Index.asp (accessed February 19, 2016).
"Combat Photographer, Filmmaker Charles 'Chick' Gallagher Dies at 88." http://highlandscurrent.com/2013/04/combat-photographer-filmmaker-charles-chick-gallagher-dies-at-88/ (accessed December 12, 2015).
Connor, Par D'Arcy. "Caribbean Time Machine." *Air Canada enRoute*, February 5, 2016, 48–56.
Cuff, Daniel F. "Business People." *New York Times*, February 1, 1984.
"Davies Will Inspect South Russian Areas." *New York Times*, May 16, 1938, 6.
"Davies Yacht Released." *New York Times*, September 28, 1944, 15.
"Davieses Land at Miami." *New York Times*, January 16, 1936, 18.
Decatur, Stephen. "Marblehead Man Not Afraid to Make Waves at Sea." *Marblehead Community*, December 14, 2000.
Delta Upsilon. "The Cornerstone." http://www.deltau.org/aspnet_clientFreeTextBox/upload/documents/Cornerstone%202015web.pdf (accessed January 29, 2016).
Department of the Navy, Bureau of Naval Personnel. "Guide to Command of Negro Naval Personnel." NAVPERS-15092, February 12, 1945. https://www.history.navy.mil/research/library/online-reading-room/title-list-alphabetically/g/guide-command-negro-naval-personnel-navpers-15092.html (accessed November 12, 2015).
Dinsmore, R. P. "Ocean Weather Ships, 1940–1980." https://www.uscg.mil/history/webcutters/rpdinsmore_oceanstations.asp (accessed February 23, 2016).
Donner, Suzanne. "A Four-Masted Barque That Sails the Caribbean." *New York Times*, January 6, 1980, 5.

Dubois, Jules. "For Sale: One Used Yacht." *Sarasota Herald Tribune*, March 11, 1962, 7.

Durdin, Tillman. "Civilian Rule Set Friday for Guam." *New York Times*, June 24, 1950, 5.

"Edward F. Hutton, Financier, 86, Dies." *New York Times*, July 12, 1962, 29.

"Ensign Rowe Is Bride of Lieut. Skinner." *Washington Post*, May 4, 1943.

"Eugene Duffield, Publisher, Editor." *New York Times*, September 22, 1974, 57.

Evanson, Christopher. "Looking Back: A Veteran Remembers the First Steps to Racial Equality." *Coast Guard*, July 1, 2007, 46–47.

"Ex-Reporter Appointed Guam Civilian Governor." *New York Times*, September 4, 1949, 14.

Fagan, Kevin. "Carlton Skinner—Broke Racial Barriers in Navy." *SF Gate*, August 29, 2004. https://www.sfgate.com/bayarea/article/Carlton-Skinner-broke-racial-barriers-in-Navy-2729705.php (accessed September 28, 2016).

"Few Big Yachts Left." *New York Times*, June 19, 1959, 29.

"First Civilian Chief of Guam Designated." *New York Times*, August 25, 1949, 15.

Fractal Foundation. "What Is Chaos Theory?" http://fractalfoundation.org/resources/what-is-chaos-theory/ (accessed March 4, 2016).

"Francis C. Pollard." https://valor.militarytimes.com/hero/308610 (accessed November 17, 2016).

"Friedrich Krupp Germaniawerft." https://en.wikipedia.org/wiki/Friedrich_Krupp_Germaniawerft (accessed December 5, 2015).

"Germania-Werft Actien-Gesellschaft [Fried Krupp]." http://www.globalsecurity.org/military/world/europe/de-kaiserliche-marine-germania.htm (accessed January 5, 2016).

Goetzfridt, Nicholas J. "Governor Carlton Skinner." https://www.guampedia.com/governor-carlton-skinner/ (accessed November 3, 2015).

"Governor Carlton Skinner: Pacific." http://www.carltonskinner.com/pacific.html (accessed November 10, 2015).

"Governor of Guam Quits; Nebraskan May Get Post." *New York Times*, February 13, 1953, 2.

"Great Lady of the Sea Arrives in Fiji." *Sunday Times* (Fiji), May 31, 1987, 7.

"Gresham, 1897." http://www.uscg.mil/history/webcutters/Gresham1896.pdf (accessed March 18, 2016).

"Guam Charges Denied." *New York Times*, June 21, 1951, 8.

"Guam Corruption Denied." *New York Times*, June 4, 1952, 10.

"Guam Governor Due in Capital." *New York Times*, November 26, 1949, 7.

"Guam Greets Skinner." *New York Times*, September 27, 1949, 12.

"Guam Head Steps Out Today." *New York Times*, February 20, 1953, 6.

"Guam Paper for Sale." *New York Times*, December 16, 1949, 2.

"Guam Radio-Phone Open." *New York Times*, November 22, 1951, 39.

"Guam Storm Cost Large." *New York Times*, November 20, 1949, 3.

“Guam Transfer Signed.” *New York Times*, September 8, 1949, 9.

“Guam’s House Elected.” *New York Times*, November 9, 1950, 2.

“Guamanians Seek to Enlist.” *New York Times*, August 8, 1950, 4.

Gugilelmo, Ernestine. “School Days on the Bounding Main.” *Rome News-Tribune*, October 4, 1972, 6D.

“History of Gibbs & Cox.” http://www.gibbscox.com/about/history-of-gibbs-cox (accessed December 6, 2015).

“History—SPC—Secretariat of the Pacific Community.” http://www.spc.int/en/about-spc/history.html (accessed November 11, 2015).

Howes, Durward, ed. “BEACH, Marian Weymouth.” In *American Women: The Official Who’s Who among the Women of the Nation*, 37. Los Angeles: Richard Blank Publishing, 1935.

“Huge Luxury Yacht, Owned by Mrs. Post, Unused but Manned.” *Sunday Star*, March 27, 1955, A22.

Hull, Michael D. “A Black Hero’s Courage under Fire.” *Naval History*, February 2016, 56–61.

“Hussar.” http://www.bruzelius.info/Nautica/Ships/Fourmast_ships/Hussar(1931).html (accessed December 19, 2015).

“Jacob A. Lawrence.” https://www.history.uscg.mil/Browse-by-Topic/Notable-People/Celebrities-and-Famous-People/ (accessed February 13, 2017).

“Jeanne R. Skinner.” *Marin Independent Journal*, April 23, 1988.

“Joseph E. Davies Quits Bermuda.” *New York Times*, July 15, 1947, 5.

“Julius A. Krug Advised to Rest.” *New York Times*, November 2, 1947, 26.

Kaplan, Hyman R. “Half a Century of Coast Guard Wings.” *Proceedings of the Merchant Marine Council*, September 1966, 177.

Kigar, Paul D. “Fair Wind to Martinique: The Atlantic Crossing of the Sea Cloud.” *Sea Classics*, November 1983, 32–40.

“Krug Appoints Carlton Skinner.” *New York Times*, April 39, 1946, 4.

Laughlin, Lauren. “Mapping the Way to Equality.” *Coast Guard Compass*, February 17, 2014. http://coastguard.dodlive.mil/2014/02/mapping-the-way-to-equality/ (accessed November 21, 2016).

“Lost Jacksonville: Gibbs Corporation Shipyards.” *Metro Jacksonville*, March 12, 2013. https://www.metrojacksonville.com/article/2013-mar-lost-jacksonville-gibbs-corporation-shipyards (accessed December 22, 2015).

Lovejoy, Clarence E. “Few Big Yachts Left.” *New York Times*, June 19, 1959, 29.

Lythgoe, Darrin. “Macy Millmore SKINNER.” Andrea Genealogy Pages. https://ancestry.omnes.ovh/getperson.php?personID=I31&tree=bmds (accessed May 30, 2020).

Maritime Administration (MARAD). “A Short History of the Maritime Administration.” https://maritime.dot.gov/outreach/history/short-history-maritime-administration (accessed December 5, 2015).

“Marjorie P. Hutton Receives A Divorce.” *New York Times*, September 8, 1935.

McCormick, Patricia. "Ocean-going School Gives 'Life Experience.'" *Montreal Gazette*, October 5, 1972, 17.

Miller, John. "The Art of History." *Coast Guard*, April 1, 2009, 24–27.

Mizrachi, Robert. "350-Foot Yacht Angelita, 1958." *San Diego Reader*, November 8, 2007. https://www.sandiegoreader.com/news/2007/nov/08/350-Foot-Yacht-Angelita-1958/ (accessed December 7, 2015).

Morris, Edmund. "Luffing toward Ravenna." *Forbes*, March 8, 1999. https://www.forbes.com/forbes-life-magazine/1999/0308/074.html#171f18a055f5 (accessed November 5, 2016).

"Mrs. Marion Beach, 84, Dies." *Marin Independent Journal*, April 27, 1966.

"Mrs. Marjorie Merriweather Post Is Dead at 86." *New York Times*, September 13, 1973, 50.

"Mrs. Max Mandellaub." *New York Times*, May 1, 1953, 21.

"Mrs. Post Hutton Wed to J. E. Davies." *New York Times*, December 16, 1935.

"Mrs. M. P. Hutton to Wed." *New York Times*, December 14, 1935, 3.

Murphy, Joe. "Carlton Skinner: Governor Extraordinaire." *Pacific Daily News*, November 19, 1996, 29.

———. "Skinner Shaped Guam's Future, Fought Injustice with Integrity." *Pacific Daily News*, August 30, 2004.

"Nauru Appoints Honorary Consul." *Charleston Daily Mail*, December 7, 1971.

Naval History and Heritage Command. "DANFS: Gresham." https://www.history.navy.mil/research/histories/ship-histories/danfs/g/gresham.html (accessed March 18, 2016).

———. "DANFS: Hoquiam (PF-5)." https://www.history.navy.mil/content/history/nhhc/research/histories/ship-histories/danfs/h/hoquiam.html (accessed April 2, 2016).

———. "DANFS: Sea Cloud." https://www.history.navy.mil/content/history/nhhc/research/histories/ship-histories/danfs/s/sea-cloud.html (accessed October 24, 2010).

———. "U.S. Ship Force Levels, 1886–Present." http://www.history.navy.mil/research/histories/ship-histories/us-ship-force-levels.html#1945 (accessed February 15, 2016).

"Navy Aids Guam in Strike." *New York Times*, July 15, 1952, 14.

"Navy Celebrates African-American/Black History Month." http://www.cnic.navy.mil/regions/ndw/news/navy-celebrates-african-american-black-history-month.html (accessed February 22, 2016).

"New Chairman Elected by Pratt & Whitney Co." *New York Times*, July 19, 1962, 40.

"New Values Stir the South Pacific." *New York Times*, August 9, 1962, 14.

"No Double Tax on Guam." *New York Times*, January 4, 1951, 19.

"North Florida Notes." *Motor Boating*, February 1950, 62, 64.

"Northland, 1927." http://uscg.mil/history/webcutters/Northland_1927.pdf (accessed November 16, 2015).

"Nourmahal, USS." https://www.uscg.mil/history/webcutters/Nourmahal_PG72.pdf (accessed February 27, 2016).
"Oceanics Schools." GuideStar. https://www.guidestar.org/profile/13-2680697 (accessed November 29, 2016).
"PepsiCo Chairman's Award 2017." https://pepsicochairmansaward.com/ca/hraward1.shtml (accessed November 21, 2016).
Perrin, Noel. "Under Full Sail on the Barque Sea Cloud." *New York Times*, May 30, 1982.
Polmar, Norman. "If It Flies Like a Duck . . ." *Naval History*, October 2015, 14–15.
"President Picks New Labor Aide after Signing Bill Creating Post." *New York Times*, August 12, 1961, 42.
"Presidente Trujillo frigate (1944/1946)." http://www.navypedia.org/ships/dominicanrep/dom_es_presidente_trujillo.htm (accessed July 14, 2016).
Priolo, Gary P. "Hoquiam (PF 5)." http://www.navsource.org/archives/12/08005.htm (accessed April 2, 2016).
"Private Services Were Held for Dr. Selby M. Skinner, 96, of Kirtland." *News-Herald* (Willoughby, OH), May 8, 2002.
"Reederei Nord Group." http://reederei-nord.com/ (accessed December 19, 2015).
"Refitted for Peacetime Luxury Service." *New York Times*, April 8, 1947, 55.
Roberts, Stephen S. "Appendix 2: The Auxiliary Vessels Board, 1941–1948." http://www.shipscribe.com/usnaux/auxvessboard.html (accessed May 25, 2020).
———. "Class: Sea Cloud (IX-99)." http://shipscribe.com/usnaux/IX3/IX099.html (accessed December 31, 2015).
"Robert Earl Hammond." *Courier News*, October 7, 2013.
Robinson, Bill L. "Transatlantic by Square-Rigger." *Yachting*, April 1982, 76–79.
Rosenfeld, Stanley. "2 Picture Boats Tell Tale of Social Change." *New York Times*, January 23, 1973, 3.
"Sailing Yacht Now a School." *Boca Raton News*, December 8, 1971, 12.
"Salt Air to Add Zest to High School Lessons." *Toledo Blade*, December 12, 1971, 43.
"Sea Cloud." http://castlesoftheseas.nl/sea-cloud-1.html (accessed December 10, 2015).
Sea Cloud Cruises. "The Renaissance of an Extraordinary Yacht." https://www.seacloud.com/en/yachts/sea-cloud/history/the-renaissance/.
Sea Cloud Cruises. "A Windjammer Writes History." http://www.seacloud.com/en/yachts/sea-cloud/history/ (accessed January 5, 2016).
"Shipyards: Germaniawerft, Kiel." https://uboat.net/wwi/types/shipyards.html?yard=Germaniawerft%2C+Kiel (accessed January 5, 2016).
"Silberstein Resigns Directorship in the Penn-Texas Corporation." *New York Times*, August 19, 1958, 37, 39.
Skinner, Carlton. "Arctic Navigation." *Yachting*, May 1943, 28–29, 90.
———. "Greenland, North Atlantic and North Pacific." In *World War II Reminiscences*, ed. Col. John H. Roush Jr., 57–59. San Rafael, CA: Xlibris, 2013.

Skinner, Carlton. "The Lost Wartime Paintings of Jacob Lawrence." https://www.uscg.mil/history/people/bios/SkinnerC/SkinnerC_LostPaintings-JacobLawrence.pdf (accessed March 7, 2016).

———. "Nauru: The Remarkable Community." *Oceanistes* 32, no. 50 (1976): 105–9.

———. "Self-Government in the South Pacific." *Foreign Affairs*, October 1963, 137–47.

———. "U.S.S. Sea Cloud, IX-99, Racial Integration for Naval Efficiency." https://media.defense.gov/2018/Jun/04/2001926386/-1/-1/0/CARLTON_SKINNER.PDF (accessed November 16, 2015).

"Skinner, Guam's Governor, Quits." *New York Times*, December 19, 1952, 4.

Slater, Shirley, and Harry Basch. "Sailing in Style on the Sea Cloud." *Los Angeles Times*, March 1, 1992.

"Solange Petit Skinner." http://solangepetitskinner.com/ (accessed November 21, 2016).

Stark, Louis. "Lewis Signs Soft Coal Terms with U.S." *New York Times*, May 30, 1946, 1–2.

Stewart, Stanley. "Siren of the Seas." *Weekend Australian*, November 16, 2013.

Temin, Christine. "Kathie Lee Need Not Apply: The Luxurious Sea Cloud Has a Cruising Style All Its Own." *Boston Globe*, September 7, 1997, 8.

Thiesen, William H. "Change Hastened by Conflict." *Naval History*, February 2015, 26–31.

———. "The Long Blue Line: Carl Christian von Paulsen—Coast Guard Aviation Pioneer and War Hero." *Coast Guard Compass*, April 21, 2016. http://coastguard.dodlive.mil/2016/04/the-long-blue-line-carl-christian-von-paulsen-coast-guard-aviation-pioneer-and-war-hero/ (accessed November 17, 2016).

———. "The Long Blue Line: Clarence Samuels—Coast Guard Trailblazer." *Coast Guard Compass*, February 4, 2016. https://coastguard.dodlive.mil/2016/02/the-long-blue-line-clarence-samuels-coast-guard-trailblazer/ (accessed November 17, 2016).

———. "Pioneers of Ethnic Diversity in the American Sea Services." http://www.uscg.mil/history/articles/Bulletin_HistoryLesson_Oct_11.pdf (accessed February 22, 2016).

Tidwell, Mike. "The Best Democracy I've Known." *American Legacy*, Summer 2000, 31–40.

Tilton School. "Affording Tilton." https://www.tiltonschool.org/admissions/affording-tilton (accessed May 22, 2020).

———. "Our Mission and Vision." https://www.tiltonschool.org/about/mission-and-vision (accessed May 25, 2020).

"Trujillo Buys Sea Cloud." *New York Times*, October 7, 1955, 49.

"Trujillo Presents Medal to Mrs. Davies." *St. Petersburg Times*, March 11, 1948, 7.

"Trujillo's Yacht Firmly Anchored." *Florence Times*, June 25, 1958, 4.

"Trujillo's Yacht Gets a New Name." *Tuscaloosa News*, July 16, 1958, 7.

"Trujillo's Yacht Up for Sale." *Tuscaloosa News*, March 28, 1966.
"23 Yachts Given to 3 U.S. Services." *New York Times*, February 8, 1942, 8.
"Typhoon Hits Guam." *New York Times*, November 17, 1949, 14.
"U-Boat Fates." http://uboat.net/fates/losses/1942.htm (accessed February 4, 2016).
UCLA. "Mission & Values." http://www.ucla.edu/about/mission-and-values (accessed January 29, 2016).
US Coast Guard. "Two Buildings Named for Coast Guard Heroes." ALCOAST 227/19, July 8, 2019. https://content.govdelivery.com/accounts/USDHSCG/bulletins/2501bbe.
"U.S. Coast Guard Cutter Northland 1927–1947, 1944 Configuration" (line drawing). https://www.uscg.mil/history/docs/plans/Northland001.jpg (accessed December 30, 2015).
"U.S. Coast Guard Cutter Sea Cloud 1942–1943" (line drawing). https://www.uscg.mil/history/docs/plans/CGCSeaCloud002.jpg (accessed December 30, 2015).
US Coast Guard Historian's Office. "African Americans in the U.S. Coast Guard." https://www.history.uscg.mil/Browse-by-Topic/Notable-People/Minorities/African-Americans/ (accessed November 16, 2015).
US Department of Labor. "A Brief History." https://www.dol.gov/general/aboutdol/history/dolhistoxford (accessed May 22, 2020).
US Department of State, Office of the Historian. "Joseph Edward Davies." http://history.state.gov/departmenthistory/people/davies-joseph-edward (accessed December 6, 2015).
"USS Hoquiam, PF-5." https://www.uscg.mil/history/cutters/USN/PF/PF5_Hoquiam.pdf (accessed November 16, 2015).
"USS Sea Cloud, 1942." http://www.uscg.mil/history/webcutters/Sea_Cloud_IX99.asp (accessed February 23, 2016).
Valbuena, Jose A. "For Sale: Yacht with Memories." *Desert Sun*, June 28, 1963, 7.
"A Vessel Built in Germany Is Chartered to U.S. Navy." *New York Times*, January 8, 1942, 8.
"Wallace B. Bishop, Cartoonist of 'Muggs and Skeeter' Strip." *New York Times*, January 18, 1982.
"Warde's Role at Airline." *New York Times*, February 3, 1984.
Wesleyan University. "Wesleyan University: A Brief History." https://www.wesleyan.edu/about/history-traditions/index.html (accessed January 29, 2016).
Whitney Museum of American Art. "Jacob Lawrence 1917–2000." https://whitney.org/artists/759 (accessed March 23, 2016).
"Windsors Visit Bahamas." *New York Times*, April 1, 1948, 35.
Winegar, Karin. "Elegance under Sail Sea Cloud: Luxury Cruise Aboard a Floating Palace." *Orlando Sentinel*, July 30, 1989.
Wisner, Bill. "The Golden Age of Yachts." *Motor Boating & Sailing*, December 1975, 29, 66.
"World City America President Stephanie Gallagher Dies June 10." *Highlands*

Current (Cold Spring, NY), June 22, 2013. https://highlandscurrent.org/2013/06/22/world-city-america-president-stephanie-Gallagher-dies-june-10/ (accessed December 12, 2015).
"Yacht Return Is Demanded." *Milwaukee Journal*, November 25, 1961, 2.
Zumwalt, Elmo R., Jr. "Equal Opportunity." Z-Gram 66, December 17, 1970. https://www.history.navy.mil/research/library/online-reading-room/title-list-alphabetically/z/list-z-grams/z-gram-66.html (accessed May 26, 2020).

Archival and Miscellaneous Material

Department of the Navy. "Navy to Accept Negroes for General Service." Press release, April 7, 1942.
Executive Order 9981. July 26, 1948. Harry S. Truman Library. https://www.trumanlibrary.gov/library/executive-orders/9981/executive-order-9981 (accessed November 29, 2016).
"Log of President Truman's Trip to Puerto Rico, the Virgin Islands, Guantanamo Bay, Cuba, and Key West, Florida." http://www.Trumanlibrary.org/calendar/travel_log/pdfs/Keywest4.pdf (accessed August 14, 2016).
May v. Commissioner of Internal Revenue. Docket No. 72983, March 8, 191, 35 T.C. 865 (U.S.T.C. 1961). https://www.leagle.com/decision/196190035cstc8651804 (accessed December 19, 2015).
McEnery, John P. Interview by James R. Fuchs, March 11, 1970, Monterey, CA. Oral History Interviews, Truman Library. https://www.trumanlibrary.gov/library/oral-histories/mcenery1 (accessed August 17, 2016)
Oceanics Schools Inc. v. Clifford E. Barbour Jr. March 14, 2003. No. E2002-00181-COA-R3-CV. Tenn. Court of Appeals. https://caselaw.findlaw.com/tn-court-of-appeals/1450245.html (accessed December 12, 2015).
Oceanics Schools Inc. v. Clifford E. Barbour Jr. April 22, 2003. http://www.tsc.state.tn.us/sites/default/files/OPINIONS/TCA/PDF/032/OceanicsSchools2.pdf (accessed December 12, 2015).
Oceanics Schools Inc. v. Operation Sea Cruise Inc. November 19, 1999. www.tba.org/tba_files/TCA/1999/Oceanics.pdf (accessed December 1, 2015).
Skinner, Carlton. 1943 notebook. Collection of the US Coast Guard Historian's Office, Washington, DC.
———. Interview by James A. Oesterle, November 17, 1970, San Francisco, CA. John F. Kennedy Oral History Program, John F. Kennedy Library, Boston, MA.
———. Interview by Morris J. MacGregor Jr., June 29, 1975. Summary transcript, Chief of Military History/Historical Services Division files, RG 0319, container 11, National Archives and Records Administration, College Park, MD.

———. Lecture delivered on board *Sea Cloud* (transcript), n.d. Collection of the US Coast Guard Historian's Office, Washington, DC. The author believes this lecture was delivered by Skinner in 1983 during a voyage across the Atlantic. (For background, see Kigar, "Fair Wind to Martinique.")

———. Letter to James C. Bunch, March 31, 1999. Collection of the US Coast Guard Historian's Office, Washington, DC.

———. Testimony before the President's Committee on Equality of Treatment and Opportunity in the Armed Forces, April 25, 1949, Washington, DC. Collection of the US Coast Guard Historian's Office, Washington, DC.

Skinner, Solange P. Interview by Ian P. Hurley, December 12, 2015, Boston, MA. Transcript in author's files.

Snyder, John W. Interview by Jerry N. Hess, April 9, 1969, Washington, DC. Oral History Interviews, Truman Library. https://www.trumanlibrary.gov/library/oral-histories/snyder35 (accessed December 1, 2016).

Index